THE BEER SELECT- O-PEDIA

CAMRA
CAMPAIGN
FOR
REAL ALE

**CAMPAIGN
FOR
REAL ALE**

First published in the UK in 2014 by
Campaign for Real Ale Ltd
230 Hatfield Road, St Albans, Hertfordshire AL1 4LW
www.camra.org.uk

A Marshall Edition
Conceived, edited, and designed by
Marshall Editions
The Old Brewery
6 Blundell Street
London N7 9BH

www.marshalleditions.com
© 2014 Marshall Editions

Editorial Director Sorrel Wood
Design Rawshock Design
Editor Cathy Meeus
Editorial Assistants Philippa Davis, Lucy Kingett
Photography Simon Pask
Production Nikki Ingram

For CAMRA Books
Head of Publishing Simon Hall
Editor Katie Button
Consultant Editor Roger Protz

The publishers will be grateful for any information that will assist them in keeping future editions up to date.
Although all reasonable care has been taken in the preparation of this book, neither the publishers nor the authors
can accept any liability for any consequence arising from the use thereof, or the information contained therein.

The views and opinions expressed in this book are those of the author alone and not
necessarily those of the Campaign for Real Ale.

ISBN 978-1-85249-318-9

Originated in Singapore by Pica Digital Pte Ltd
Printed and bound in China by 1010 Printing International Ltd

For other CAMRA Books titles please visit: **www.camra.org.uk/books**

THE BEER SELECT-O-PEDIA

MICHAEL LARSON

The Beer Select-O-Pedia:
A Periodic Table of Beer Origins

22 Go — English Golden

24 Ob — Ordinary Bitter	36 Ir — Irish Red Ale	44 Eo — English Old Ale	52 Bn — English Brown Ale	60 Ss — Sweet Stout	72 Wit — Witbier	80 Spa — Belgian Strong Pale Ale	88 Tr — Tripel	98 Bli — Belgian IPA
26 Bb — Best Bitter	38 Mac — Scottish Ales	46 Es — English Strong Old Ale	54 Ep — English Porter	62 Os — Oatmeal Stout	74 Gs — Gose	82 Ch — Bière de Champagne	90 Bpa — Belgian Pale Ale	100 S — Saison
28 Sb — Strong/Extra Special Bitter	40 Bar — English Barley Wine	48 Ww — Winter Warmer	56 Bp — Baltic Porter	64 Fs — Foreign/Extra Stout	76 Be — Berliner Weisse	84 Kw — Kristalweizen	92 L — Lambic	102 Bdg — Bière de Garde
30 Pa — Pale Ale	42 We — Strong Scotch Ale	50 Mi — Dark Mild	58 Ds — Irish Dry Stout	66 Ims — Imperial Russian Stout	78 Kol — Kölsch	86 Wb — Weissbier	94 G — Gueuze	104 Dk — Dunkelweizen
32 Ipa — India Pale Ale							96 Lf — Fruit Lambic	106 Fl — Flanders Red
34 Lm — Light/Pale Mild								

158 Aml — American Lager	164 Ppl — Pre-Prohibition Lager	170 Gf — Gluten-free	176 Apa — American Pale Ale	182 Si — Single Hop IPA	188 Pu — Pumpkin Ale	194 Cc — California Common
160 Pl — Pale Lager	166 Ab — American Blonde/Golden Ale	172 Aw — American Style Wheat	178 Ai — American IPA	184 Aal — American Amber Lager	190 Amb — American Amber	196 Ft — Fruit Beers
162 Am — American Malt Liquor	168 Cr — Cream Ale	174 Ry — Rye Beer	180 Wh — Wet Hop	186 Di — Double/Imperial IPA	192 Wi — American Wild Ale	198 Usb — American Barley Wine

The periodic table is grouped according to where different styles of beer most famously originate – most types of beer are available from craft brewers the world over. Use the numbers to find out more about each style: turn to that page to discover recommended brewers, tasting notes and also three beers to try.

142 **Smk** Rauchbier			
108 **Alt** Altbier	126 **Gp** German Pilsner	132 **De** Dortmunder Export	144 **Tb** Traditional Bock
110 **Rg** Roggenbier	128 **Bop** Bohemian Pilsner	134 **Mk** Maibock	146 **Md** Munich Dunkel
112 **Du** Dubbel	130 **H** Helles	136 **Mo** Märzen/Oktoberfest	148 **Db** Doppelbock
114 **Fb** Flanders Brown	118 **Wz** Weizenbock	138 **Vl** Vienna Lager	150 **Eib** Eisbock
116 **Bs** Belgian Strong Dark Ale	120 **Bba** Belgian Black Ale	140 **Kb** Kellerbier	152 **Swb** Schwarzbier

200 **Asa** American Strong Ale		
202 **Aba** American Brown Ale	206 **Bi** Black IPA	210 **I** Imperial and Hyper Beers
204 **Ap** American Porter	208 **Bg** Barrel-aged Beers	212 **Ast** American Stout

HOW THE TABLE WORKS

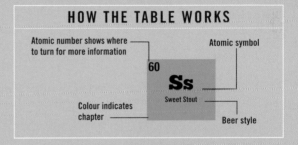

Atomic number shows where to turn for more information

Atomic symbol

60 **Ss** Sweet Stout

Colour indicates chapter

Beer style

HOW THE TABLE IS ORGANISED

Each chapter runs from the lightest to the darkest beer.

KEY TO THE CHAPTERS

Ales of British or Irish Origin **1**

Ales of Continental European Origin **2**

Lagers of Continental European Origin **3**

Beers of American Origin **4**

... *also indicated by coloured bars on each page.*

Introduction

From its illustrious history to its current renaissance, beer has refreshed and intrigued the masses through the ages. Using a few simple ingredients, craft breweries, multinational brewing companies and novice home brewers alike produce drinks of complexity that rival the satisfaction bestowed by any other beverage.

All too often, beer is taken for granted, dismissed as a quick refresher lacking the grandeur of wine – a misconception fostered by ubiquitous, bland, mass-market beer. However, beer has an unparalleled scope for dramatically different varieties in a rainbow of possible colours and with infinite, heady mixtures of aromas, flavours and textures. Increasing numbers of consumers are coming to appreciate this delicious, flourishing world of beer and are keen to explore it. This book will guide you through the bewildering variety of beer styles and the exciting possibilities they offer.

Covering scores of traditional and innovative new styles from Britain and Ireland, Continental Europe and America, this book will become your companion as you venture through a jungle of malt and hops, of stout and IPA, of bière de garde and pilsner. It will give you the tools to navigate your way along the bar and through the beer aisles, and the confidence to build on your personal likes and dislikes to find your own perfect pint.

The modern-day beer renaissance is a remarkable success story. In Britain, the Campaign for Real Ale (CAMRA) was founded in the early 1970s to save traditional cask-conditioned beer from extinction at the hands of giant national brewers. So successful has CAMRA been that real ale is now the only growth sector of the British brewing industry, with astonishing numbers of new breweries opening to meet demand. This consumer-led revival of the brewing industry in Britain helped inspire beer lovers and craft brewers in other countries and the revival has spread worldwide.

Although CAMRA's focus is on real ale (cask-conditioned beer) – Britain's native beer style and a totally natural, live product that can be the ultimate expression of the brewer's craft – CAMRA does not live in a real ale bubble. The Campaign revels in the worldwide explosion of new breweries and new beers, and appreciates good beer wherever it comes from. However, not all beer is equal. This book takes an inclusive approach to beer styles in order to represent the beer world as it is but, inevitably, some styles offer greater rewards than others.

Despite its variety and complexities, beer remains an approachable drink – one enjoyed both a sip at a time and glass after glass. Beer is a drink that creates and fosters community rather than exclusivity or snobbery – a community founded on shared interests, passion for the craft of brewing and sheer enjoyment of unique handcrafted brews. Journeying through the world of craft beer one discovers a virtual village of people – not vying for attention or thriving on competition, but a dedicated group devoted to producing, selling, buying, sharing and most importantly, drinking, the world's most intriguing, versatile beverage.

Beer is a world to be explored at your own pace. Hopefully, these pages will help you wander a little less aimlessly, a little more pointedly, and will help you discover moments with beer that you never thought you would have. Cheers!

How to Use This Book

The **BEER SELECT-O-PEDIA** lists 90 different styles of beer (see page 4). These are grouped in four chapters according to the geographical origin of that style.

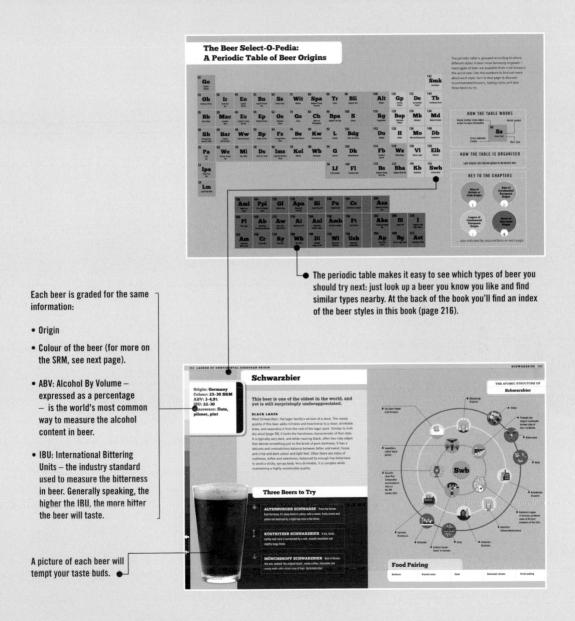

The periodic table makes it easy to see which types of beer you should try next: just look up a beer you know you like and find similar types nearby. At the back of the book you'll find an index of the beer styles in this book (page 216).

Each beer is graded for the same information:

- Origin
- Colour of the beer (for more on the SRM, see next page).
- ABV: Alcohol By Volume — expressed as a percentage — is the world's most common way to measure the alcohol content in beer.
- IBU: International Bittering Units — the industry standard used to measure the bitterness in beer. Generally speaking, the higher the IBU, the more bitter the beer will taste.

A picture of each beer will tempt your taste buds.

How to Use This Book ... continued

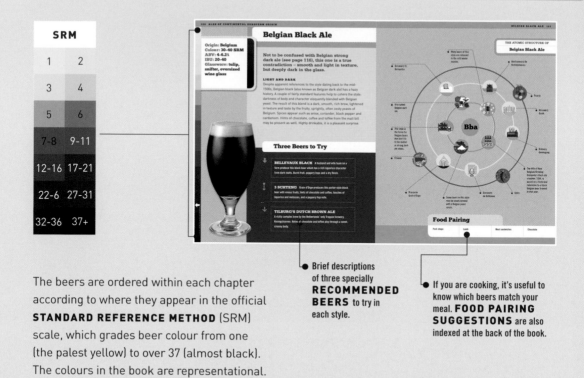

The beers are ordered within each chapter according to where they appear in the official **STANDARD REFERENCE METHOD** (SRM) scale, which grades beer colour from one (the palest yellow) to over 37 (almost black). The colours in the book are representational.

Brief descriptions of three specially **RECOMMENDED BEERS** to try in each style.

If you are cooking, it's useful to know which beers match your meal. **FOOD PAIRING SUGGESTIONS** are also indexed at the back of the book.

Each style of beer has an **ATOMIC STRUCTURE DIAGRAM** that tells you more about each beer, lists breweries to watch out for and gives tasting notes on the style of beer.

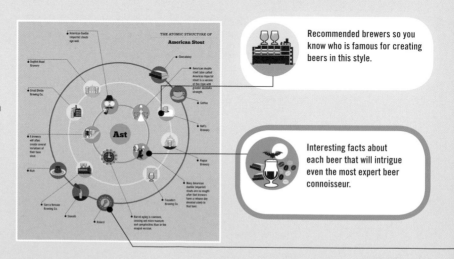

Recommended brewers so you know who is famous for creating beers in this style.

Interesting facts about each beer that will intrigue even the most expert beer connoisseur.

The **TASTING NOTES** are divided into four groups: malt flavours, hop characteristics, fermentation, and body and mouthfeel. Sample tasting notes in each category are shown on the diagram below. For some beers, spice flavours are also notable.

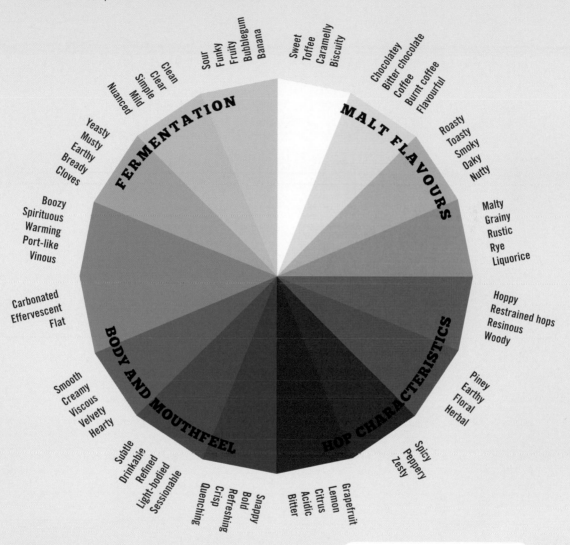

Diagram to show positions of tasting notes on the **ATOMIC DIAGRAMS** in this book.

Tasting notes help you identify and enjoy the full flavour of every beer. Tasting notes appear in the same place on each page so if you know you like citrus-flavoured beers you can watch out for the same symbol as you flick through the book.

Once you know what you like to taste in a beer the **TASTING NOTES** allow you to track that flavour through the book. This diagram shows how the icons are organised.

AN INTRODUCTION TO DRINKING BEER

Whether you are looking at it from a glass half empty or glass half full perspective, drinking beer is not a complicated process – unlike many pastimes, you don't need any expert knowledge to get started. That said, the more you know, the more you will enjoy. This section will whet your appetite before you dive into the different styles.

What is beer?

There are scores of different styles of beer, often so different from one another that it is hard to tell they are created from the same ingredients. And that is the simple beauty of this beverage – while crafted from just a few simple ingredients – water, malt, yeast and hops – the results are hugely varied. Beers can look like sunshine or midnight. They can be as clear as glass or as opaque as engine oil. They can be spritzy like champagne, viscous like maple syrup or creamy as a milkshake.

INGREDIENTS

• **WATER** makes up the highest proportion of beer volume, generally around 90 per cent. Its chemical and mineral composition has an impact on the end result, so it is crucial that the source is clean and pure. Some brewers alter the mineral content of the water to produce specific qualities in the end product.

• **MALT** begins as barley, a cereal grain grown worldwide. The origin and variety of the barley used affect the flavour profile of the beer. For use in brewing, barley must be malted, a process in which the raw grain is steeped in water until it begins to sprout and then placed into a kiln to dry. It is this process that breaks down the hard husk of the barley and changes it into a soft, usable product. Kilning occurs in a roasting drum or on a heated floor and the temperature and length of this process governs whether the malt is light, both in colour and flavour, or a dark, heavily roasted malt. A brewer chooses a particular malt in order to achieve the desired flavour and colour of beer. Depending on the style, other grains, such as oats, rye, wheat and special brewing sugars, may be added.

• **HOPS** are inextricably associated with beer – more than any other ingredient. It is surprising to some that a flower produces bitterness, and certain flavours and aromas, in beer. Hops help to preserve the beer and also provide a crucial balance to the malt, without which beer would be overly sweet and cloying. The hop plant is a vine on which small flower cones form in the late summer and early autumn. There are dozens of types of hops and the brewer selects a specific variety based on the desired flavours and aromas. Hops can be spicy, citric, woody, piney, grapefruity, earthy and/or floral. Usually hops are added during the boiling process. However, they are sometimes added later in the brewing process.

• **YEAST**, a living microorganism, is essential to brewing, as it converts the wort – the liquid produced in the early part of the brewing process – into beer. As the yeast eats the sugar in the wort, it creates a multitude of flavours – and produces alcohol. There are two commonly-used species: *Saccharomyces cerevisae*, the yeast used in ales, which ferment at warmer temperatures, and *Saccharomyces uvarum*, the yeast used in lagers, which ferment in cooler temperatures.

Ale yeast ferments more quickly than lager yeast, and during fermentation, rises to the top, hence the term 'top-fermenting'. By contrast, when a lager yeast has completed its task of fermentation, it settles on the bottom, and is therefore dubbed 'bottom-fermenting.' There are many strains within these species, each one having a different impact on the beer – some in significant and intriguing ways.

How Beer is Brewed

The first step in **BREWING** is to make **WORT**, by steeping crushed malt in hot water in a mash tun to form the **MASH**, a porridge-like substance. During this stage, starches are broken down into sugars, which are then drawn away from the grain in the water as the mash is filtered and transferred into a copper or kettle. This liquid can now be called wort. At this point, it is brought to a vigorous **BOIL**, which helps to sterilise the wort. During the boil, hops are added to the wort, which help to create the bitterness, flavours and aromas in the final product. The first additions primarily affect the bitterness of the beer while later additions form the aroma. Spices may also be added. After the boil, the hops and any protein solids are removed using a strainer or a whirlpool. At this point, the wort is rapidly cooled to temperatures suitable for **FERMENTATION**.

The transformation of malt sugar to alcohol takes place in a fermentation vessel, where yeast is mixed with the hopped wort. Fermentation creates both alcohol and natural carbonation. When the process is complete, the 'green beer' is pumped to **CONDITIONING** vessels to rest and purge itself of unwanted rough alcohols. Some beers may undergo a further period of **MATURATION**. Next, the beer is dispensed, or 'racked' into casks, kegs or bottles for distribution.

REAL ALE (cask-conditioned beer) is racked directly into casks (or bottles) without filtration or pasteurisation so the beer retains important flavours and some live yeast, which is crucial for a secondary fermentation in the cask. Hops may be added for extra aroma while finings are added to help clear the beer. In the cask,

the yeast turns remaining sugars to alcohol, consumes unwanted oxygen and creates a gentle, natural carbonation. The beer is served by drawing it from cellar to bar by a handpump.

Other beers are filtered (thus removing any yeast) and often pasteurised before being racked into sealed kegs (or bottles) along with extraneous gas to provide carbonation (creating higher levels than in real ale). These **KEG BEERS** are served from bar founts by applied gas. Filtering and pasteurisation can remove important flavour compounds from keg beer.

Current trends in brewing

The production of mass-market, light lagers is a feature of modern times. Yet creative, passionate craft brewers have continued to produce unique beers of high quality. In recent times, their patience has been rewarded. The historic brews of England, Germany and Belgium are receiving renewed and well-deserved attention, while the American styles are becoming standards in their own right. New styles are being created and established styles are being given new twists. Conservatism and caution have been thrown aside and replaced with ingenuity and brash creativity. At the same time, the classic styles of past centuries have been revived by new breweries revisiting their beer heritage.

Serving and Storing Beer

GLASSWARE

A flute for champagne and a mug for coffee. Tea in a china cup and cola in a can. Every drink seems to have its signature vessel, and beer is no exception to the rule. While Belgium takes the art of serving beer to an unprecedented level, even the most basic home-bar setup can benefit from a small makeover to the glassware department. With a few different glasses, beer can be tasted as it was intended. Some beers present best in a tall, thin cylinder, others find themselves comfortably contained in a sturdy nonic pint glass. In almost every case, there is an ideal way for beer to be served.

• **FLUTE** Tall, slender and stemmed, the flute typically conjures up images of wedding toasts and New Year's Eve. However, this delicate glass can be the perfect vessel for beer. The tall, thin shape is ideal for highly carbonated brews that are light in colour and extremely translucent. The design tends to force the aroma upwards and outwards, giving the drinker a strong burst of bouquet before the first sip is taken.

• **GOBLET/CHALICE** Recommended for certain Belgian styles in particular. A glass of this type can be thin and delicate or solidly thick. It allows for splendid head retention. Many breweries produce their own customised designs.

• **MUG/STEIN** Sturdy and with a large capacity, a mug begs for a quenching beer. The design is simple and practical, easy to use, and can hold plenty of beer.

• **IPA GLASS** This glass, marketed as recently as 2013, has yet to see wide acceptance. However, it was designed with India pale ales specifically in mind. The shape allows room for a foamy head and glass ridges aid head retention.

• **PILSNER GLASS** This thin, tall and slender glass is an ideal match for the pilsner beer after which it is named. Its height shows off the rushing stream of carbonation, while keeping

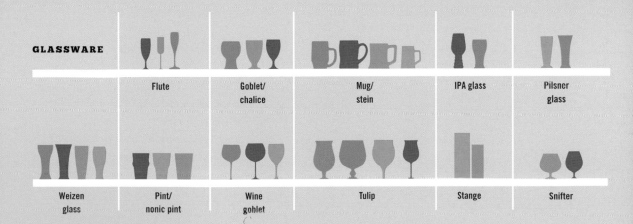

GLASSWARE

Flute | Goblet/chalice | Mug/stein | IPA glass | Pilsner glass

Weizen glass | Pint/nonic pint | Wine goblet | Tulip | Stange | Snifter the beer cool – a quality essential to a style best served on the cooler side. With the height to show off a bright-coloured body and a brilliantly white cap, a proper pour into this glass can create a mouth-watering picture.

• **WEIZEN GLASS** With a narrow base spreading to a wider mouth, this glass is designed to enhance wheat beer. The size accommodates the desired volume of beer and the characteristic fluffy head.

• **PINT/NONIC PINT** Either straight sided (pint), or with a bulge near the top (nonic pint), these glasses are the default option for many brews. The design focus is less on the drinking experience than the ease of storage. Pint glasses are cheap to make and therefore an ideal choice for many drinking establishments.

• **WINE GOBLET** Another glass borrowed from beyond the world of beer, this large-bowled design can be used for a variety of beer styles. The body is wide enough to display the colour and viscosity of heavier brews and, like the snifter, allows room for a fluffy head and an assertive swirl that will release the aromas easily through the wide mouth.

• **TULIP** Its shape echoes that of the eponymous flower, the wide body narrowing near the top and then fanning out, allowing for the formation of a billowing head, harnessing and then projecting the aroma.

• **STANGE** Straight sided, this specialised glass, meaning 'stick' in German, focuses the aromatics of more delicate styles of beer and helps to concentrate flavours.

• **SNIFTER** With a slight stem and a wide bowl, this glass style is borrowed from the world of brandy. Easy to swirl, the glass gives the drinker an invitingly forward bouquet and allows the formation of 'legs', which indicate the viscosity of the particular beer. Perfect for bigger, heavier, darker brews.

HOW TO STORE BEER

After you have chosen the proper glassware, there are a few easy steps to consider to maximise your tasting experience. First, ensure the beer is being stored and served at the proper temperature. Generally speaking, beer is kept best in cold, dry, dark spaces. The fridge is the obvious choice for many beers. Some beers should be served slightly warmer and others at cooler temperatures, but with some experimentation, these differentiations will become clear. Light, refreshing, lower alcohol beers tend to appreciate cooler temperatures, while complex, rich and dark brews may be at their best when slightly warmer. Strong, complex ales are most effectively aged in a cool, but not cold, location. A cool cellar at around 13°C (55°F) is ideal for long-term storage and can heighten and accentuate the more subtle aromas and flavours.

HOW TO POUR BEER

Pouring requires consideration, but this is another area that can be overthought. Typically, you can achieve an adequate pour by angling the glass and pouring slowly down the side. At about two-thirds full, tilt the glass upright and finish the pour. This will help to build the head, which adds to the look, feel and aroma of most beers.

How to Taste Beer

Tasting beer should be fun. You shouldn't be searching for proper vocabulary or awkwardly mimicking a supposed connoisseur. Your hands shouldn't sweat – your mouth should water. That said, even the most casual tasting session can be refined with a few simple steps. The brewer who crafted that lovely pint in your hand wants you to taste everything that he or she intended, so here are a few suggestions to help you do just that.

• **APPEARANCE** After pouring the beer into the recommended and clean glass, it is time to take it all in. When gauging its appearance take note of the colour, clarity and carbonation of the body. Also look at the head: is it light and airy or dense and firm? Does it linger or disappear? A tall, thick head will produce more lace. Also referred to as Brussels lace, this term describes the foam left sticking to the side of the glass. Take the glass in your hand and swirl it slightly, noting the texture of the brew and its viscosity. All of this thinking time will prepare your palate for what is to come.

• **AROMA** The fragrance of a beer is a crucial element of the taste – just consider how little you can taste when your nose is blocked by a head cold. Swirl the glass to release the bouquet and, with your nose in the glass, inhale. With experience, the nuances intended by the brewer will become more apparent, but even a beginner can easily distinguish some different aromas.

• **TASTE AND MOUTHFEEL** Next, take a drink. Don't be bashful, the intention of the brewer is that you will take a mouthful, not just a nip. Wash it around on your tongue to absorb the weight and texture. Take note of the thickness, viscosity and carbonation. All these are aspects of what is known as 'mouthfeel'. Finally, taste the beer and search for the initial flavours, then the centre and the finish. The many flavours are what make beer such a consistently intriguing drink. After you swallow, you can form an overall impression. How do the pieces knit together to form the final complete tapestry of taste?

BEER TASTINGS

When tasting several beers in succession, as part of a beer dinner or a 'flight' (several small servings of different beers), it is best to sample them in a particular order. Aim to try the lighter, less complex and powerful styles first, then work through your lineup towards the richer, more impactful brews. This will allow you to perceive the delicate flavours of the lighter styles before the heavier styles overshadow them. A perfect pilsner can seem watery and flavourless following a Russian imperial stout.

Pairing Food with Beer

While wine has always taken centre stage at the dinner table, beer has an incredible, and generally untapped, potential. Many diners adhere to the perception that beer belongs in a pub, with crisps, or from a can at a rowdy party. While some beers belong in these places, there have always been others with a well-earned spot at a dinner party. Fine beers, paired well, poured well, and drunk with appreciation, have the potential to pleasantly surprise and impress. The primary goal should be a marriage of beer and food resulting in a flavour experience impossible to attain with either item on its own. In essence, the sum is greater than its parts.

CHOOSING FOOD FOR BEER

Complementary pairings of beer and food aim to match similarities in both. Some obvious examples could include a light pilsner served with a summer salad or a dark Russian imperial stout served with a rich chocolate dessert. The similarities in the beer and the accompanying food create harmony and cohesion that amplify the flavours of both. A few useful tips that will help to develop complementary tasting combinations: fatty and sweet foods do well with high alcohol beers that have hop bitterness, sweetness or roasted malt notes. Highly carbonated beers tend to cut rich foods and cleanse the palate. At the back of the book you will find the recommended food pairings indexed by food, so you can easily find a beer to match what you are eating.

• **STYLE** In crafting a pairing, you first must know what style of beer you will be tasting.

Generally the brewer has made this an easy job, boldly emblazoning the style across the bottle. Armed with this bit of information you can look up the beer style in this book and use the atomic diagram to discover more about how it will taste (plus some recommended pairings).

• **FLAVOUR FOCUS** Beer can be many things at once. It can be sweet, caramelly, malty and heavy. It can be bitter, citric and bright. It can be light, effervescent and refreshingly cleansing. Attention to these individual nuances is essential when attempting to make a memorable pairing. Your taste buds have already experienced the vast array of flavours in food, it is now simply time to take note of those specifics and properly partner them with beer. A particularly effective way of doing so is to narrow down one focal point on which to build your pairing. Focus on the primary characteristic of the beer or the food with which you are attempting to pair it, and your choices become more obvious.

• **BALANCE** The backdrop to attaining a successful pairing is to consistently maintain balance. The strength and flavours in both the food and beer should create an interplay that is not dominated by either. Hearty, robust, rich foods should be matched with beers of a similar quality. Light, refreshing and delicate dishes are best suited to beers with the same characteristics. However, achieving overall balance does not mean that the pairing will necessarily involve like flavours in both beer and food. In fact, some of the most impressive beer and food pairings result from opposing flavours.

• **COMPLEMENTARY** If a beer is light, fruity, and crisp, perhaps a fresh salad would be a

match. If it has a robust, toasty quality with a chewy malt backbone, a chargrilled steak would delight the taste buds.

• **CONTRAST** Often the best matches in food and beer are ones in which the most prominent flavour in the beer contrasts with the focal point in the food. When choosing contrasting pairings, however, you must be careful not to overdo it. A light, bright beer will be stripped of its flavours if served with a dark chocolate torte. However, a hoppy IPA will cut through the sweetness of carrot cake for a surprisingly delicious result.

THE FOOD PAIRINGS IN THIS BOOK

The recommended food pairings in this book are guided by a basic principle: taking note of the style of beer and the focal flavour points, the beer is then paired to food with similar balance to either complement underlying flavours or contrast with them. Many pairings will have both elements and it is this interplay of flavours that creates intriguing and complex food and beer interactions.

ALES OF BRITISH OR IRISH ORIGIN

ALES OF BRITISH OR IRISH ORIGIN

Britain has had an indelible influence on modern beer styles. It is on these shoulders that so many other nations, brewers and fantastic beers now stand. Beers with origins in Britain and Ireland that are still produced on home turf retain distinctive differences from the same historic styles that have been adapted and translated to fit a new nation's tastes. Contemporary British and Irish brewers typically still guide their brewing processes along traditional lines, making beers today that mimic styles brewed decades before.

A crucial category of British beer is bitter, considered the nation's drink of choice. After ordinary bitter comes best bitter, and then strong/extra special bitter – amped up versions with added malt and hops and increased alcohol content. For the domestic British beer drinker, the latter are the favoured styles and, when in fine form, a definite English treat. While the term 'bitter' invokes images of assaulting assertive hops, bitters are well-balanced and in a camp far from the American pale ales and IPAs of such hop-based bitterness. It's not just the paler spectrum of beer on which Britain has had a notable influence. The rich English brown ale, the warming old ale and the deep, luscious porters and stouts have all been the cradles from which beers worldwide have been born.

Cask-conditioned ales remain a significant and unique ingredient of British beer culture, thanks in no small part to the Campaign for Real Ale (CAMRA), whose passionate work has helped to inspire a national cask-beer revival. The United Kingdom remains one of the few nations where ale is served directly from the cask it was aged in – at cellar temperatures and with no added carbonation – and using either the natural force of gravity or a pump to conjure it from the taps. This method of serving beer is beginning to gain some momentum in other countries as well. While great examples of British beers are exported to the four corners of the globe, to truly understand the greatness of these heritage-rich styles, one must experience them as they were meant to be: from the cask in a traditional pub.

North of the border, Scotland has long produced distinct ales that are as reflective of their home country as any style the world over. With a climate unsuited to growing hops, Scotland's rich, seductive ales are malt forward, complex, and warming – the perfect foil to a blustery Scottish eve. Scottish ales, sessionable and substantial, range in strength from the so-called 60-shilling to 80-shilling brews – the more expensive the better quality the beer, traditionally. Its stronger 90-shilling brother, the strong Scotch ale, or 'wee heavy', is a real sipper, as high in alcohol as it is in flavour, and now more commonly brewed outside of the United Kingdom.

It can be argued that no country is so represented by a single brewer than Ireland. The popularisation of Irish dry stout by the Guinness company has, over time, solidified into an eternal bond between a nation and a drink. It is said that no Guinness tastes so good as in Dublin at the original St. James's Gate Brewery. From that seed of brewing genius, foreign extra stout was spawned, an export to quench the thirst of the British Empire as it explored the vast corners of the world. Ireland's other beer of note is Irish red ale. Dubbed as such by the late beer expert and writer Michael Jackson, red ale's history and specific origin are hazy, but its fine examples are undeniably delicious.

English Golden

Origin: England
Colour: 3-9 SRM
ABV: 3.8-5%
IBU: 40-55
Glassware: pint, nonic pint

It's often said that necessity is the mother of invention. The hot English summer of 1995 called for the popularisation of this quenching brew, to rival the popularity of imported lagers.

INTENSELY QUENCHING

Also called summer ale, this refreshing beauty pours bright, light golden, and is topped with a thin layer of white. It looks perfectly refreshing – which is the intention, with a low ABV and a clean, cool hop bite. The nose is fresh and spicy. The flavour leans on the hops, but in true English fashion still maintains a core of biscuity maltiness. After a nicely hopped, intense body, the finish is long, clean and dry. A great summer beer served cooler than many English brews for a wonderfully thirst-quenching pint.

Three Beers to Try

HOP BACK SUMMER LIGHTNING This has a powerful aroma of peppery Goldings hops and citrus fruit, with lightly toasted malt, tart fruit and earthy hop resins on palate and finish.

CASTLE ROCK HARVEST PALE Brewed with three American hops and pale malt, this ale offers tart citrus fruit, biscuit malt and tangy hop resins.

CUMBRIAN LEGENDARY ALES LOWESWATER GOLD Brewed with pale malt and Brewers Gold hops, the creamy malt character is balanced by lemon fruit and cedar-like hops.

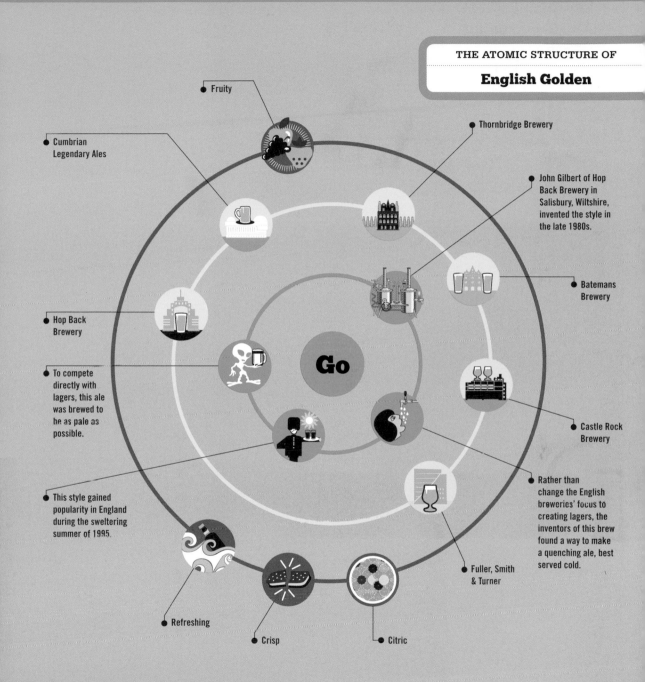

THE ATOMIC STRUCTURE OF

English Golden

Fruity

Thornbridge Brewery

Cumbrian
Legendary Ales

John Gilbert of Hop
Back Brewery in
Salisbury, Wiltshire,
invented the style in
the late 1980s.

Batemans
Brewery

Hop Back
Brewery

Go

To compete
directly with
lagers, this ale
was brewed to
he as pale as
possible.

Castle Rock
Brewery

This style gained
popularity in England
during the sweltering
summer of 1995.

Rather than
change the English
breweries' focus to
creating lagers, the
inventors of this brew
found a way to make
a quenching ale, best
served cold.

Fuller, Smith
& Turner

Refreshing

Crisp

Citric

Food Pairing

| Lightly spiced dishes | Salads | Seafood |

Ordinary Bitter

Origin: England
Colour: 4-14 SRM
ABV: 3-3.9%
IBU: 20-35
Glassware: pint, nonic pint

Anything but ordinary, this English staple has a strong history and a stronger following.

SURPRISINGLY COMPLEX

A beer drinker from outside of the United Kingdom may be reluctant to order a pint of anything dubbed 'ordinary', but there is very good reason to do so. The lightest in alcohol of the bitter family, this quite sessionable ale is served often – and best – from a cask in a quintessential English pub. It is bitter, but with a central, often caramelly, malt character. There are surprising complexities, especially when served on cask, that come through as spicy, peppery, and even grassy hop flavours. The hops make for a quenching body and end in a dry finish, with a smooth mouthfeel throughout. There is just a thin sheath of a head, typically off-white, and an ever-so-slight level of carbonation. Colour ranges from light orange to amber.

Three Beers to Try

CONISTON BLUEBIRD BITTER   A great example of the style, Bluebird pours golden amber, with a thinly layered head. There are notes of caramel blended with floral hops and a dry finish.

ADNAMS SOUTHWOLD BITTER   Brewed by Adnams since 1967, this is a classic in the brewer's core lineup. Copper in colour, lingering floral hops in taste.

TRIPLE FFF ALTON'S PRIDE   Brewed with pale and cara gold malts and First Gold and Northdown hops, this beer has a resinous, nutty character with a hint of butterscotch.

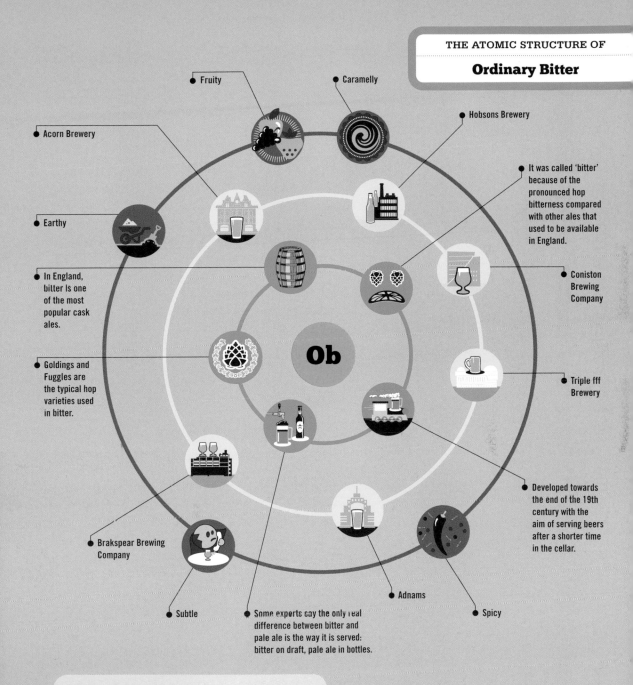

THE ATOMIC STRUCTURE OF
Ordinary Bitter

Ob

Fruity

Caramelly

Hobsons Brewery

Acorn Brewery

It was called 'bitter' because of the pronounced hop bitterness compared with other ales that used to be available in England.

Earthy

Coniston Brewing Company

In England, bitter is one of the most popular cask ales.

Goldings and Fuggles are the typical hop varieties used in bitter.

Triple fff Brewery

Brakspear Brewing Company

Developed towards the end of the 19th century with the aim of serving beers after a shorter time in the cellar.

Subtle

Adnams

Spicy

Some experts say the only real difference between bitter and pale ale is the way it is served: bitter on draft, pale ale in bottles.

Food Pairing

| Lightly spiced Thai food | Mild English cheese | Seafood | Shepherd's pie | Bangers and mash |

Best Bitter

Origin: England
Colour: 5-16 SRM
ABV: 3.8-4.6%
IBU: 25-40
Glassware: pint,
nonic pint

The middle child of the bitter family, the best bitter is traditionally just that – the brewery's finest crafted brew.

A BALANCED CORE

Stuck between ordinary and extra special, this style compiles the best from both siblings, producing a remarkably drinkable, strong-but-sessionable English ale. It is generally medium gold to copper and quite clear, with a thin head that lingers just slightly above a minimally carbonated body. While maintaining an overarching theme of bitterness, it has an elevated maltiness when compared to ordinary bitter. Best bitter can be caramelly and fruity, but is always well-balanced. At times quite filling, this beer quenches while it satisfies. A favourite in England, this delicious brew is best savoured on cask at an English pub!

Three Beers to Try

 FULLER'S LONDON PRIDE Smooth and characteristically balanced, the herbal, floral hops meld deliciously into the malt base. Perfectly sessionable.

 TIMOTHY TAYLOR'S LANDLORD Multi-award-winning beer from Yorkshire, with an intense bitterness achieved by circulating the hopped wort over a deep bed of Styrian Goldings.

 SKINNER'S BETTY STOGS Cornish malt and English and Slovenian hops combine to produce a beer with rich biscuit and fruity bitterness on the aroma, followed by juicy malt and tangy hops in the finish.

THE ATOMIC STRUCTURE OF

Best Bitter

The greatest number of bitters produced are best bitters.
Caramelly
Timothy Taylor & Co.
Skinner's Brewery
Also sometimes called special or premium bitter.
Earthy
Mordue Brewery
100%
Bb
1
This style is often the finest product in the brewery's overall bitter lineup.
Fresh hops
In England, the bitter family is most typically served on cask as a 'real ale'. Real ales are conditioned in the cask, imparting a light carbonation, and are served at cellar temperature – coaxing out complexities unmatched by a bottle of the same.
Drinkable
Uley Brewery
Hogs Back Brewery
Fuller, Smith & Turner
Well-balanced
Within England, specific geography plays a significant role in the prominent flavours of bitters.

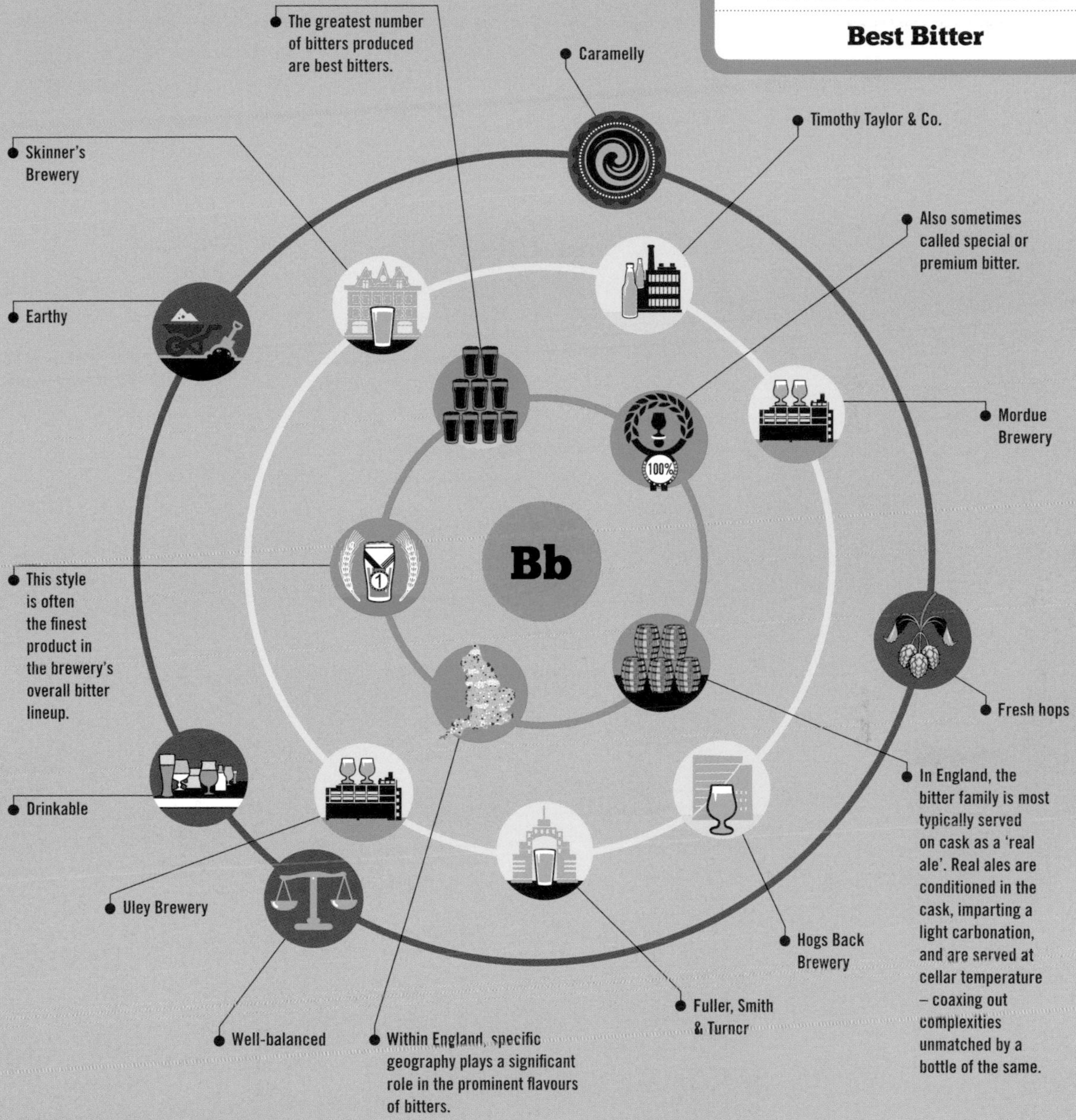

Food Pairing

Roast chicken	Curry	Blue cheese

Strong/Extra Special Bitter

Origin: England
Colour: 6–18 SRM
ABV: 4.6–6.2%
IBU: 30–50
Glassware: pint, nonic pint

The biggest of the bitter bunch, this fine brew climbs the ABV scale, but maintains drinkability – gaining an enhanced complexity from the elevated amount of raw materials used.

CROWN JEWELS

If it were just about names, extra special bitter would get all the attention. It would be the belle of the ball and poor, old ordinary bitter would be the wallflower. But in truth, extra special stands on the shoulders of ordinary, with just enough added hops, malt and alcohol to be fitting for the title. While the style is broad, the typical strong bitter is medium-bodied, complex and well-balanced. They can be as light as gold or as dark as copper, and are usually capped with a layer of white foam. Despite more full hop and malt flavour than other bitters, they still come in fairly drinkable. Typically chock-full of fresh English hops, they are balanced by the rich, nutty malts so critical to a true English brew. In some, dark fruits and spice enter in both aroma and taste.

Three Beers to Try

MOORHOUSE'S PENDLE WITCHES BREW   Pale bronze beer with pale and crystal malts and Fuggles hops, offering vanilla and pear-like fruit, balanced by spicy hops.

YORK CENTURION'S GHOST   Three hops and three malts combine in this beer to produce roasted grain, chocolate and berry fruits aromas and flavours.

FULLER'S ESB   One of the first of the style to export to America, its influence abroad is ongoing and far-reaching. A fruit-caramel blend on the nose, the body is full-flavoured and bursting with English hoppiness.

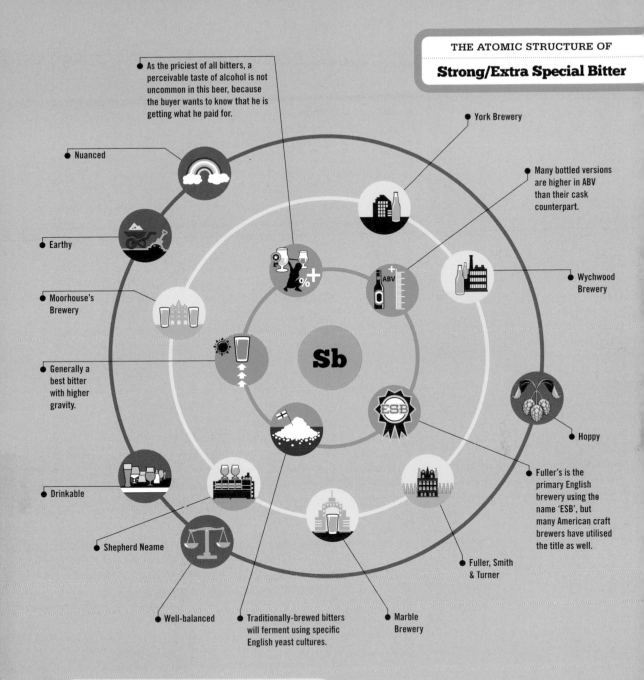

THE ATOMIC STRUCTURE OF

Strong/Extra Special Bitter

Sb

As the priciest of all bitters, a perceivable taste of alcohol is not uncommon in this beer, because the buyer wants to know that he is getting what he paid for.

Nuanced

Earthy

Moorhouse's Brewery

Generally a best bitter with higher gravity.

Drinkable

Shepherd Neame

Well-balanced

Traditionally-brewed bitters will ferment using specific English yeast cultures.

Marble Brewery

Fuller, Smith & Turner

York Brewery

Many bottled versions are higher in ABV than their cask counterpart.

Wychwood Brewery

Hoppy

Fuller's is the primary English brewery using the name 'ESB', but many American craft brewers have utilised the title as well.

Food Pairing

| Pork | Full-flavoured pasta | Game meats | Curry | Strong blue cheese |

Pale Ale

**Origin: England
Colour: 5–14 SRM
ABV: 3.8–6.2%
IBU: 20–50
Glassware: pint,
nonic pint**

Once dubbed 'pale' simply because it wasn't dark, pale ale has now become a style with boundaries as wide as the world that brews it.

BITTER'S BIGGER BROTHER

English pale ale has been described as a bottled bitter. While the distinctions between these two styles can be ever so slight, there are a few. Generally, a member of the pale ale family is bigger, stronger and more substantial than its brother in the bitter family. A glass of pale ale can be golden to deep orange to amber. The head is most consistently off-white and thin – just a fine layer remaining through the life of the pint. On the nose, sweet, caramel notes are mixed with spicy or herbal hop aromas. On first sip, there is a blend of nutty and toasted malts and a solid hop bitterness, but dark fruits, sweetness and caramel can be present as well. Its smooth body has a lingering, clean finish. For American pale ale, see page 176.

Three Beers to Try

ADNAMS GHOST SHIP Stunning beer from Adnams with violets, citrus fruit and 'malt biscuit' grain on aroma and a palate with dry and bitter finish.

DARK STAR AMERICAN PALE ALE Three American hops and a yeast culture from the US help produce Dark Star's fruity beer.

MARSTON'S PEDIGREE Classic Burton pale ale fermented in oak casks. Sulphur on the nose is followed by spicy hops, apple fruit and a dry, salty finish.

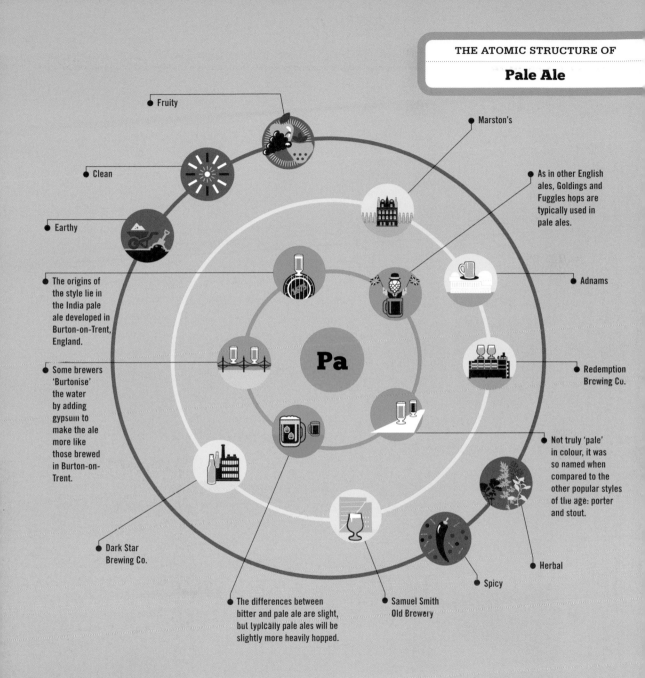

Pale Ale

Fruity

Clean

Earthy

Marston's

As in other English ales, Goldings and Fuggles hops are typically used in pale ales.

Adnams

The origins of the style lie in the India pale ale developed in Burton-on-Trent, England.

Some brewers 'Burtonise' the water by adding gypsum to make the ale more like those brewed in Burton-on-Trent.

Pa

Redemption Brewing Co.

Not truly 'pale' in colour, it was so named when compared to the other popular styles of the age: porter and stout.

Dark Star Brewing Co.

Herbal

Spicy

The differences between bitter and pale ale are slight, but typically pale ales will be slightly more heavily hopped.

Samuel Smith Old Brewery

Food Pairing

| English cheese | Grilled meats | Cream-based pasta dishes | White fish |

India Pale Ale

Origin: England
Colour: 6–14 SRM
ABV: 4.5–7.5%
IBU: 40–60
Glassware: pint, nonic pint

IPAs have become a significant feature of the craft beer world. English IPAs, however, differ greatly from their American cousins.

HOPS AND MORE HOPS

With a past littered with myth and legend, the truth about India pale ale's history is hazy. As a thirsty beer drinker, however, you only need to know a few simple things. It is hoppy – generously, bitterly and sometimes assaultingly so. The English style of IPA is earthy, spicy and herbal, with a solid malt backbone that, while obviously present, takes a backseat to the hops. In fine examples, the hops aren't simple, but layered with distinct spice – separate, but working in perfect orchestration and harmony. It is scented with spice and herbal hops, yet also has an undercurrent of malt. English IPAs can be intensely bitter with a long, lingering finish.

Three Beers to Try

FULLER'S BENGAL LANCER   Fuller's faithful recreation of a 19th century IPA with pale and crystal malts, Fuggles, Goldings and Target hops.

ST AUSTELL PROPER JOB   *Proper job* means 'well done' in the Cornish dialect and St Austell deserves the praise for this superb IPA brewed with local barley malt and three American hops.

THORNBRIDGE JAIPUR IPA   Maris Otter pale malt combines with Cascade and Chinook hops to produce a beer packed with juicy malt, tart fruit and bitter hop resins.

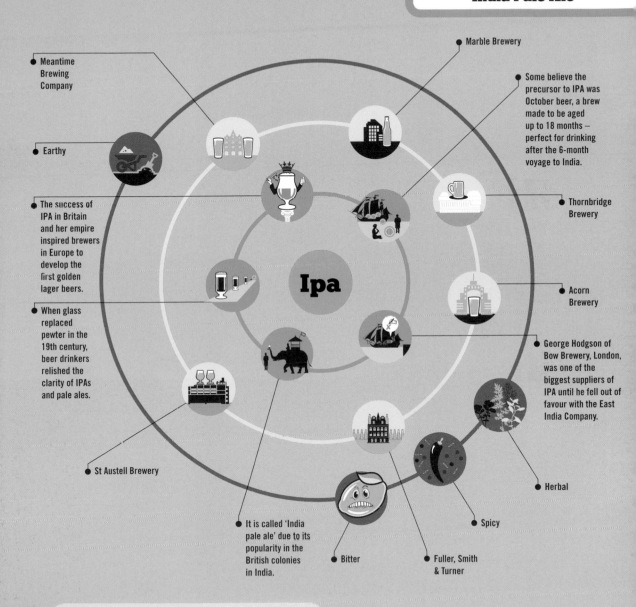

Marble Brewery

Meantime Brewing Company

Some believe the precursor to IPA was October beer, a brew made to be aged up to 18 months — perfect for drinking after the 6-month voyage to India.

Earthy

The success of IPA in Britain and her empire inspired brewers in Europe to develop the first golden lager beers.

Thornbridge Brewery

Ipa

When glass replaced pewter in the 19th century, beer drinkers relished the clarity of IPAs and pale ales.

Acorn Brewery

George Hodgson of Bow Brewery, London, was one of the biggest suppliers of IPA until he fell out of favour with the East India Company.

St Austell Brewery

Herbal

Spicy

It is called 'India pale ale' due to its popularity in the British colonies in India.

Bitter

Fuller, Smith & Turner

Food Pairing

| Spicy food | Carrot cake | Thai food | Curry | Aged Cheddar |

Light/Pale Mild

Origin: England
Colour: 8–17 SRM
ABV: 2.8–4%
IBU: 10–20
Glassware: pint, nonic pint

The characteristic thread of English maltiness weaves its way through this style, but the tell-tale hops of the bitter family manifest here slightly softer and more restrained.

ENGLAND'S OLD FAVOURITE

What used to be a house favourite, on tap at every pub across the English countryside in the 1960s, has seen drastic decline in the last several decades. This softer, less hoppy brew has relinquished much of its former following to bitters. However, these low-alcohol, light-coloured ales are perfect session brews and still have a place in the English beer family. They have experienced a recent resurgence and are quite fittingly served on cask. Without a great variety of specific distinctions, this style is pleasant, often with lightly fruity notes mixing harmoniously with the soft, English-style hops. The malt backbone is consistent and sturdy, without being overpowering.

Three Beers to Try

TIMOTHY TAYLOR'S GOLDEN BEST Light amber and clear, a slight aroma of bready malts mix with fruit. Light in body, it is refreshing and quaffable.

MCMULLEN'S AK This is a classic light mild, brewed at McMullen's family brewery with pale malt and a touch of chocolate malt. Rich and fruity with a gentle hop character balancing juicy malt.

OLD CHIMNEYS RAGGED ROBIN Amber coloured, it has a sharp lemon and tangerine aroma and palate with a gentle but persistent balance of floral hops. There's a hint of caramel in the finish.

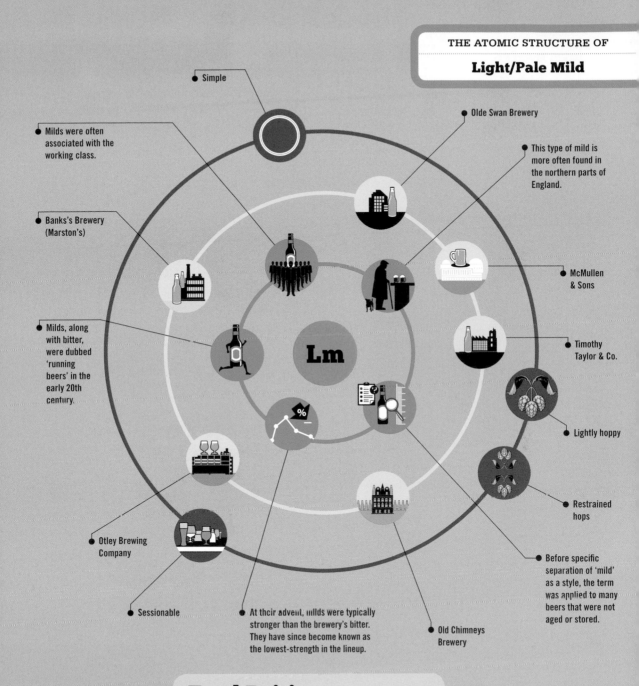

Simple

Milds were often associated with the working class.

Banks's Brewery (Marston's)

Milds, along with bitter, were dubbed 'running beers' in the early 20th century.

Otley Brewing Company

Sessionable

At their advent, milds were typically stronger than the brewery's bitter. They have since become known as the lowest-strength in the lineup.

Olde Swan Brewery

This type of mild is more often found in the northern parts of England.

McMullen & Sons

Timothy Taylor & Co.

Lightly hoppy

Restrained hops

Before specific separation of 'mild' as a style, the term was applied to many beers that were not aged or stored.

Old Chimneys Brewery

Lm

Food Pairing

| Shellfish | Salad | Light chicken dishes | Curry |

Irish Red Ale

Origin: Ireland
Colour: 9–18 SRM
ABV: 4–6%
IBU: 17–28
Glassware: pint, nonic pint

This brew has mostly been overshadowed by stout, Ireland's signature style, but the lesser-known Irish red ale deserves a place on any beer lover's list.

WARM COLOUR, RICH FLAVOUR

With its rich red pour, one can immediately see this beer's potential. The colour is a hearty blend of bronze, amber and even edges of blood orange. The head is an advertisement for the malt, looking rich, frothy and tan. And yet, an undercurrent of light, earthy hops comes off on the nose as well. From the scent to the body and taste, this brew is a well-rounded, balanced treat. It has decent body and a moderate level of carbonation followed by a typically roasted, dry finish. On the palate, there are light hops and toasted or caramel notes in many examples of the style. It's an easy-drinking pint, one that can be enjoyed with a warm, hearty meal, or as a meal itself.

Three Beers to Try

CARLOW O'HARA'S IRISH RED A complex beer with a big roasted grain and herbal and spicy hops character.

FRANCISCAN WELL REBEL RED Brewed with a large proportion of crystal malt, with East Kent Goldings and Fuggles, it has bitter orange fruit, caramel and grassy hops on aroma and palate.

PORTERHOUSE RED With three bars in Dublin plus a brewery, Porterhouse kick-started the Irish beer revival. This offering is big and assertively hoppy for the style.

THE ATOMIC STRUCTURE OF

Irish Red Ale

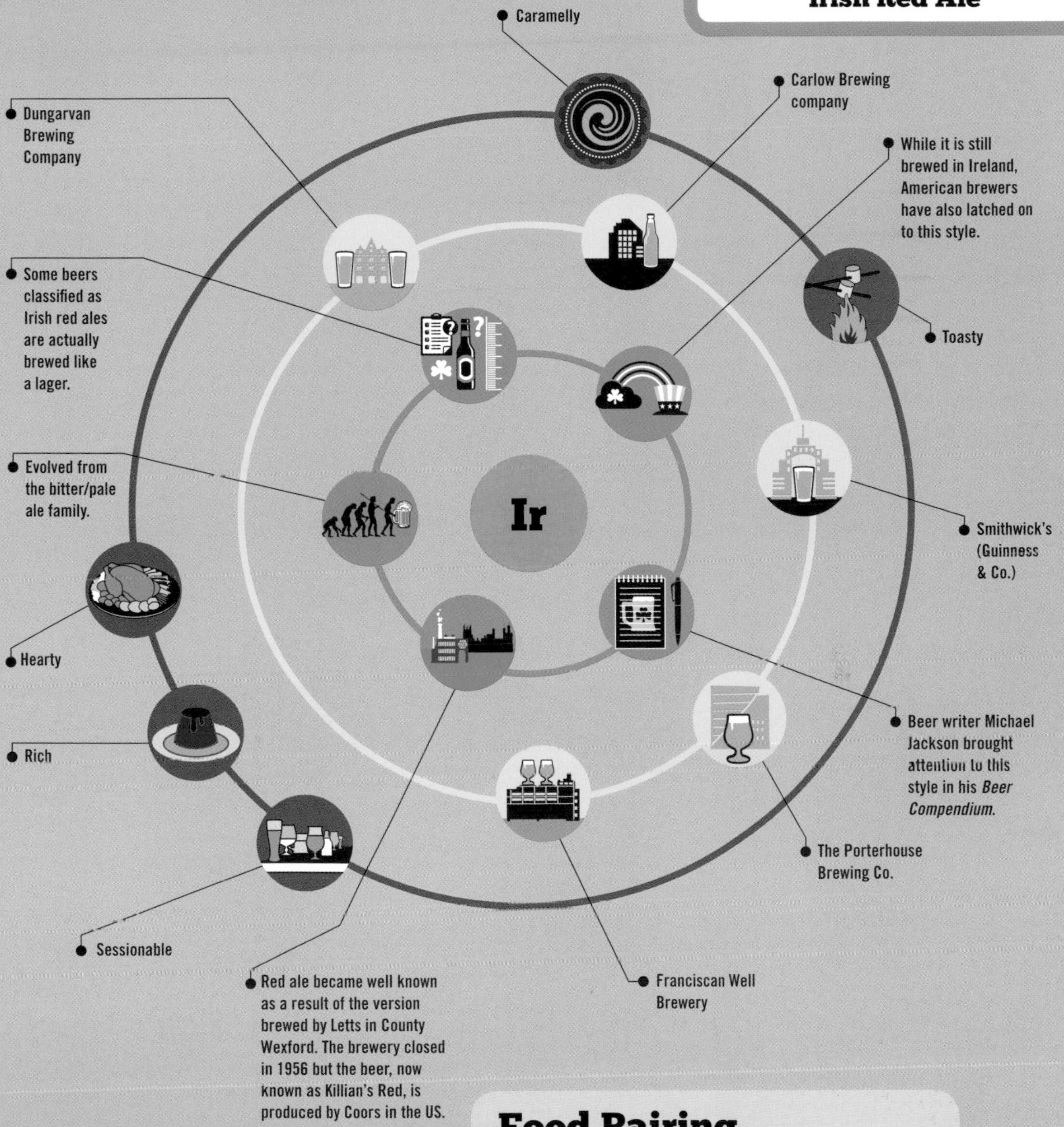

Caramelly

Carlow Brewing company

While it is still brewed in Ireland, American brewers have also latched on to this style.

Dungarvan Brewing Company

Toasty

Some beers classified as Irish red ales are actually brewed like a lager.

Ir

Smithwick's (Guinness & Co.)

Evolved from the bitter/pale ale family.

Hearty

Beer writer Michael Jackson brought attention to this style in his *Beer Compendium*.

Rich

The Porterhouse Brewing Co.

Sessionable

Red ale became well known as a result of the version brewed by Letts in County Wexford. The brewery closed in 1956 but the beer, now known as Killian's Red, is produced by Coors in the US.

Franciscan Well Brewery

Food Pairing

| Pork | Shepherd's pie | Beef stew |

Scottish Ales

Sociable beers with subtle nuances, Scottish ales are founded on smooth, rich maltiness.

MAKING THE MOST OF THE CLIMATE

Typically pouring amber to dark ruby, a pint of Scottish ale screams malt. And for good reason: Scotland's climate precludes the growth of hops, naturally encouraging brewers to accentuate what is more easily available. A solid crown of off-white to light brown laces down the glass. The base is solidly set on the malts, with some examples displaying notes of caramel, light chocolate, vanilla, dark fruits, sweetness and sometimes even slight smokiness. A medium body makes for a sessionable yet substantial brew, perfectly matched for cool weather. A finish of light hops bitterness is not uncommon – enough for balance, but generally understated. The ales are traditionally classified '60/-' or 'light'; '70/-' or 'heavy'; '80/-' or 'export'. For '90/-' ales also called 'wee heavy', turn to strong Scotch ale on page 42.

Three Beers to Try

STEWART'S 80 SHILLING A fine interpretation of a true '80 bob' with chocolate, crystal and cara malts alongside pale, along with four hops. It has roasted grain and burnt fruit on aroma and palate.

ORKNEY DARK ISLAND Dark red-brown with a well-layered nose of roast malt, chocolate, earth and slight peat, this lightly hopped Orkney Brewery beer has a dry finish.

HIGHLAND SCAPA SPECIAL Highland Brewery's pale ale is named after Scapa Flow Viking harbour in the Orkney Islands. It offers citrus fruit and herbal aromas with honeyed malt.

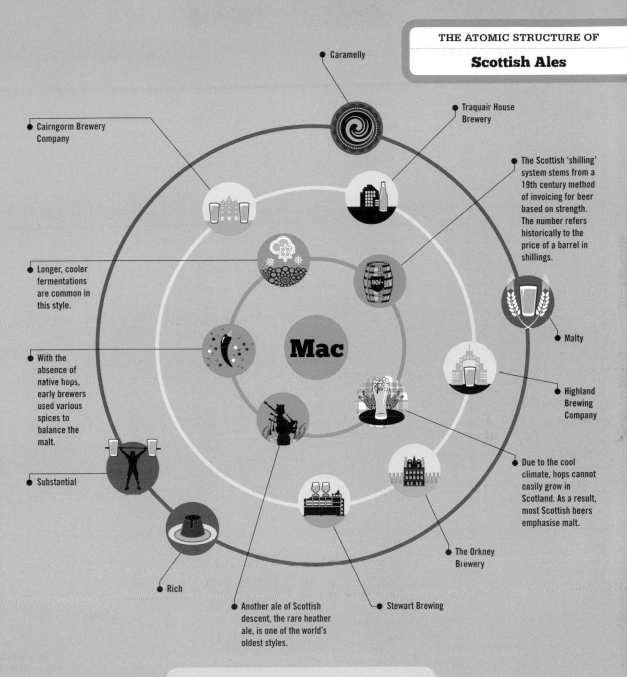

THE ATOMIC STRUCTURE OF

Scottish Ales

Caramelly

Traquair House Brewery

Cairngorm Brewery Company

The Scottish 'shilling' system stems from a 19th century method of invoicing for beer based on strength. The number refers historically to the price of a barrel in shillings.

Longer, cooler fermentations are common in this style.

Malty

Mac

With the absence of native hops, early brewers used various spices to balance the malt.

Highland Brewing Company

Substantial

Due to the cool climate, hops cannot easily grow in Scotland. As a result, most Scottish beers emphasise malt.

Rich

The Orkney Brewery

Another ale of Scottish descent, the rare heather ale, is one of the world's oldest styles.

Stewart Brewing

Food Pairing

| Lamb chops | Mild cheeses | Arbroath smokies | Haggis |

English Barley Wine

Origin: England
Colour: 8–22 SRM
ABV: 8–12%
IBU: 35–70
Glassware: snifter

Big and bold, yet also subtle and soft, barley wines are the perfect contradiction and make a beautiful evening sipper.

MOUTH-FILLING AND MALTY

Prepare yourself. With an ABV of up to 12 per cent and complexities in every category, barley wines can be unexpected and delicious. The colours vary, but typically it is medium-dark, with some examples starting on the orange side of amber and others creeping towards mahogany. It has a bit of a head, but not one to linger, and veils, just for a moment, the blend of incredible aromas below – from caramel to dark fruits, spices, apples, toffee and oak. The palate can show just as vast an array, with a mouthfeel that is smooth, coating and chewy. There is a balance, but typically the malt nuances shine.

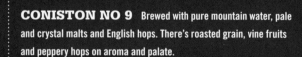

Three Beers to Try

CONISTON NO 9 Brewed with pure mountain water, pale and crystal malts and English hops. There's roasted grain, vine fruits and peppery hops on aroma and palate.

BURTON BRIDGE TICKLE BRAIN Tickle brain is a Shakespearean term for someone who overindulges, so sip this beer with reverence.

FULLER'S VINTAGE ALE This beer is brewed annually and will improve in bottle over several years. English malts and hops combine to produce a beer with woody, orange fruit and spicy hop notes.

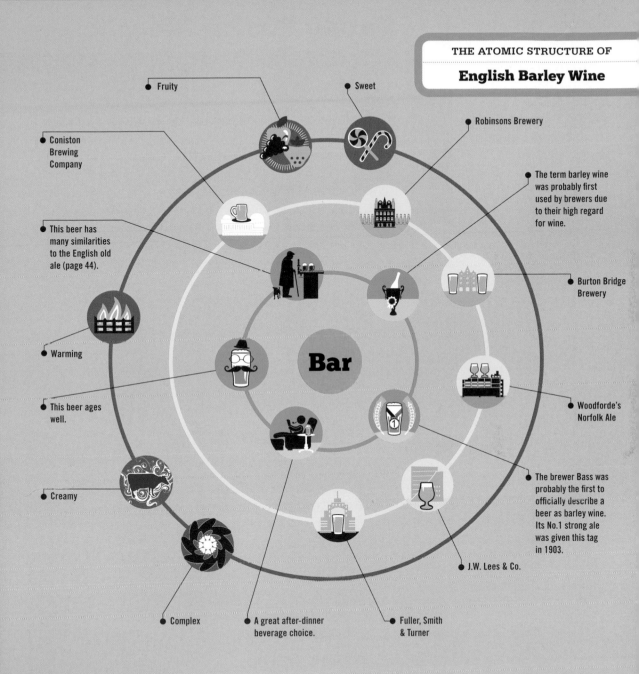

THE ATOMIC STRUCTURE OF
English Barley Wine

Fruity

Sweet

Robinsons Brewery

Coniston
Brewing
Company

The term barley wine
was probably first
used by brewers due
to their high regard
for wine.

This beer has
many similarities
to the English old
ale (page 44).

Burton Bridge
Brewery

Warming

Bar

This beer ages
well.

Woodforde's
Norfolk Ale

Creamy

The brewer Bass was
probably the first to
officially describe a
beer as barley wine.
Its No.1 strong ale
was given this tag
in 1903.

J.W. Lees & Co.

Complex

A great after-dinner
beverage choice.

Fuller, Smith
& Turner

Food Pairing

Stilton cheese	Bread pudding	Hearty foods	Goat's cheese	Crème brûlée

Strong Scotch Ale

Origin: Scotland
Colour: 14–25 SRM
ABV: 6.5–10%
IBU: 17–35
Glassware: thistle, tulip, snifter

Also known as 'wee heavy', this ale has a thick, creamy mouthfeel and layer upon layer of rich malts. It is a beer that stands alone and makes a perfect after-dinner sipper.

SWEET WITHOUT BEING CLOYING

As the glass fills up you can tell it is a rich, sweet, undeniably intriguing brew. Aromas of toffee, malt, fruits and caramel are common and mouth-watering. The head is dense and light brown and sits on a body of copper to deep brown, with edges and accents of amber. The mouthfeel is full-bodied, juicy and often viscous, but with just a slight bite of hops to avoid an unpleasant cloying feel. The relatively high alcohol content is warming and appropriately gauged to keep the drinker at a pace that ensures pure enjoyment without excess.

Three Beers to Try

ISLE OF SKYE CUILLIN BEAST A 7% ABV ale packed with ripe fruits, toasted grain and peppery hops with a powerful hint of caramel: a beer to deter the winter chill.

BROUGHTON OLD JOCK This beer is a rare example of wee heavy, brewed with pale malt and roasted barley and hopped with three English varieties. It delivers vine fruits, roasted grain and spicy hops.

ORKNEY SKULL SPLITTER This island ale is well-balanced, smooth, creamy and dry. It is named for the 7th Viking Earl of Orkney – and maybe for its 8.5% ABV.

THE ATOMIC STRUCTURE OF
Strong Scotch Ale

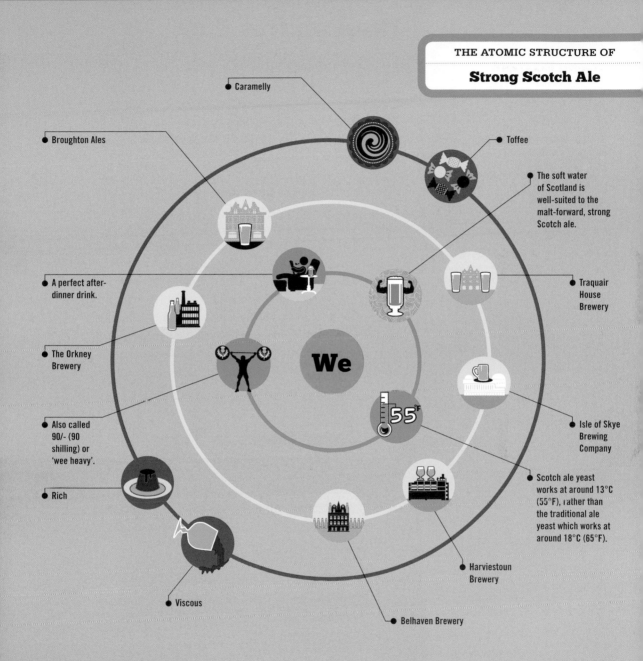

Caramelly

Broughton Ales

Toffee

The soft water of Scotland is well-suited to the malt-forward, strong Scotch ale.

A perfect after-dinner drink.

Traquair House Brewery

The Orkney Brewery

We

Also called 90/- (90 shilling) or 'wee heavy'.

Isle of Skye Brewing Company

55°F

Rich

Scotch ale yeast works at around 13°C (55°F), rather than the traditional ale yeast which works at around 18°C (65°F).

Harviestoun Brewery

Viscous

Belhaven Brewery

Food Pairing

| Heavy desserts | Crème brûlée | Mild cheese | Game | Beef ribs |

English Old Ale

Origin: England
Colour: 10–30 SRM
ABV: 4.5–6%
IBU: 30–60
Glassware: snifter, pint

Old ale has become a catch-all category for many sweet and complex beers, but was historically a beer that was aged for months to achieve myriad complexities.

A RICH AND INTRIGUING BREW

Likely a descendent of the historic Burton ale, old ales tend to be sweeter and darker than barley wines, with less hopping. In colour, they vary widely, from pale amber to dark ruby. They have layers of flavour that span the palate: treacle, raisins, dark fruits, nuts, chocolate and molasses in the darker versions, and tart fruit and spicy hops in the lighter. Often sherry and port-like notes appear in both flavour and feel and hints of leather and tobacco further intensify the experience. The texture is critical and often intriguing. Chewy, vinous and intense, old ales can make for great, sipping brews that finish with an alcoholic warmth.

Three Beers to Try

THEAKSTON OLD PECULIER   The yardstick of the style, this beer by Theakston is a mix of sweet caramel, dark fruits and chocolate. Earthy hops balance the malts and it finishes dry.

DURHAM EVENSONG   A recreation of a 1930s beer using five malts and three English hops. Toasted malts, dark fruits and floral hop aromas and flavours.

HOBSONS OLD HENRY   A tangy, fruity ale with toffee notes and a drying bitterness.

THE ATOMIC STRUCTURE OF

English Old Ale

Dark fruity esters
Sweet
The Durham Brewery
George Gale & Co. (Fuller, Smith & Turner)
This style typically ages wonderfully and makes for interesting comparisons after periods of cellaring.
Vinous
A close kin to barley wine.
Harviestoun Brewery
Eo
Also known as stock, strong or stale ale.
Daniel Thwaites
Originally, much of the character of old ales came from the *Brettanomyces* yeast present in the barrels.
Chewy
Hobsons Brewery
T&R Theakston
Traditionally used as stock ale to blend with a younger beer before serving.

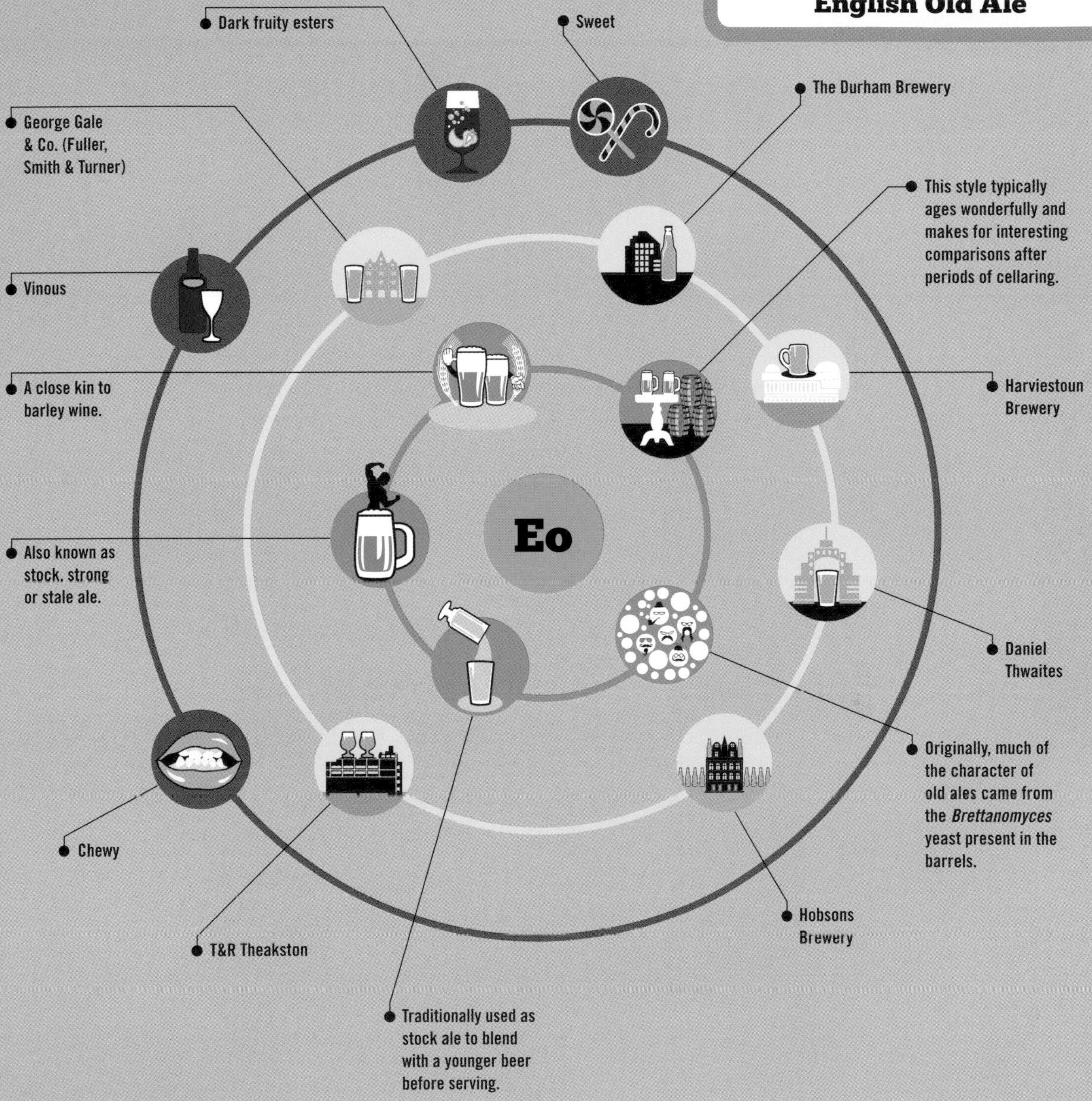

Food Pairing

Roast beef	Roast game	Stilton cheese	Serve as a digestif

English Strong Old Ale

Origin: England
Colour: 8–22 SRM
ABV: 6.5–12%
IBU: 20–75
Glassware: snifter

In many ways similar to English barley wine, English strong old ale takes on a darker hue and a rich, malty character.

BIG, BOLD AND SATISFYING

While distinct differences separate English barley wine and English old ale, this style bridges the gap, borrowing characteristics from both of its sister styles. Dark like old ale, but strong like barley wine, the end result is a palpable depth and complexity. Hops are typically slight, but perhaps present as an earthy bitterness. There can be a fruitiness that lends to the mix of flavours as well as a big malty sweetness. Varied notes of caramel, vanilla, raisins, plums, wood, earth and spices are just a few of the many potential nuances found in this style. Overall, rich and viscous, these deliciously big brews are practically a meal in themselves!

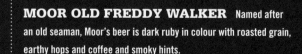

Three Beers to Try

MOOR OLD FREDDY WALKER   Named after an old seaman, Moor's beer is dark ruby in colour with roasted grain, earthy hops and coffee and smoky hints.

GALE'S PRIZE OLD ALE   Close in style to a lambic, Gale's 10% ABV beer is acidic, with flavours of roasted grain, toffee, vinous fruit and a spritzy, lightly-hopped finish.

BLUE ANCHOR SPINGO SPECIAL   This ancient Cornish brewpub uses just pale malt and one hop to produce a massively fruity ale with earthy and spicy hop resins.

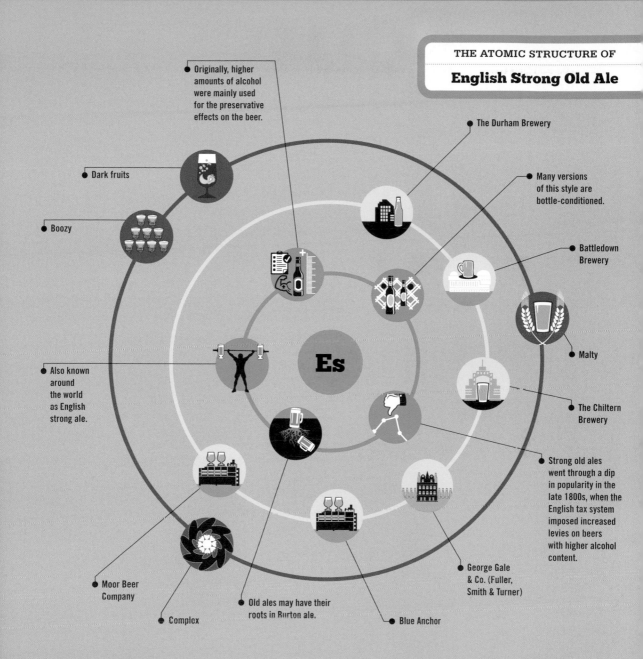

Originally, higher amounts of alcohol were mainly used for the preservative effects on the beer.

Dark fruits

Boozy

The Durham Brewery

Many versions of this style are bottle-conditioned.

Battledown Brewery

Malty

Also known around the world as English strong ale.

The Chiltern Brewery

Strong old ales went through a dip in popularity in the late 1800s, when the English tax system imposed increased levies on beers with higher alcohol content.

Es

Moor Beer Company

Complex

Old ales may have their roots in Burton ale.

Blue Anchor

George Gale & Co. (Fuller, Smith & Turner)

Food Pairing

| Heavy stews | Grilled game meats | Stilton cheese | Rich desserts |

Winter Warmer

Origin: England
Colour: 18–22 SRM
ABV: 4.4–7.5%
IBU: 30–50
Glassware: pint

The aroma of gingerbread, mulling spices and freshly baked treats evoke images of warm fires and Christmas tidings. A winter warmer is a beer fitting for just such a time.

COOKIES AND SPICE

Nutmeg, cinnamon, cloves and allspice. While it may sound like a recipe for Christmas biscuits or festive gingerbread, it is actually the list of spices you may encounter on the bouquet and palate of a winter warmer. The style is most often dark in colour, ranging from deep amber to dark brown and topped with a well-suited beige head. The inviting nose is a well-crafted blend of spices, mixed with malts and typically lacking any hoppiness. Winter warmers are rich in mouthfeel and flavour, a chewy maltiness and scattered dark fruits are not uncommon.

Three Beers to Try

VALE GOOD KING SENSELESS This winter offering includes chocolate malt and four hops. It's fruity and malty but with a gentle underpinning of peppery hops.

GRAIN WINTER SPICE Ruby coloured ale flavoured with orange peel and spices. It's aged for a month and has a fruity, spicy appeal with hints of spice and chocolate.

YOUNG'S WINTER WARMER Pale and crystal malts, dark brewing sugar and Fuggles and Goldings hops combine to produce a port wine, toffee, caramel and spicy delight.

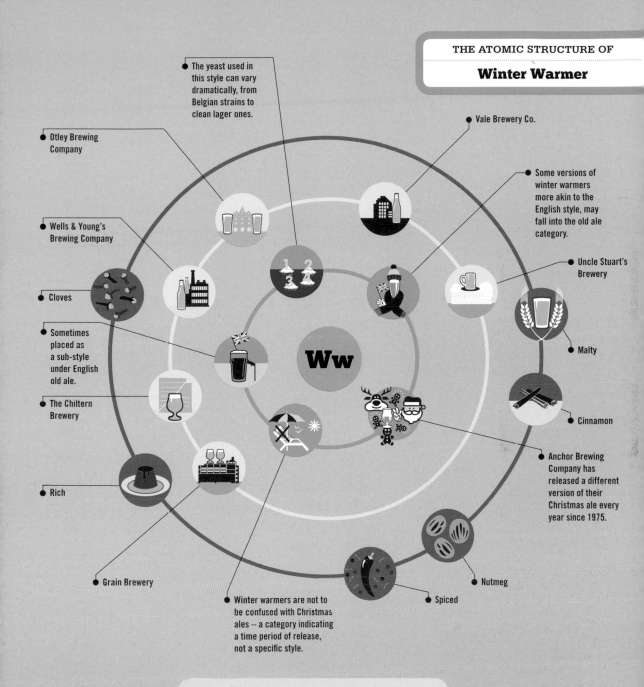

The yeast used in this style can vary dramatically, from Belgian strains to clean lager ones.

Otley Brewing Company

Vale Brewery Co.

Some versions of winter warmers more akin to the English style, may fall into the old ale category.

Wells & Young's Brewing Company

Uncle Stuart's Brewery

Cloves

Sometimes placed as a sub-style under English old ale.

Malty

The Chiltern Brewery

Cinnamon

Rich

Anchor Brewing Company has released a different version of their Christmas ale every year since 1975.

Grain Brewery

Ww

Winter warmers are not to be confused with Christmas ales — a category indicating a time period of release, not a specific style.

Nutmeg

Spiced

Food Pairing

| Roast meats | Robust cheeses | Spiced desserts | Apple pie |

Dark Mild

**Origin: England
Colour: 15–34 SRM
ABV: 2.8–5%
IBU: 10–25
Glassware: pint,
nonic pint**

As a low-gravity beer, sessionable but well-built, dark milds are the perfect accompaniment to a hearty lunch.

PLEASINGLY MELLOW

In true English beer-naming fashion, mild is an understated style. With a low ABV, but still flavourful and solid, this beer becomes the perfect choice for many occasions. This mellow, almost flat, ruby/dark-coloured brew is a chameleon of style. It is said that "if the brewer calls it a mild – then, by Jove, it is". Generally speaking, hops are on the light side and malts are prevalent, bringing roasty, chocolatey notes. The best of the dark mild family are low in alcohol, but still flavourful, rich and interesting beers.

Three Beers to Try

MOORHOUSE'S BLACK CAT Chocolate malt and Fuggles hops combine to produce a beer with rich dark fruit, spicy hops and chocolate/coffee undertones.

ELGOOD'S BLACK DOG Pale and crystal malts and Fuggles hops combine in this succulent mild. It offers roasted grain, vinous fruit and earthy hops.

MIGHTY OAK OSCAR WILDE This Essex brewery uses Cockney rhyming slang (Oscar Wilde = mild) in this 3.7% ABV beer with chocolate malt providing a rich, full flavour backed by spicy Challenger hops.

THE ATOMIC STRUCTURE OF
Dark Mild

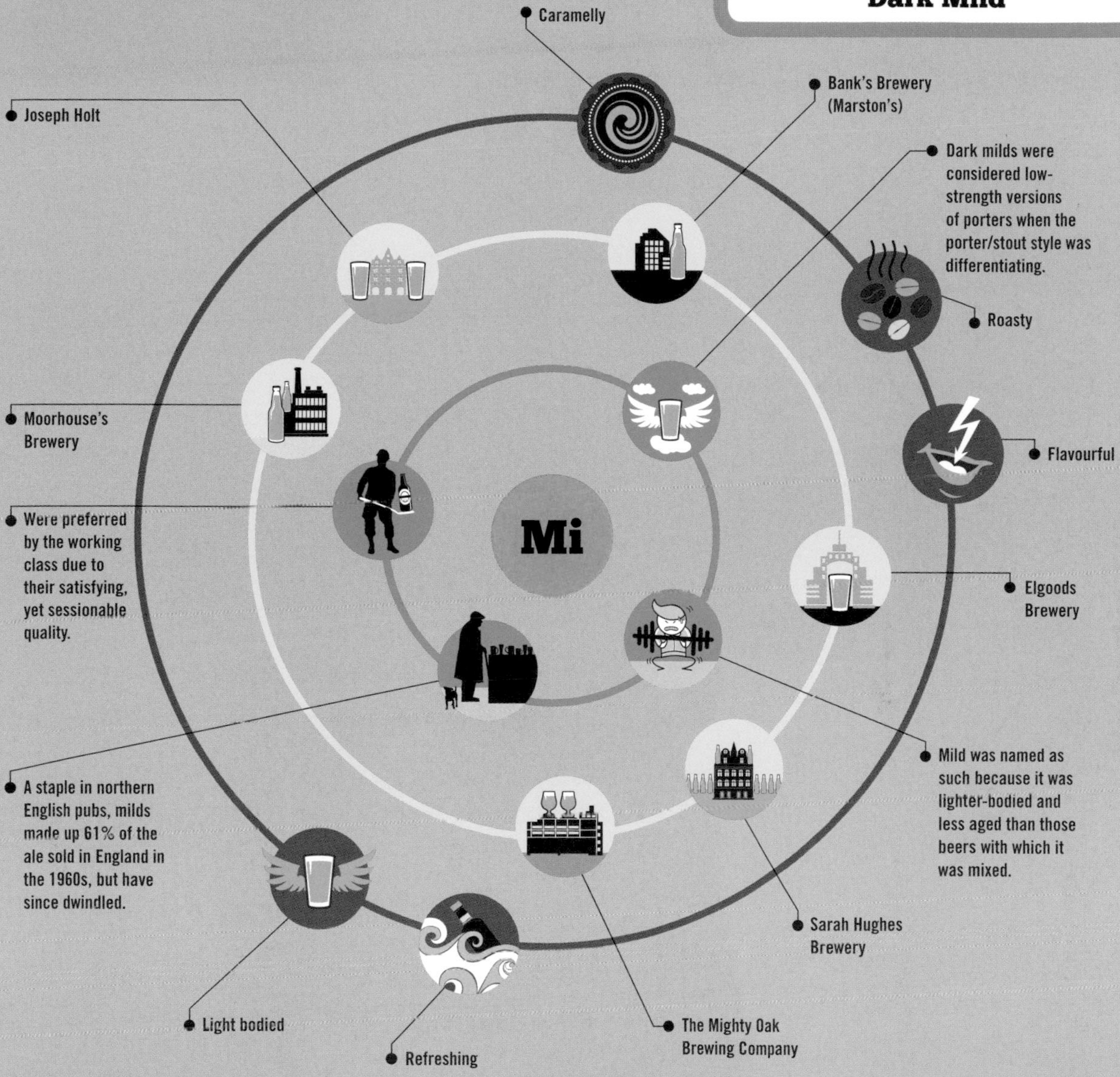

Caramelly

Joseph Holt

Bank's Brewery
(Marston's)

Dark milds were
considered low-
strength versions
of porters when the
porter/stout style was
differentiating.

Roasty

Moorhouse's
Brewery

Flavourful

Were preferred
by the working
class due to
their satisfying,
yet sessionable
quality.

Mi

Elgoods
Brewery

Mild was named as
such because it was
lighter-bodied and
less aged than those
beers with which it
was mixed.

A staple in northern
English pubs, milds
made up 61% of the
ale sold in England in
the 1960s, but have
since dwindled.

Sarah Hughes
Brewery

Light bodied

The Mighty Oak
Brewing Company

Refreshing

Food Pairing

| Barbecue | Cured meats | Meat sandwiches | Mushroom dishes | Cassoulet |

English Brown Ale

Origin: England
Colour: 12–35 SRM
ABV: 3–6%
IBU: 12–30
Glassware: pint, nonic pint

Originally a working man's brew, brown ale has now found favour with beer lovers from all walks of life.

LIGHT AND DARK

A brown ale is for those on the fence. Less weighty than a porter, but more toasty and malty than a pale ale, brown ales have settled comfortably into a between-ales niche in beerland. The range in colour within this style is significant, from a translucent light brown, almost amber, to a rich, hearty brown, almost black. These differences stem from geography: the darker brews come from the south of England and the lighter come from the north. In both styles, however, the malts steal the show, with just a hint of hops in most examples. With this comes toasty flavours and nuttiness, caramel and even fruit.

Three Beers to Try

TEIGNWORTHY EDWIN TUCKER'S CHOICE OLD WALNUT BROWN ALE
A strong 6% ABV version of the style, brewed in an old maltings, offering chocolate, vinous fruits and light hops notes.

BUTTS GOLDEN BROWN   Organic bottle-conditioned beer packed with rich caramel and fruit notes and a gentle underpinning of hops.

MAXIM DOUBLE MAXIM   A fine example of northern brown ale, brewed with pale, crystal and cara malts with Fuggles hops. Apricots and plums on the palate with spicy hop notes.

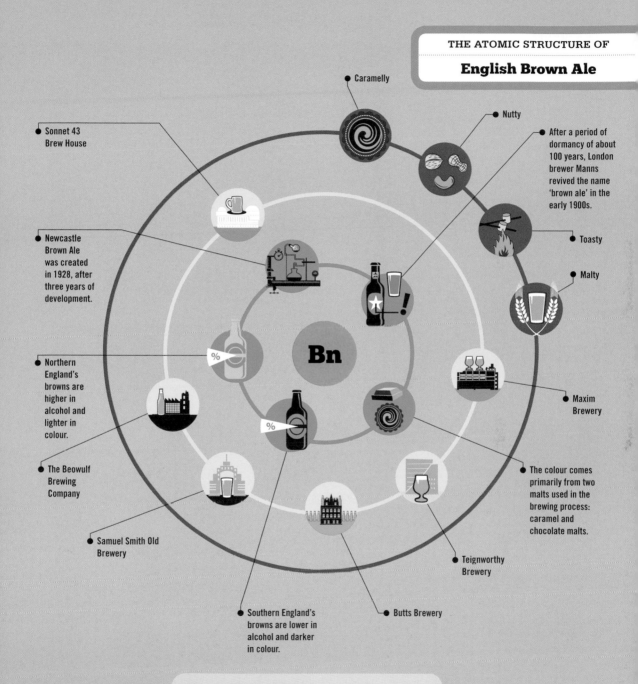

Caramelly

Nutty

Sonnet 43
Brew House

After a period of
dormancy of about
100 years, London
brewer Manns
revived the name
'brown ale' in the
early 1900s.

Newcastle
Brown Ale
was created
in 1928, after
three years of
development.

Toasty

Malty

Bn

Northern
England's
browns are
higher in
alcohol and
lighter in
colour.

Maxim
Brewery

The Beowulf
Brewing
Company

The colour comes
primarily from two
malts used in the
brewing process:
caramel and
chocolate malts.

Samuel Smith Old
Brewery

Teignworthy
Brewery

Southern England's
browns are lower in
alcohol and darker
in colour.

Butts Brewery

Food Pairing

| Roasted meats | Hearty dishes | Beef stew | Pork loin |

English Porter

Origin: England
Colour: 20–30 SRM
ABV: 4–6.5%
IBU: 18–40
**Glassware: pint,
nonic pint**

The original choice of London's market and dock workers was a blend of three beers. The style has changed constantly since its advent and remains ambiguous even today.

A VARIED STYLE

From a light chestnut to a black-edged deep brown, English porters have a vast and varied style guideline. Generally less full-bodied than a stout, some push even this boundary. Typically an off-white head may approach tan, and generally has decent weight and retention. The texture is soft and smooth, with just enough carbonation to leave a dry, malty, bready finish. In many examples there are caramel, toffee, chocolate and light coffee notes – all blended eloquently with the malt core. With its reasonably light alcohol content, this is a perfect partner for hearty dinners of grilled and roasted meat.

Three Beers to Try

ELLAND 1872 PORTER Elland Brewery has recreated a 19th-century porter using three dark malts and two English hops. It has coffee, bitter chocolate, vinous fruit and peppery hops.

RED SQUIRREL LONDON PORTER Brewed with dark crystal and chocolate malts, and Goldings and Magnum hops, for a dark berry fruitiness, chocolate and piny flavours.

WICKWAR STATION PORTER Crystal and black malts and Fuggles combine to offer port wine, liquorice, chocolate and earthy hops.

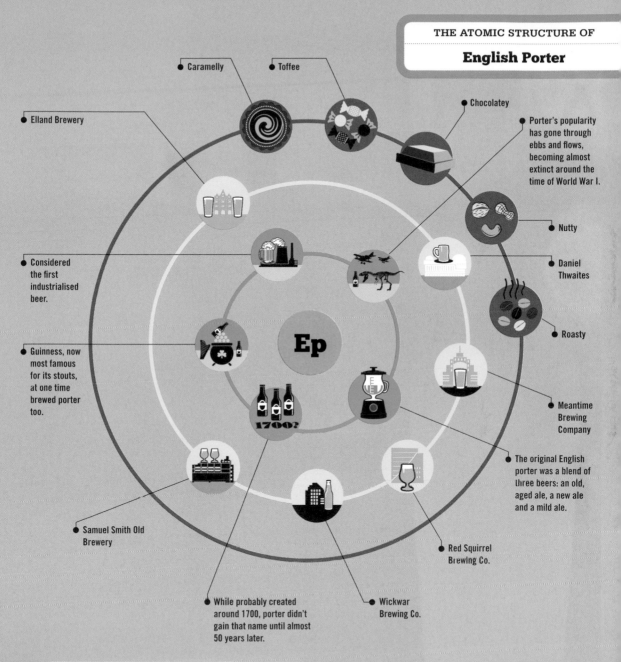

Caramelly

Toffee

Chocolatey

Elland Brewery

Porter's popularity has gone through ebbs and flows, becoming almost extinct around the time of World War I.

Nutty

Considered the first industrialised beer.

Daniel Thwaites

Roasty

Guinness, now most famous for its stouts, at one time brewed porter too.

Meantime Brewing Company

The original English porter was a blend of three beers: an old, aged ale, a new ale and a mild ale.

Ep

1700?

Samuel Smith Old Brewery

Red Squirrel Brewing Co.

While probably created around 1700, porter didn't gain that name until almost 50 years later.

Wickwar Brewing Co.

Food Pairing

Roasted foods	Light chocolate desserts	Burgers	Steak	Sausages

Baltic Porter

Origin: England
Colour: 17–30 SRM
ABV: 5.5–10.5%
IBU: 20–40
Glassware: pint,
nonic pint, mug

Originally brewed in England, this beer was exported to countries in the Baltic and Scandinavia, and then adopted by its recipients and crafted into what it is today.

A HARDY TRAVELLER

This dark, smooth beauty was brewed bigger and bolder in order to survive the journey from England to the Baltic countries. Since the original journey, however, it has become a distinct, stand-alone style. Dark mahogany to black, it is smooth, full-bodied and almost coating – nearing stout in character. The malt-forward introduction can be a bevy of flavours: caramel, chocolate, roasty notes, liquorice, raisins, prunes and molasses. There is no flavour from the hops, but a balance and a bitterness is attained in their presence. It is sweet on the finish and overall a velvety treat. Unknown to many, Baltic porters are worth discovering.

Three Beers to Try

GREEN JACK BALTIC TRADER Based in Lowestoft, a major port for the Baltic. This beer uses roasted barley and chocolate malt and has dark fruits, chocolate and peppery hop notes.

TEIGNWORTHY EDWIN TUCKER'S EMPRESS RUSSIAN PORTER A mighty 10.5% ABV beer with smoky malt, leather, liquorice, dark chocolate and burnt fruit notes with light hop resins

HOPSHACKLE BALTIC PORTER Intensely fruity (blackberries and lemons) with dark chocolate and peppery hop notes.

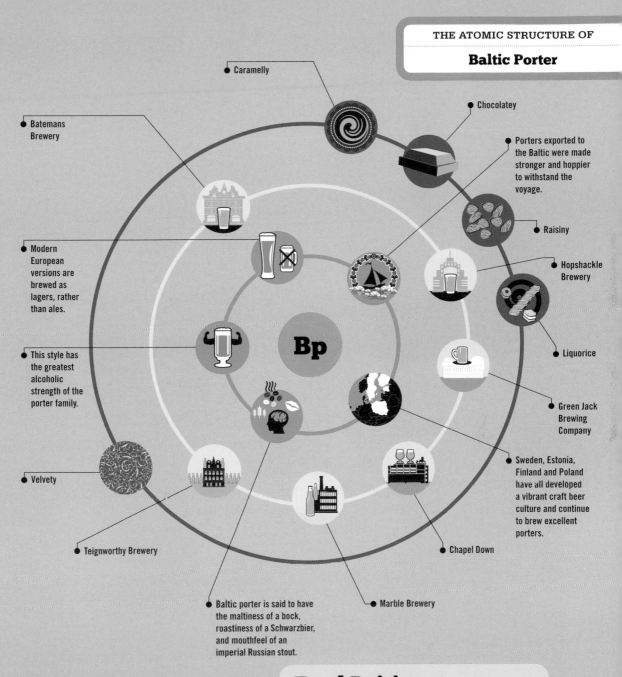

THE ATOMIC STRUCTURE OF
Baltic Porter

Bp

- Caramelly
- Chocolatey
- Porters exported to the Baltic were made stronger and hoppier to withstand the voyage.
- Batemans Brewery
- Raisiny
- Hopshackle Brewery
- Modern European versions are brewed as lagers, rather than ales.
- Liquorice
- This style has the greatest alcoholic strength of the porter family.
- Green Jack Brewing Company
- Sweden, Estonia, Finland and Poland have all developed a vibrant craft beer culture and continue to brew excellent porters.
- Velvety
- Chapel Down
- Teignworthy Brewery
- Marble Brewery
- Baltic porter is said to have the maltiness of a bock, roastiness of a Schwarzbier, and mouthfeel of an imperial Russian stout.

Food Pairing

| Barbecue | Roasted meats | Chocolate cake |

Irish Dry Stout

Origin: Ireland
Colour:
25–40+ SRM
ABV: 4–5%
IBU: 30–45
Glassware: pint,
nonic pint, mug

This style was refined and typified in Ireland, and today few beers are so closely tied to a single nation.

ROASTED BARLEY

Simply the mention of dry stout conjures images of Irish pubs and Arthur Guinness. Evolving from the porters brewed in London, stouts were stronger and more full-bodied. Dry stout is typified by the use of roasted barley instead of black roasted malt. This gives the characteristic core of sharp, espresso-like roastiness. It is an opaque deep brown to pure motor-oil black with a thick, creamy head. There can be a hint of hop bitterness, but this is usually overcome by the bitterness of dark chocolate, cocoa or coffee. From a keg or a can with a nitrogen widget, the creaminess makes this brew smooth and chewy. Deceivingly refreshing and highly sessionable, Irish dry stout is known to be the perfect choice for a long evening in the pub.

Three Beers to Try

GUINNESS DRAUGHT STOUT   The world's most famous dry stout. The fluffy brownish head is the focal point. On first sip, there is an almost burnt bitter espresso flavour.

O'HARA'S IRISH STOUT   Brewed by Carlow Brewing Company, this stout has a rich chocolate aroma with smoky roasted grain, followed by peppery hops on the palate and a bittersweet finish.

FRANCISCAN WELL SHANDON STOUT
A big aroma of chocolate and coffee gives way to roasted grain and peppery hops in the mouth, with a smoky malt and coffee finish.

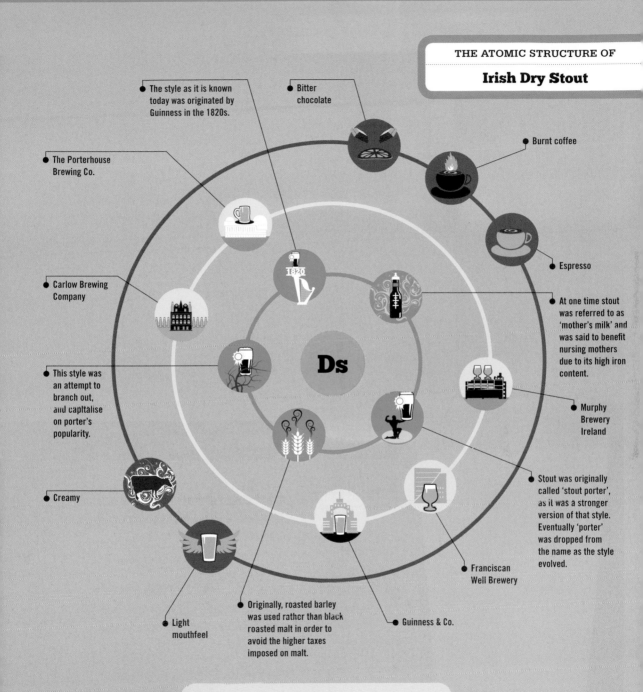

THE ATOMIC STRUCTURE OF

Irish Dry Stout

- Bitter chocolate
- Burnt coffee
- The style as it is known today was originated by Guinness in the 1820s.
- The Porterhouse Brewing Co.
- Espresso
- Carlow Brewing Company
- At one time stout was referred to as 'mother's milk' and was said to benefit nursing mothers due to its high iron content.
- This style was an attempt to branch out, and capitalise on porter's popularity.
- Murphy Brewery Ireland

Ds

- Creamy
- Stout was originally called 'stout porter', as it was a stronger version of that style. Eventually 'porter' was dropped from the name as the style evolved.
- Franciscan Well Brewery
- Light mouthfeel
- Originally, roasted barley was used rather than black roasted malt in order to avoid the higher taxes imposed on malt.
- Guinness & Co.

Food Pairing

Oysters	Seared scallops	Beef stew	Chocolate soufflé

Sweet Stout

Origin: England
Colour:
30–40+ SRM
ABV: 3–6%
IBU: 15–40
Glassware: pint,
nonic pint, mug,
snifter

While the health effects of beer are rarely touted today, not long ago sweet stout was marketed as just that – a nutritious choice for the masses.

SWEET AND COMFORTING

This one pours deep, oily and opaque. Its intimidating black colour seems to bid the drinker beware. In contrast, the aroma is inviting, with sweet maltiness and creamy, burnt sugar notes rising from the glass and light layers of vanilla, chocolate, dark fruit and coffee are not uncommon. After a sip, inhibitions are gone – it is a comforting brew with a viscous mouthfeel meant for sipping, but an ABV that allows for a few pints at a time. The addition of milk sugar, or lactose, counters the dry mouthfeel of other stouts. Initially an alternative to bitter dry stouts or boozy Russian imperials, sweet stout still finds its niche drinker today.

Three Beers to Try

ST. PETER'S CREAM STOUT Bitter and burnt, with notes of espresso and dark chocolate, its mouthfeel is soft and creamy, finishing in a full circle at bittersweet.

BRISTOL BEER FACTORY MILK STOUT
This is a recreation of an English classic, with lactose added during the copper boil. Creamy and chocolatey but with a touch of spicy hops.

BEOWULF DRAGON SMOKE STOUT
This stout is named after the dragon that is slain by the hero, Beowulf, in the famous Anglo-Saxon epic poem. It has smoked malt, chocolate and coffee notes.

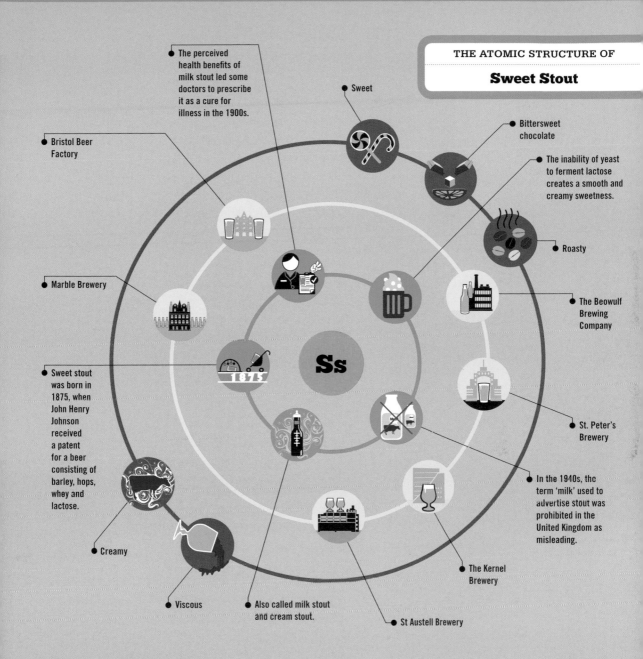

THE ATOMIC STRUCTURE OF
Sweet Stout

The perceived health benefits of milk stout led some doctors to prescribe it as a cure for illness in the 1900s.

Bristol Beer Factory

Marble Brewery

Sweet stout was born in 1875, when John Henry Johnson received a patent for a beer consisting of barley, hops, whey and lactose.

Creamy

Viscous

Also called milk stout and cream stout.

St Austell Brewery

Sweet

Bittersweet chocolate

The inability of yeast to ferment lactose creates a smooth and creamy sweetness.

Roasty

The Beowulf Brewing Company

St. Peter's Brewery

In the 1940s, the term 'milk' used to advertise stout was prohibited in the United Kingdom as misleading.

The Kernel Brewery

Ss

1875

Food Pairing

| Beef ribs | Mexican mole-based dishes | Ice cream | Chocolate |

Oatmeal Stout

**Origin: England
Colour:
22–40+ SRM
ABV: 3.8–7%
IBU: 20–40
Glassware: pint,
nonic pint, mug**

A bowl of piping-hot porridge can be a comforting morning ritual. The addition of oats to stout has the same effect, creating a soft, creamy and delicious beer.

ADDED CREAMINESS

In brewing, it's the simplest, sometimes seemingly insignificant, changes that can entirely shift the final product. The addition of oats to stout is just such an example. Adding a rich creaminess, the mouthfeel is soft and the flavours complex. The roastiness becomes rounded around the edges, and the dryness of other beers within this style becomes slightly sweeter. There can be notes of dark chocolate, roastiness, dark fruits and even nuttiness, but the mouthfeel steals the show. Creamy, smooth and soft, this brew seems made to accompany dessert.

Three Beers to Try

BELVOIR OATMEAL STOUT This is a rich, creamy and delectable dark stout with a coffee, chocolate and sweet grain character.

BLACK ISLE HIBERNATOR This is an organic beer from Scotland, with pale and chocolate malts, oats and First Gold hops. Creamy malt, chocolate and dark fruits coat the mouth.

ST. ANDREWS OATMEAL STOUT Another Scottish brewery, St. Andrews, offers this version with five malts and American and New Zealand hops delivering creamy malt, chocolate, coffee and spicy hop notes.

THE ATOMIC STRUCTURE OF

Oatmeal Stout

Pairs nicely with chocolate chip cookies.
Black Isle Brewing Co.
St. Andrews Brewing Co.
Chocolatey
An overuse of oats in the brewing process can lead to poor head retention.
In the late 1800s, oats were perceived as a healthy addition to beer.
Belvoir Brewery
Os
Brighton Bier
Creamy
Smooth
Brewing with oats can be difficult, as the consistency in the mash can become sticky.
Wells & Young's Brewing Company
Rich
Soft
Oats are a staple crop in Britain, and this adjunct found its initial place in brewing there during the Middle Ages.
Peerless Brewing Company

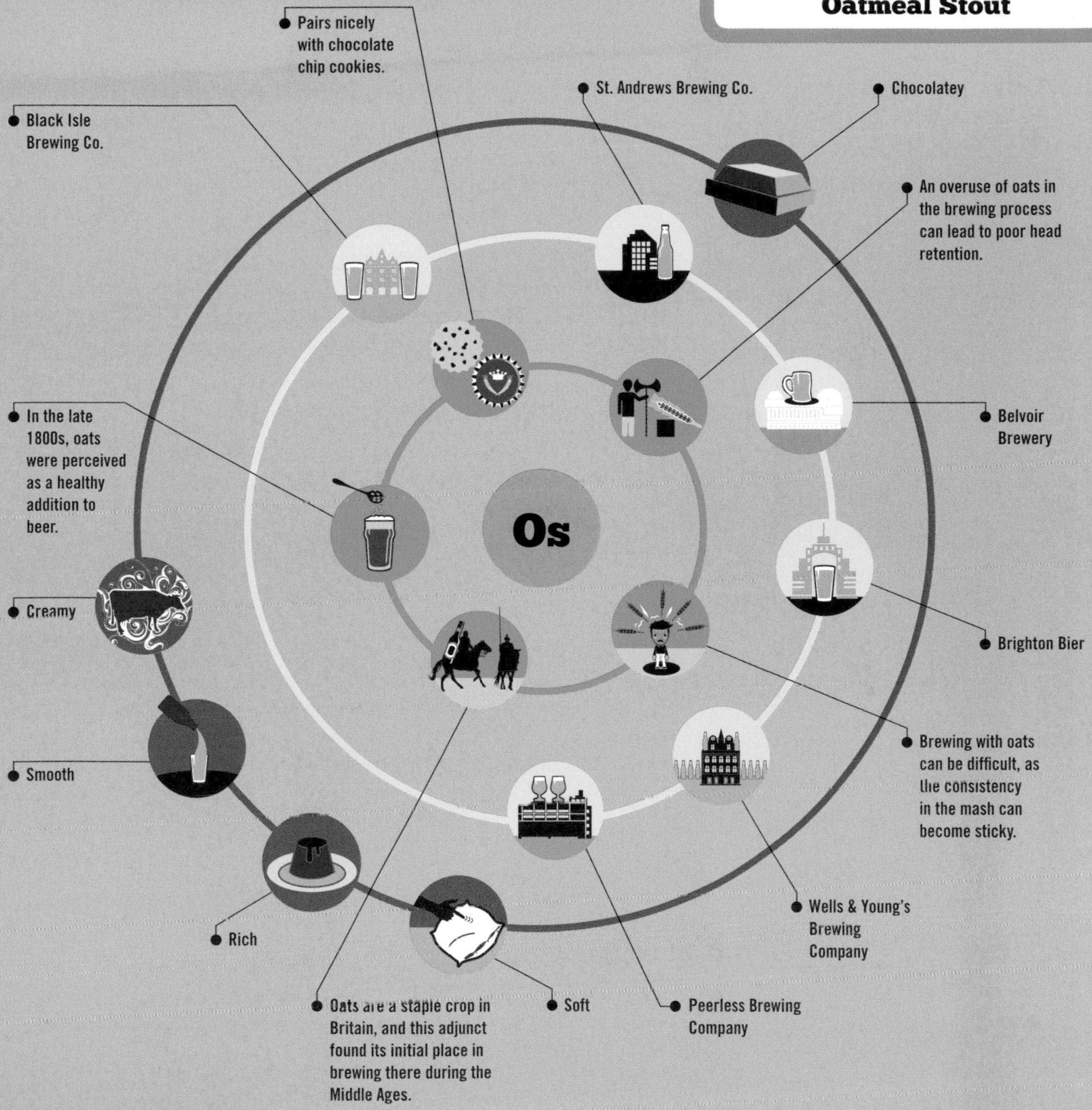

Food Pairing

Chocolate desserts	Ice cream	Rich fruit desserts	Cheesecake

Foreign/Extra Stout

Origin: Ireland
Colour:
30-40+ SRM
ABV: 5.5-8%
IBU: 30-70
Glassware: pint,
nonic pint, snifter

This broad style has variety, but it all started with the intention to get good beer to people who were far away.

TROPICAL VOYAGER

Another stout with just enough differences from the base to qualify as a style. Originally, foreign stout was brewed stronger and hoppier in order to withstand the voyage to the more tropical parts of the British Empire. The style is typified by bittersweet roastiness and smooth darkness, but it can vary from there. Some are sweet and fruity, while others lean more bitter and dry. Even within the style there are subsets: tropical versions evoke sweeter notes of an almost rum quality, and exports tend to focus on bitterness and roasted malt. Generally both of these sub-styles show signs of coffee, bitter chocolate and no hop flavour.

Three Beers to Try

GUINNESS FOREIGN EXTRA STOUT
Pours a deep black with a well-suited light brown head. Full-bodied roastiness blends with layers of dark fruit, caramel and dark bitter chocolate. Smooth, and a must-try for the style.

ACORN GORLOVKA Acorn Brewery's stout marks
Barnsley's twinning with Gorlovka in Ukraine. It has liquorice, coffee, burnt fruit and peppery hop aromas and flavours with a bitter finish.

RIDGEWAY FOREIGN EXPORT STOUT
This complex 7% ABV stout uses roasted barley and oats as well as dark malts and delivers smoky, chocolate and espresso flavours.

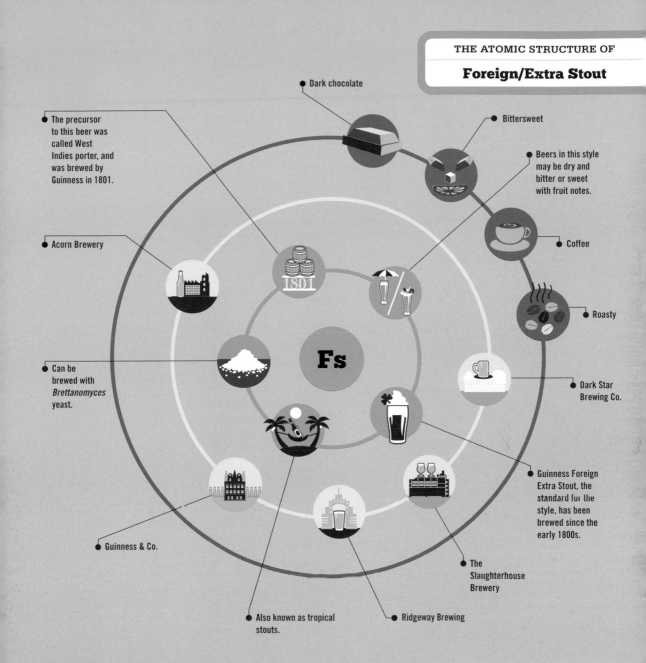

THE ATOMIC STRUCTURE OF
Foreign/Extra Stout

- Dark chocolate
- Bittersweet
- The precursor to this beer was called West Indies porter, and was brewed by Guinness in 1801.
- Beers in this style may be dry and bitter or sweet with fruit notes.
- Acorn Brewery
- Coffee
- Can be brewed with *Brettanomyces* yeast.
- Roasty
- Dark Star Brewing Co.
- Guinness Foreign Extra Stout, the standard for the style, has been brewed since the early 1800s.
- Guinness & Co.
- The Slaughterhouse Brewery
- Also known as tropical stouts.
- Ridgeway Brewing

Fs

Food Pairing

| Oysters | Smoked or grilled meats | Dark chocolate |

Imperial Russian Stout

Origin: England
Colour:
30–40+ SRM
ABV: 7–13%
IBU: 50–90
Glassware: snifter

It's no wonder the Russian tsars of the 1700s loved this brew. Hugely roasty, it coats as you sip – practically a liquid dessert.

A HUGE BEER

In many ways, imperial Russian stouts are the biggest of beers. Consistently high in alcohol content, they hide it well between a massive malt bill and flavours that range from soft vanilla to dark chocolate and bitter coffee. The mouthfeel is coating, thick and rich, and the colour an opaque black. There is a prevalent forward roastiness that provides the foundation on which each brewer's unique creation is built. A huge beer, and if you're bold enough – or simply intrigued – there is a wealth of amazing beers in this category to try.

Three Beers to Try

COURAGE IMPERIAL RUSSIAN STOUT
The original imperial exported to Catherine II of Russia. Revived in 2011 by Wells & Young's, it boasts a smooth mouthfeel mingled with rich espresso notes, fruit and a dark chocolate finish.

THORNBRIDGE SAINT PETERSBURG
An outstanding stout, aged for 55 days, with aromas and flavours of smoke, oak, chocolate, espresso, and fruity and spicy hops.

HARVEYS IMPERIAL EXTRA DOUBLE STOUT
Based on a genuine Victorian recipe, Harvey's beer has vinous fruits, leather, tobacco, smoky malt and peppery hops.

THE ATOMIC STRUCTURE OF
Imperial Russian Stout

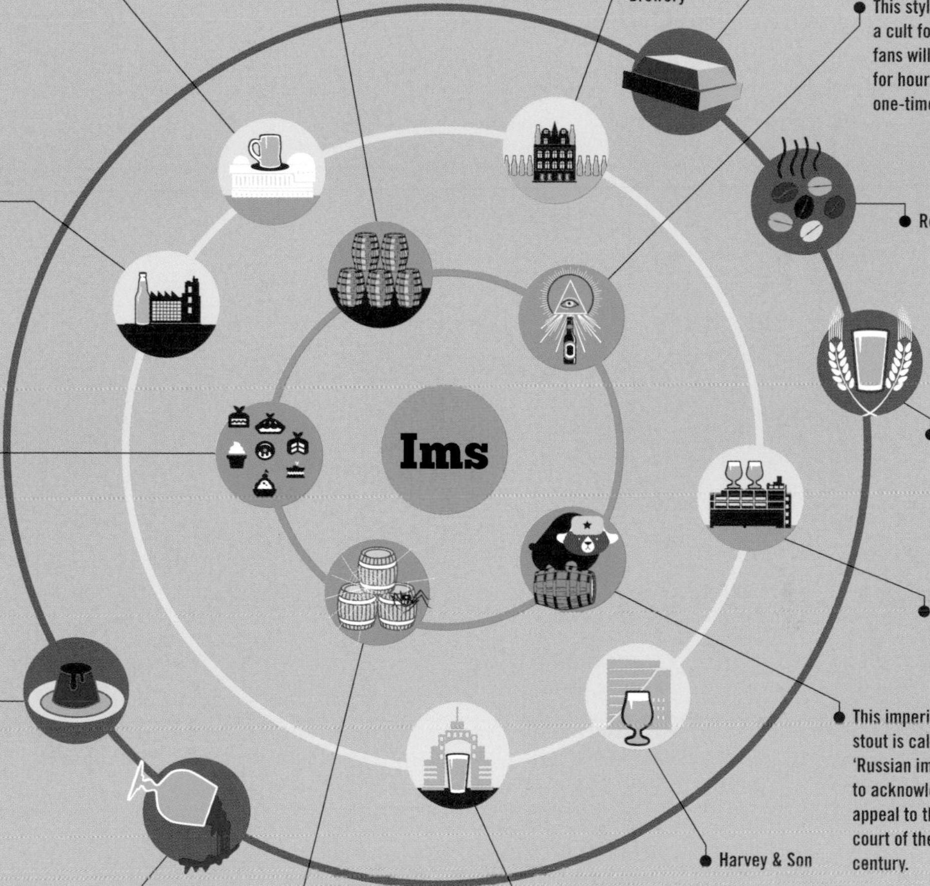

Barrel-aged versions are increasingly popular.

Acorn Brewery

Bartrams Brewery

Chocolatey

This style has bred a cult following with fans willing to queue for hours for special one-time releases.

Hopshackle Brewery

Roasty

Malty

Pairs surprisingly well with desserts.

Ims

Thornbridge Brewery

Rich

This imperial stout is called 'Russian imperial' to acknowledge its appeal to the Russian court of the 18th century.

Harvey & Son

Viscous

Courage Russian Imperial Stout is said to be drinkable – even improved – after up to 13 years of aging.

Wells & Young's Brewing Company

Food Pairing

Chocolate	Crème brûlée	Ice cream	Fruit tarts

ALES OF CONTINENTAL EUROPEAN ORIGIN

ALES OF CONTINENTAL EUROPEAN ORIGIN

Beyond the United Kingdom and Ireland, the birthplace of most European beers is primarily one of two dominating countries on the Continent. As different in beer styles as two nations could be, Germany and Belgium have historically exerted the strongest influence on the Continental brewing scene. Belgium, with its ever-influential yeast, full of nuance and complexity, continues to defy style groups and rigid classifications, while maintaining excellence in product and beer culture. Germany, on the other hand, with roots in the *Reinheitsgebot* brewing purity law, continues to produce an impressive stable of ales, most still strictly adhering to traditional styles and brewing guidelines.

Belgium has passionately embraced beer through the ages, and that historic devotion and attention to excellence still seeps through in both the brewing and the drinking culture. Most Belgian beers have a particular style of serving glass and many cafés, anchored deeply in rich traditions, forbid the serving of beer in any glass but its intended. The Belgian brewer is considered a creative – an artist continually perfecting his craft – and it is the drinker's pleasure to imbibe their delicious work.

In Belgian beer, yeast is the prominent player. Where a taste for bold and brash may be yearned for elsewhere in the world, the complex, nuanced and intricate aromas and flavours of Belgian beer is what attracts the attention of the drinker willing to take the first adventurous sip. It is a journey that few will regret. Many Belgian ales come packed with a sleeping alcoholic punch that hides coyly beneath the array of intriguing flavours. Most beers, when paired correctly with food, create a memorable culinary experience.

Trappist ales are brewed on a monastery properly and under direction of the monks that live there. The term 'Trappiste' is an appellation and legally protects eight breweries – Achel, Chimay, La Trappe/ Koningshoeven, Orval, Rochefort, Westmalle, Westvleteren and Stift Engelszell. All are held in justifiably high regard, each excellent, and many of the beers produced mark the apex of their style. While other secular brewers have crafted similar styles, they cannot bear the Trappiste title, and are instead dubbed Abbey ales. These too are not to be overlooked – many rival their sacred counterparts.

With some of the greatest and longest-standing beer traditions in the world, Germany continues to produce brews that are the standard for their style. While pale lagers have stolen the spotlight of modern-day brewing in Germany, until the 16th century the nation only produced ales.

Wheat beers – Weissbiers – dominate German ales, ranging from the light, tart and spritzy Berliner Weisse all the way to the rich and warming Weizenbock. The differentiating ingredient, wheat, is the stitch that runs through this patchwork quilt of styles and flavours, yet the variance between each type is surprising, as some seem to have entirely unrelated palate profiles.

Alongside Germany's famous lagers and ales, two sister styles, Kölsch and Altbier, are the oddities – hybrids that each undergo warm fermentation followed by a period of the cold conditioning usually associated with lagers. Two beers closely connected with the cities from which they come, the ancient Altbier maintains a stronghold in its hometown of Düsseldorf, while Kölsch, Altbier's pale sister, was born in Cologne.

Witbier

Origin: Belgium
Colour: 2–4 SRM
ABV: 4.5–5.5%
IBU: 10–20
Glassware: pint, mug

Crisp, effervescent and zesty, this beer went from obscurity in the 1950s to become a style brewed and enjoyed worldwide.

A WHITER SHADE OF PALE

To the French, it's 'bière blanche', to the Belgians, it's 'witbier', to the Japanese, it's 'white ale', but to beer lovers worldwide, it's just plain good. A straw-yellow beer with a steady, billowing cap of white foam that leaves cascading sheets of lace, this brew transcends geographical barriers with its notable blend of spices and its slightly acidic, slightly sour flavour. The nose is a blend of tangy lemon and yeast, with a complex combination of cleansing bubbles and smooth mouthfeel. The finish is dry and refreshing. It's a brew full of contradictions and oddly pleasing combinations. A complexity worth simply enjoying.

Three Beers to Try

HOEGAARDEN WIT   The beer with which brewer Pierre Celis revived the long-lost style in 1966.

CARACOLE TROUBLETTE   The Caracole brewery uses wood-fired mash tuns and coppers to make its artisan beers. The white beer has tart and tangy lemon fruit on aroma and palate, with a dry finish.

ST. BERNARDUS WIT   A heavily-spiced beer from Sint Bernard, a major brewer of Abbey-style beers. A modest strength of 5.5% ABV tends to mask the rich malt, spice and hop flavours.

THE ATOMIC STRUCTURE OF

Witbier

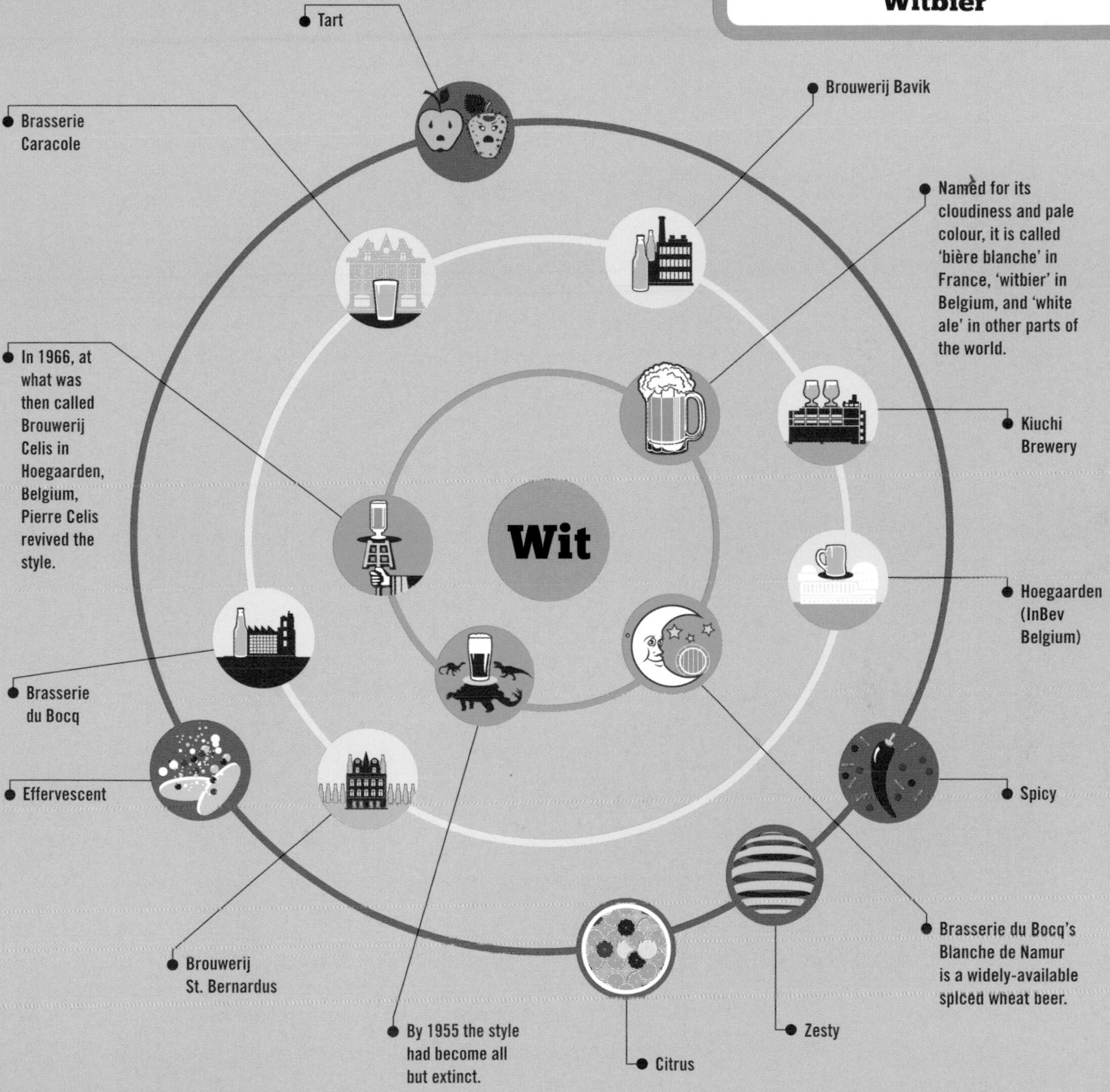

Tart

Brouwerij Bavik

Brasserie Caracole

Named for its cloudiness and pale colour, it is called 'bière blanche' in France, 'witbier' in Belgium, and 'white ale' in other parts of the world.

In 1966, at what was then called Brouwerij Celis in Hoegaarden, Belgium, Pierre Celis revived the style.

Kiuchi Brewery

Wit

Hoegaarden (InBev Belgium)

Brasserie du Bocq

Effervescent

Spicy

Brouwerij St. Bernardus

Brasserie du Bocq's Blanche de Namur is a widely-available spiced wheat beer.

By 1955 the style had become all but extinct.

Zesty

Citrus

Food Pairing

| Salmon | Poultry | Goat's cheese | Apple pie |

Gose

Origin: Germany
Colour: 2-4 SRM
ABV: 4.5-5.5%
IBU: 4-9
Glassware: stange

A rarity in the beer world, and a difficult beer to find, Gose has intriguing and unique qualities only found in this style.

THE SALTED DEEP
In the beer world there are palate-punishing hop bombs, motor-oil thick stouts, and taste-bud assaulting sour beers. Gose is none of these. Hidden behind a veil of murky gold are dancing bubbles, lightening the mouthfeel to medium, and making the sour bite refreshingly so. Gose is sour, but not mouth-puckering, and it finishes clean and dry. There can be fruity complexities with green apple notes and hints of banana, often with a reasonably prominent spicing of coriander. An oddity unique to this style, Gose is brewed with salt, adding depth to the mouthfeel and body rather than any specific flavour.

Three Beers to Try

LEIPZIGER GOSE From the Bayerischer Bahnhof, this is the classic and most common example of the style. A complex blend of fruit. Finishes dry with a slight hint of salt.

SAMUEL ADAMS VERLOREN This beer from the Boston Beer Company pours a hazy deep gold with an upfront nose of coriander and fruit. These aromas continue on the palate on a foundation of smooth fruit and slight saltiness.

UPRIGHT GOSE A dry finish preceded by a smooth body. Slight notes of lemon mix with a tactful tartness. A traditional take on the style.

THE ATOMIC STRUCTURE OF

Gose

Sour
Fruity
Brauhaus Goslar
After an almost 40-year absence, Gose began to be brewed again following the fall of the Berlin Wall.
goz-uh
Pronounced *goz-uh*.
Upright Brewing Company
Gs
Salt is added to the water used in the brewing process.
Bayerischer Bahnhof
Due to its use of salt, Gose does not meet the standards of the *Reinheitsgebot* (Bavarian Beer Purity Law) used in brewing. However, it is granted an exception as a specialty of its home region.
Dry
Named after Goslar, the town in which Gose was originally popular.
The Boston Beer Company
Cascade Brewing
Puckering
Crisp

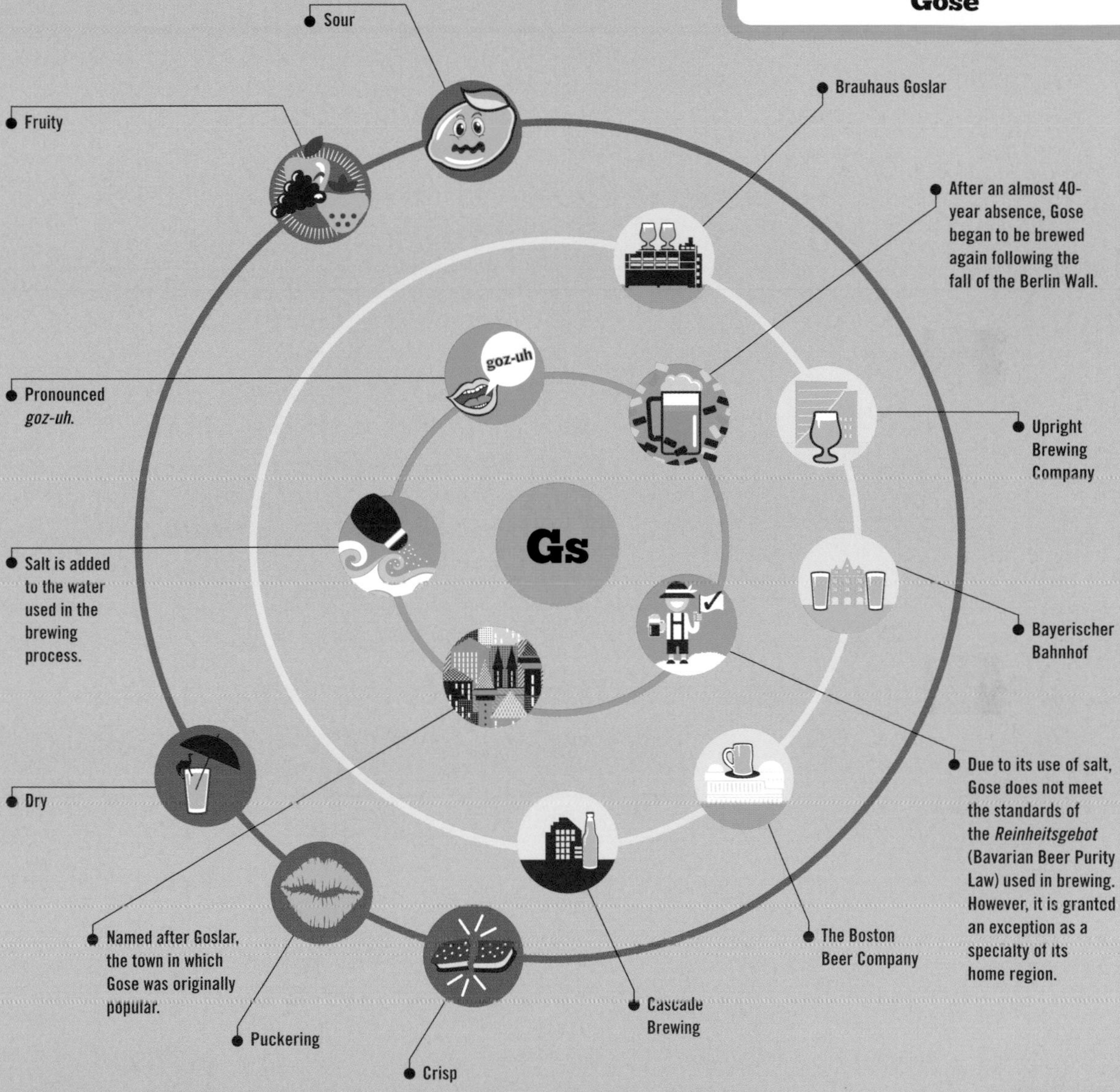

Food Pairing

Strong seafood	Light Thai food	Salmon salad

Berliner Weisse

Origin: Germany
Colour: 2-4 SRM
ABV: 2.5-3.5%
IBU: 3-8
Glassware: chalice

When it's time to toast, this brew can do the job. Bubbly, refreshing, and mouth-puckering, it shows just how vast the boundaries of beer are.

BRING OUT THE FRUIT

Napoleon declared Berliner Weisse the champagne of beers. Sprightly, bubbly and acidic to the point of sourness, this brew from Berlin has been traditionally tempered by fruit syrups – almost an adult kiddie cocktail. One of the few places where a post-brew additive is acceptable, a Berliner Weisse can be almost too much pucker without a bit of sweet fruitiness to tone it down. Raspberry syrup and herbal essence of woodruff are the most frequently chosen additives. The body is hazy, highly carbonated and capped with a white, airy head. It smells of yeast and hay with a slight, pleasant funkiness.

Three Beers to Try

BAYERISCHER BAHNHOF BERLINER STYLE WEISSE   Less sharp and acidic than the classic beer of the style. Still tart, but more mellow.

PROFESSOR FRITZ BRIEM 1809 BERLINER WEISSE   Created by Professor Fritz Briem in an attempt to revive this once almost extinct style.

BERLINER KINDL WEISSE   Even for the style, this version of Berliner Weisse has an intense, acidic sourness.

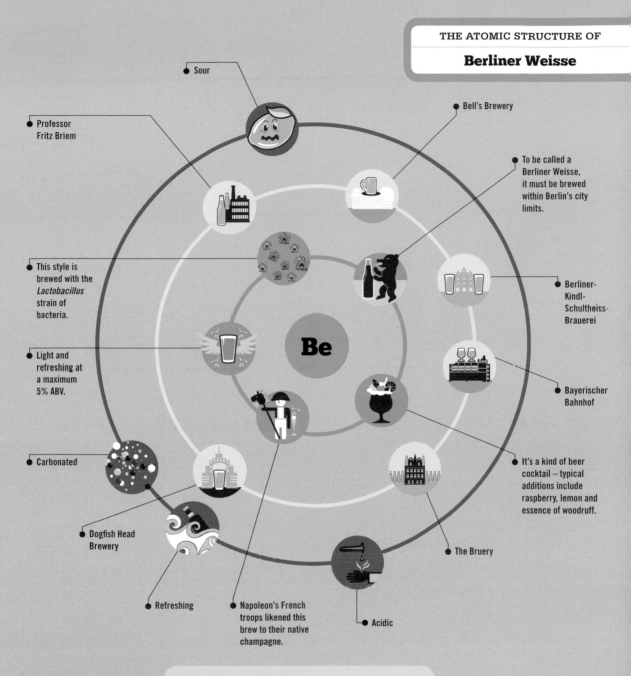

Sour

Bell's Brewery

Professor
Fritz Briem

To be called a
Berliner Weisse,
it must be brewed
within Berlin's city
limits.

This style is
brewed with the
Lactobacillus
strain of
bacteria.

Berliner-
Kindl-
Schultheiss-
Brauerei

Be

Light and
refreshing at
a maximum
5% ABV.

Bayerischer
Bahnhof

Carbonated

It's a kind of beer
cocktail – typical
additions include
raspberry, lemon and
essence of woodruff.

Dogfish Head
Brewery

The Bruery

Refreshing

Napoleon's French
troops likened this
brew to their native
champagne.

Acidic

Food Pairing

| Salads | Eggs | Citrus-flavoured fish | Chocolate (when raspberry syrup added to beer) |

Kölsch

Origin: Germany
Colour: 3.5–5 SRM
ABV: 4.4–5.2%
IBU: 20–30
Glassware: stange

A delicious crossbreed, this ale has all the characteristics of a light, quenching lager.

EFFERVESCENT AND BRILLIANTLY CLEAR

Indigenous to Köln (Cologne), Germany, Kölsch is a top-fermented, cold-conditioned hybrid. Features of both ale and lager come through: a slight ale fruitiness dances through the straw-blonde body with the clean, crisp delicacy of a lager. A soft maltiness caresses, giving an utterly smooth and refreshing character. With origins in its sister style, Altbier (see page 108), it is a young brew, its modern rendition introduced as recently as 1918. It is effervescent and brilliantly clear, and is one of the styles behind which there is little room for a brewer's mistakes to hide. Its mild flavour can contain notes of bread, fruit, hops and cereal grains.

Three Beers to Try

REISSDORF KÖLSCH A biscuity, malty nose mixes with pleasant citrus and floral notes. It is gently carbonated and very refreshing and crisp.

SÜNNER KÖLSCH The brewery responsible for designating the style 'Kölsch', created this classic. Bread and apples on the nose, floral hops play through a clean body.

GAFFEL KÖLSCH Highly effervescent, it has distinct notes of pepper strewn about a sweet maltiness. A clean finish with just a bit of fruitiness.

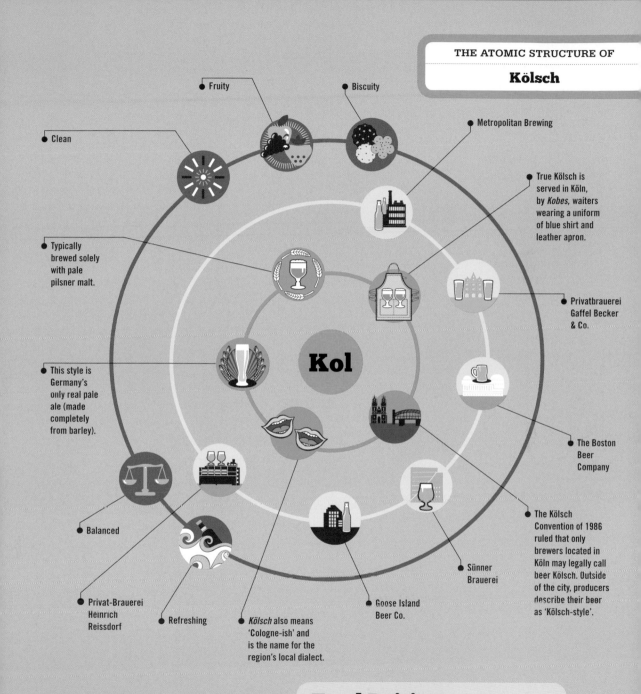

THE ATOMIC STRUCTURE OF
Kölsch

Fruity

Biscuity

Clean

Metropolitan Brewing

True Kölsch is served in Köln, by *Kobes,* waiters wearing a uniform of blue shirt and leather apron.

Typically brewed solely with pale pilsner malt.

Privatbrauerei Gaffel Becker & Co.

Kol

This style is Germany's only real pale ale (made completely from barley).

The Boston Beer Company

Balanced

The Kölsch Convention of 1986 ruled that only brewers located in Köln may legally call beer Kölsch. Outside of the city, producers describe their beer as 'Kölsch-style'.

Privat-Brauerei Heinrich Reissdorf

Refreshing

Kölsch also means 'Cologne-ish' and is the name for the region's local dialect.

Goose Island Beer Co.

Sünner Brauerei

Food Pairing

| Salads | Light pork dishes | Eggs |

Belgian Strong Pale Ale

Origin: Belgium
Colour:
3.5–5.5 SRM
ABV: 7–9%
IBU: 25–45
Glassware: tulip, snifter, oversized wine glass

The classic beers of this style are highly alcoholic but fresh, zippy, refreshing and spicy pale ales.

THE DEVIL INCARNATE

Built on a foundation laid by Brouwerij Duvel Moortgat, those brewing this style (also called strong golden or strong blonde) have traditionally been in competition to create a beer that compares to Duvel. Enticing and deceiving in pale yellow, beers of this type are dressed with an innocent linen-white cap that leaves stripes of streaked lace. Underneath this golden guise broods an intense alcohol. It is layered with fruits and spices to create a complex, crisp and enjoyable blend. This mischievous deceiver has conjured up names deserving of its ploy: Duvel (devil), Damnation and Lucifer to name a few.

Three Beers to Try

DUVEL   The absolute pinnacle of the style, this 'devil' hides a powerful 8.5% ABV in a deceptively picture-perfect bright, clear, golden body and a billowing white head.

DELIRIUM TREMENS   Beads stream upwards to create a pillowy head. Aroma of bright citrus, yeast and hops. Brewed by Brouwerij Huyghe.

ACHOUFFE LA CHOUFFE   With a profound yeasty profile, this brew made by Achouffe toes the style line, with notes of tropical fruits and moderately bitter hops.

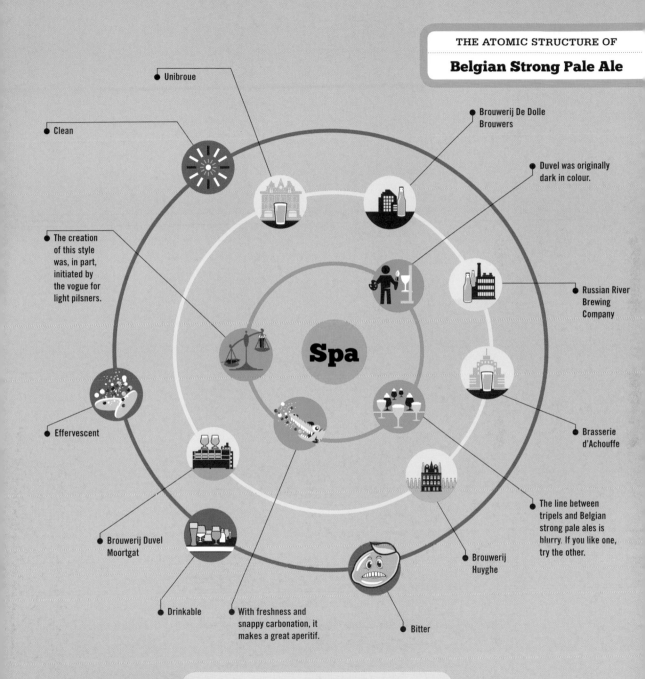

Unibroue

Clean

Brouwerij De Dolle Brouwers

Duvel was originally dark in colour.

The creation of this style was, in part, initiated by the vogue for light pilsners.

Russian River Brewing Company

Spa

Effervescent

Brasserie d'Achouffe

Brouwerij Duvel Moortgat

The line between tripels and Belgian strong pale ales is blurry. If you like one, try the other.

Brouwerij Huyghe

Drinkable

With freshness and snappy carbonation, it makes a great aperitif.

Bitter

Food Pairing

| Indian food | Pesto dishes | Chinese food | Prawns |

Bière de Champagne

Origin: Belgium
Colour: 3–6 SRM
ABV: 6.5–14%
IBU: 10–30
Glassware: flute

A different take on the time-honoured champagne toast, this beer may just begin a new tradition.

RAISE YOUR GLASS

This contemporary-style, effervescent, and toast-worthy beer has as intricate a process of production as champagne. It goes through a lengthy period of maturation and is then riddled (stored upside down and rotated) and disgorged (the settled yeast in the neck is removed), in the same manner as for sparkling wines. The result is a highly carbonated, refreshing, sparkling beer that has a high ABV. A refined selection, it is a beautiful accompaniment to light seafood or a delightful stand-alone drink before dinner.

Three Beers to Try

DEUS BRUT DES FLANDRES This beer by Brouwerij Bosteels has a golden body with an airy head. Its bright, fruity nose, full of citrus and herbs, is complemented by a smooth, but freshly bubbled feel.

ST. BERNARDUS GROTTENBIER A beer developed by the great Belgian brewer Pierre Celis, matured in caves and 'riddled' like champagne. Toasted malt and peppery hop notes.

MALHEUR BRUT RESERVE Veiling the 12% ABV dangerously well, this beer is the lightest of straw in colour and has a cap of white foam. Spicy, earthy, and tart on the nose, the alcohol surfaces on the sip, but melds into citrus and a malty but dry finish.

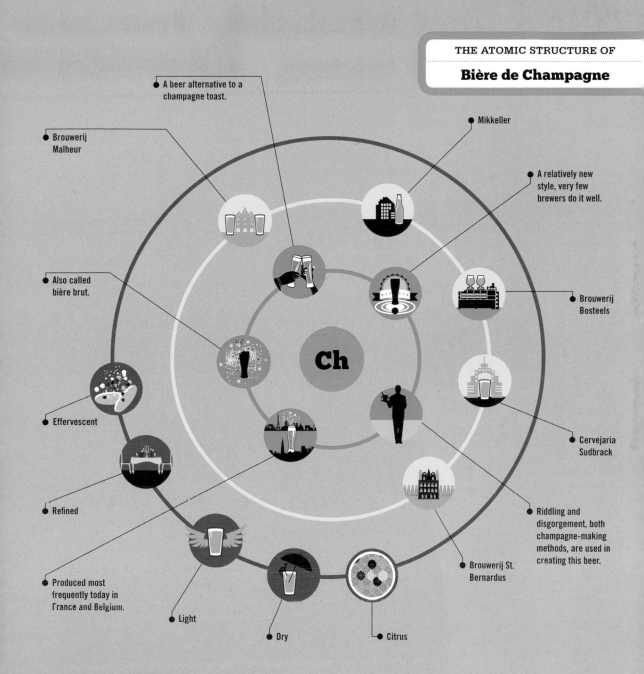

A beer alternative to a champagne toast.

Brouwerij Malheur

Mikkeller

A relatively new style, very few brewers do it well.

Also called bière brut.

Brouwerij Bosteels

Ch

Effervescent

Cervejaria Sudbrack

Refined

Riddling and disgorgement, both champagne-making methods, are used in creating this beer.

Produced most frequently today in France and Belgium.

Brouwerij St. Bernardus

Light

Dry

Citrus

Food pairing

| Shellfish | Fish | Berries |

Kristalweizen

Origin: Germany
Colour: 2-8 SRM
ABV: 4-5.5%
IBU: 10-15
Glassware: weizen

A filtered version of Weissbier (page 86), this beer is a body of refreshing complexities that suits many foods and many moods.

CLEAN AND CLEAR

In a sector of beer where cloudy styles reign supreme, this brew sticks out like a teenager with something to prove. The body of a Kristalweizen is like gold-tinted glass, busy with cascading carbonation. Almost visible notes of banana, clove and bubblegum waft out of the puffy white head, which streaks a delicate lace. It's clean and refreshing without weakness in its mouthfeel. While maintaining the classic versatility of the characteristic wheat-beer style, the filtered, clear flair of Kristalweizen makes it a very palatable transition from less interesting, light beers.

Three Beers to Try

WEIHENSTEPHANER KRISTALL WEISSBIER   As near a perfect example of the style as you will find. Refreshing, fruity, clean.

ERDINGER WEISSBIER KRISTALLKLAR
Clean and clear, medium-bodied with a touch of spice, this beer is made by a significant Weissbier brewery.

TUCHER KRISTALL WEIZEN   Light and highly effervescent with a slight, pleasant tang.

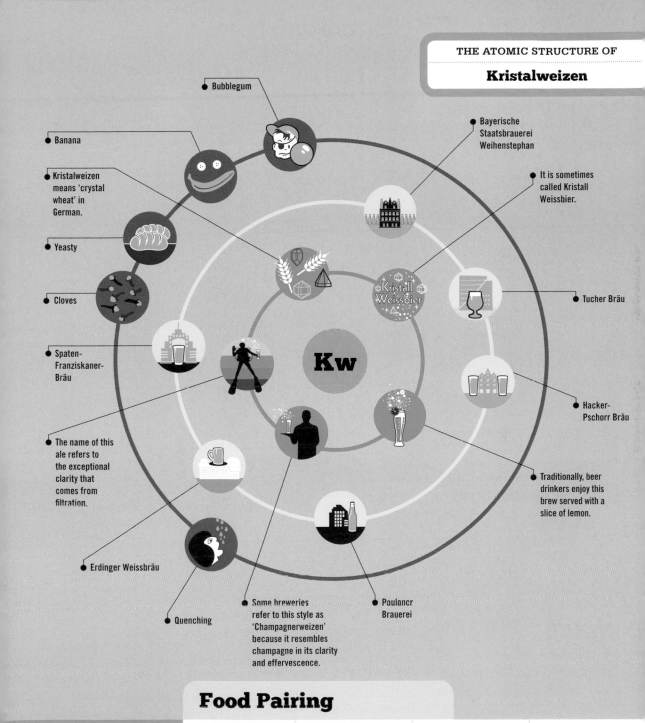

- Bubblegum

- Banana

- Kristalweizen means 'crystal wheat' in German.

- Yeasty

- Cloves

- Spaten-Franziskaner-Bräu

- The name of this ale refers to the exceptional clarity that comes from filtration.

- Erdinger Weissbräu

- Quenching

- Some breweries refer to this style as 'Champagnerweizen' because it resembles champagne in its clarity and effervescence.

- Paulaner Brauerei

- Bayerische Staatsbrauerei Weihenstephan

- It is sometimes called Kristall Weissbier.

- Tucher Bräu

- Hacker-Pschorr Bräu

- Traditionally, beer drinkers enjoy this brew served with a slice of lemon.

Kw

Kristall Weissbier

Food Pairing

| Egg dishes | Salads | Mexican food | Thai food |

Weissbier

Origin: Germany
Colour: 2–9 SRM
ABV: 4–5.5%
IBU: 10–18
Glassware: weizen

Incredibly versatile, Weissbier – the classic wheat beer – is a wonderfully satisfying brew that befits many occasions.

THE FATHER OF WHEAT BEERS

In a world where the slightest nuance signals the birth of an entirely new category of beer, Weissbier is the standard from which many new categories are born. A clear Weissbier becomes a Kristalweizen, a dark one becomes a Dunkelweizen. This father of wheat beers is a surprising contrast of pure, clear refreshment, from a hazy, unfiltered, bubbling body of orange, with a tall crown of a head sitting majestically atop. The nose and flavour are typically a pleasant mix of yeast, citrus, banana and clove. There is a power in versatility, as Weissbier can be the perfect accompaniment to many a meal. From egg dishes to spicy pad thai to homemade apple pie, this beer stands up to them all – but it's also perfect for drinking on its own.

Three Beers to Try

WEIHENSTEPHANER HEFE WEISSBIER
One of the great examples of the style, well-built in body, complex in aroma and spice – a standard for comparison.

PAULANER HEFE-WEISSBIER NATURTRÜB Beautiful body of orange and a delicately balanced blend of yeast, fruit and spice.

ERDINGER WEISSBIER The king of the wide range of beers produced by Erdinger, this bottle-conditioned beer is ready to drink after just 3–4 weeks in the bottle.

THE ATOMIC STRUCTURE OF

Weissbier

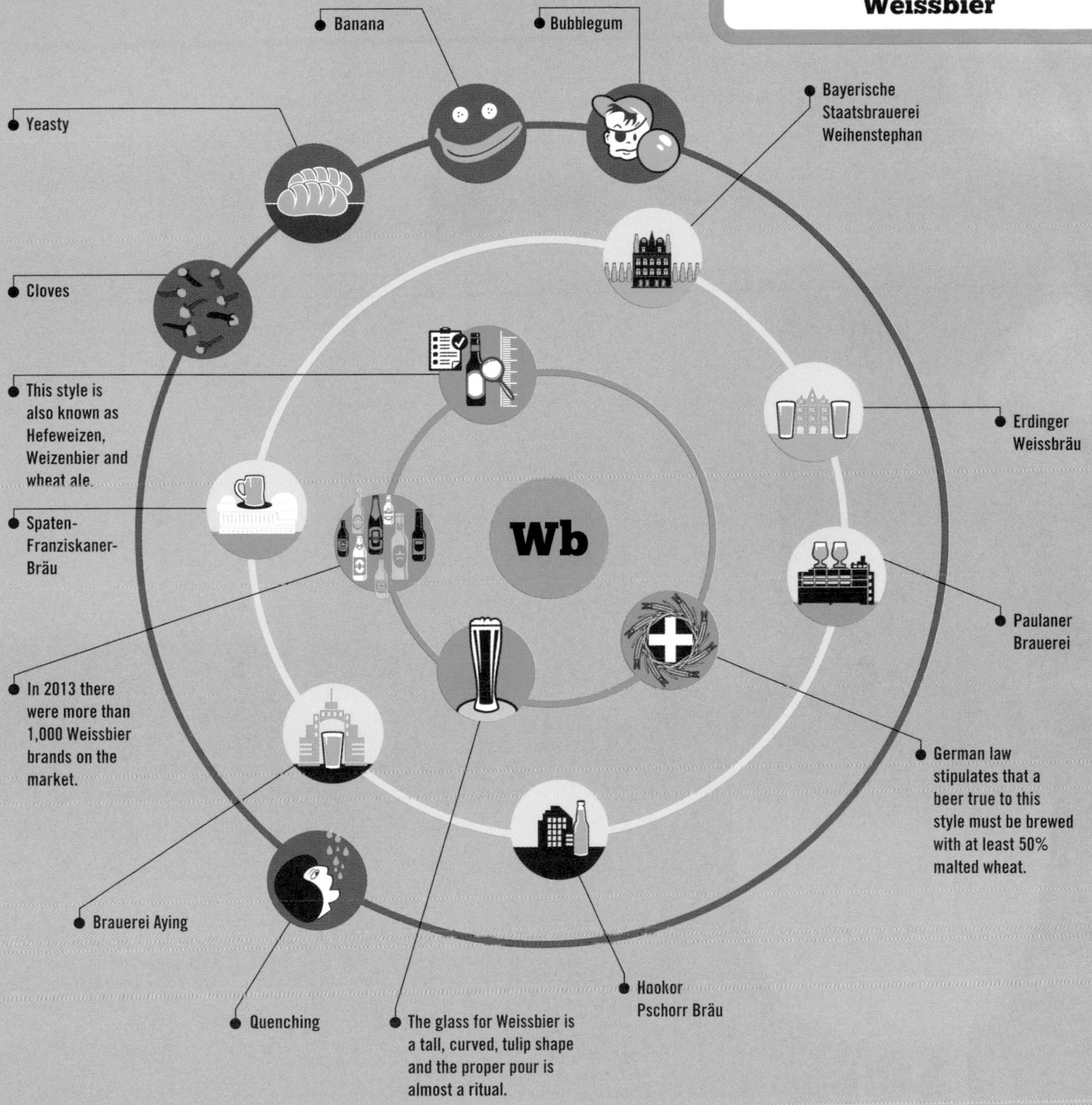
Banana
Bubblegum
Yeasty
Bayerische Staatsbrauerei Weihenstephan
Cloves
This style is also known as Hefeweizen, Weizenbier and wheat ale.
Erdinger Weissbräu
Wb
Spaten-Franziskaner-Bräu
Paulaner Brauerei
In 2013 there were more than 1,000 Weissbier brands on the market.
German law stipulates that a beer true to this style must be brewed with at least 50% malted wheat.
Brauerei Aying
Hacker Pschorr Bräu
Quenching
The glass for Weissbier is a tall, curved, tulip shape and the proper pour is almost a ritual.

Food Pairing

Egg dishes	Salads	Mexican food	Thai food	German food

Tripel

Origin: Belgium
Colour: 3.5–7 SRM
ABV: 7.5–9.5%
IBU: 20–40
Glassware: tulip, goblet

The delicately complex and surprisingly spirituous tripel is a young style that has been beautifully matured.

A GLASS OF SUNSHINE

Pouring into the glass like sunshine, its golden-yellow haze is mesmerising and the cotton-white, bulbous head literally climbs the glass to the rim. Through the thick foam rises a medley of spices, malt and yeast. The palate is complex and sweet, but can be slightly bitter. The texture feels soft and delicate. Tripel's yeast characteristics are a focal point, often a potpourri: cinnamon, clove, pepper, banana, tangerines, lemon, orange, apple and peach. Another Belgian deviant in disguise, the tripel style can be potent, yet amazingly drinkable.

Three Beers to Try

WESTMALLE TRIPEL   The benchmark for the style, this beer is bright golden with a billowing white head. It has a nose of citrus fruits, cloves and hops and a crisp, light, cleansing mouthfeel.

ANKER GOUDEN CAROLUS TRIPEL
A complex strong beer by a family-owned brewery dating from the 14th century. With five malts and rich vinous fruit and peppery hop notes.

TRIPEL KARMELIET   Family-owned for seven generations, Brouwerij Bosteels makes a fine tripel. A bursting bouquet of citrus, earth and spice meld together in a caramel-sweet body that coats before a clean finish.

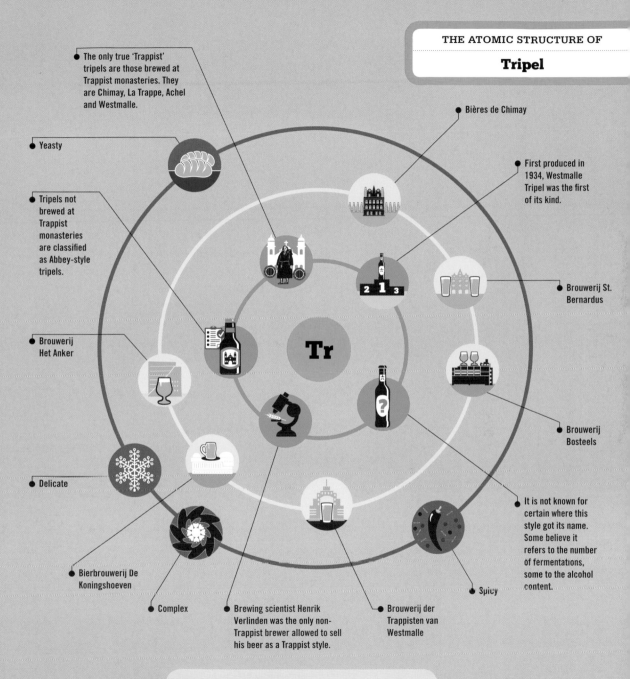

The only true 'Trappist' tripels are those brewed at Trappist monasteries. They are Chimay, La Trappe, Achel and Westmalle.

Yeasty

Tripels not brewed at Trappist monasteries are classified as Abbey-style tripels.

Brouwerij Het Anker

Delicate

Bierbrouwerij De Koningshoeven

Complex

Brewing scientist Henrik Verlinden was the only non-Trappist brewer allowed to sell his beer as a Trappist style.

Bières de Chimay

First produced in 1934, Westmalle Tripel was the first of its kind.

Brouwerij St. Bernardus

Brouwerij Bosteels

It is not known for certain where this style got its name. Some believe it refers to the number of fermentations, some to the alcohol content.

Spicy

Brouwerij der Trappisten van Westmalle

Tr

Food Pairing

| Basil-flavoured foods | Grilled salmon | Asparagus | Lobster |

Belgian Pale Ale

Origin: Belgium
Colour: 4–14 SRM
ABV: 3.9–5.6%
IBU: 20–30
Glassware: snifter, tulip, oversized wine glass

The melting pot of beers that are amber in colour and with a notable hoppiness, Belgian brews that fit in this style feature a complexity in yeast and malts that set them apart.

SHADES OF BRONZE

Belgians – brewers and drinkers alike – rarely categorise their domestic beer. Each beer has been crafted in a way that deserves its own place in the beer world. However, there is a class of ales that have the look and feel of pale ale brewed elsewhere and so have been grouped as such.

A Belgian pale is typically a light bronze to a deeper copper in colour. Generally clear, it is focused less on a bitter hopping than on the complexities shown in both the yeast and the malts. Medium in body and smooth, they are highly drinkable and with hints of light fruit, oranges, spices, cinnamon and an intriguing maltiness.

Three Beers to Try

DE KONINCK   When in Antwerp, any barkeeper knows what you want when you say a '*bolleke*' – this beer. Biscuity, fruity aromas from a deep amber body. Chewy texture of fruit and yeasty in taste.

SLAGHMUYLDER GREUT LAWAUITJ
The name of this beer means 'loads of noise', and Slaghmuylder's pale ale is heavy on peppery hops with a big malt and fruit aroma and palate, and a long bittersweet finish.

SPECIAL DE RYCK   The one word sums up DE RYCK's fine interpretation of the style, with a perfumy yeast character balanced by bitter and spicy hops and rich juicy malt.

THE ATOMIC STRUCTURE OF
Belgian Pale Ale

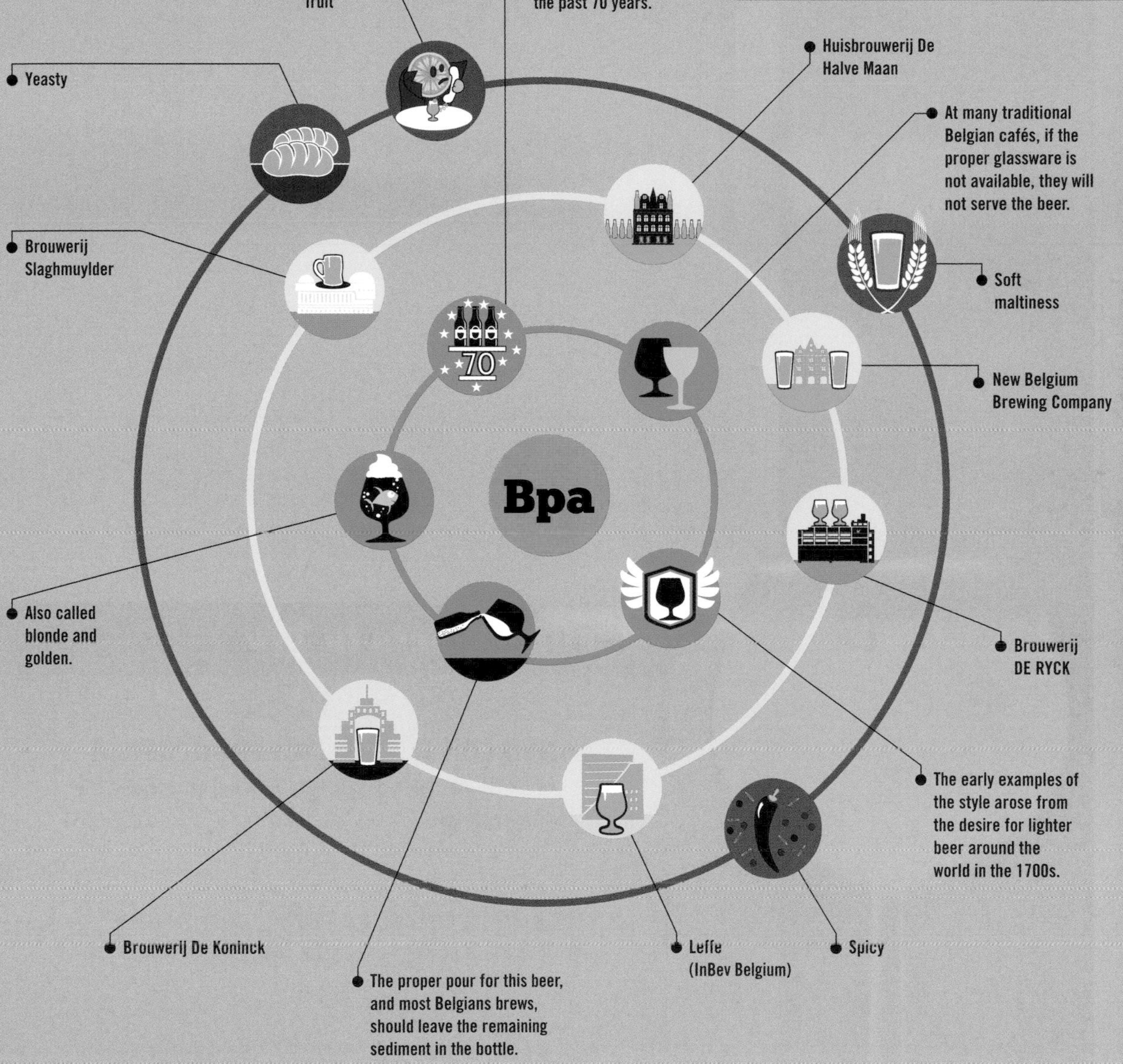

Despite its 300 year history, today's exemplars of the style were perfected in just the past 70 years.

Subtle fruit

Yeasty

Huisbrouwerij De Halve Maan

At many traditional Belgian cafés, if the proper glassware is not available, they will not serve the beer.

Brouwerij Slaghmuylder

Soft maltiness

New Belgium Brewing Company

Bpa

Also called blonde and golden.

Brouwerij DE RYCK

The early examples of the style arose from the desire for lighter beer around the world in the 1700s.

Brouwerij De Koninck

The proper pour for this beer, and most Belgians brews, should leave the remaining sediment in the bottle.

Leffe (InBev Belgium)

Spicy

Food Pairing

| Pork | Fried fish | Sausages | Thai food | Salads |

Lambic

Origin: Belgium
Colour: 3-7 SRM
ABV: 5-6%
IBU: 0-10
Glassware: flute, oversized wine glass

The lambic family is made up of three distinct sub-styles: unblended lambic, gueuze and fruit lambic. The first is the base for the others and is quite uncommon outside of Brussels.

CHARACTERFUL BACTERIA

While lambics of old are becoming increasingly rare, those still being brewed are complex and intriguing. Unblended lambics can be both young and old, depending on the amount of time spent in the barrel. Young brews are more lively and carbonated, perhaps with a slightly more puckering tartness. Mature lambics have a mellow smoothness and more of the complexities that come with the bacteria involved in the brewing process. These bacteria, intentional and desirable, give an unparalleled depth of character. It becomes pleasantly musty, lending a barnyard, leathery aroma and taste. The style is typically served from the cask and is very dry with little carbonation.

Three Beers to Try

CANTILLON GRAND CRU BRUOCSELLA
Aged on oak for three years, a funky, intense nose of earth results. It is textured and complex.

GIRARDIN OUDE LAMBIC   Farm brewery that produces a 'horse blanket' version of the style. Tart and vinous.

DE CAM OUDE LAMBIEK   A musty nose of wet hay and slight fruity notes gathers in complexity and intensity on the palate.

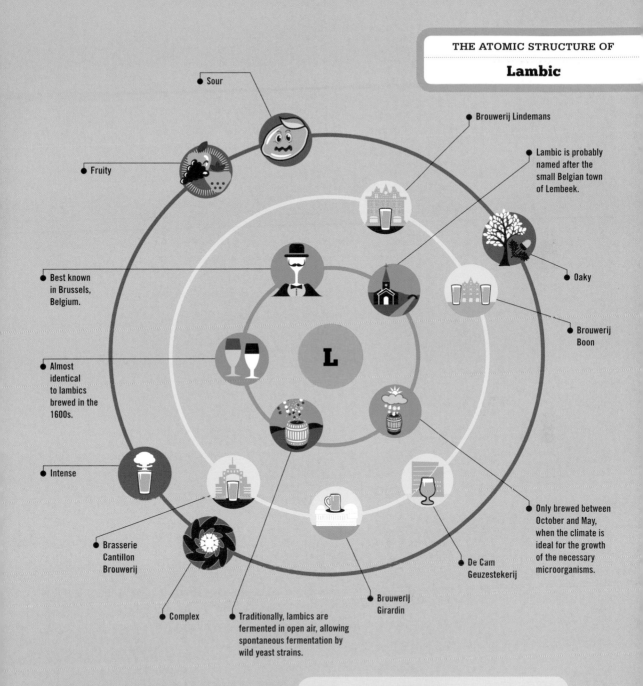

THE ATOMIC STRUCTURE OF
Lambic

Sour

Fruity

Brouwerij Lindemans

Lambic is probably named after the small Belgian town of Lembeek.

Oaky

Best known in Brussels, Belgium.

Brouwerij Boon

Almost identical to lambics brewed in the 1600s.

Intense

Only brewed between October and May, when the climate is ideal for the growth of the necessary microorganisms.

Brasserie Cantillon Brouwerij

De Cam Geuzestekerij

Complex

Traditionally, lambics are fermented in open air, allowing spontaneous fermentation by wild yeast strains.

Brouwerij Girardin

L

Food Pairing

Stews	Fish	Sauerkraut

Gueuze

Origin: Belgium
Colour: 3–13 SRM
ABV: 5–8%
IBU: 0–23
Glassware: flute

A blend of young and old lambic, gueuze is tempered but still tart, sour and involved.

BLENDED TO PERFECTION

Easier to find than unblended lambic, gueuze still bears the notable lambic complexities and characteristics. Typically three, but up to as many as seven, lambics are blended to create the brewer's perfect rendering. After the process of artistic blending, the gueuze is bottled and aged again, typically for three to nine months, but sometimes longer. The result is highly effervescent and refreshing.

Three Beers to Try

CANTILLON GUEUZE 100% LAMBIC Pours a burnt orange with a thick lace. The musty, barnyard scent blends with lemon and oak. This beer accounts for half of Cantillon's entire production.

LINDEMANS GUEUZE CUVÉE RENÉ A nose of utter complexity characterises this brew by Lindemans. Sweetness of honey mixes with sour fruit and a barnyard aroma. Refreshingly tart from beginning to end.

HANSSENS OUDE GUEUZE A tart and refreshing gueuze produced by a family of blenders based on a farm.

THE ATOMIC STRUCTURE OF
Gueuze

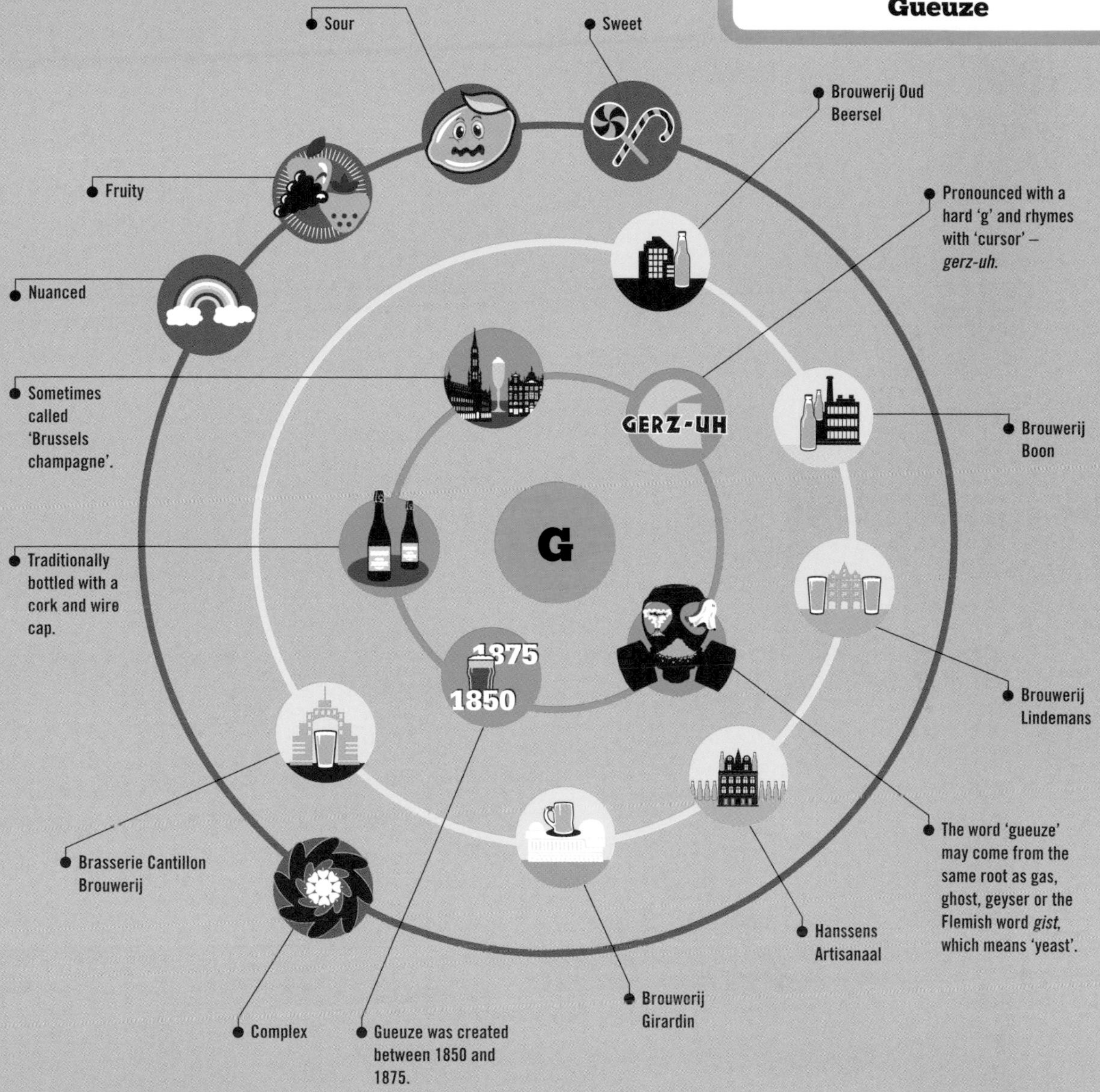

Sour

Sweet

Fruity

Nuanced

Brouwerij Oud Beersel

Pronounced with a hard 'g' and rhymes with 'cursor' — *gerz-uh*.

Sometimes called 'Brussels champagne'.

GERZ-UH

Brouwerij Boon

G

Traditionally bottled with a cork and wire cap.

1875
1850

Brouwerij Lindemans

Brasserie Cantillon Brouwerij

The word 'gueuze' may come from the same root as gas, ghost, geyser or the Flemish word *gist*, which means 'yeast'.

Complex

Gueuze was created between 1850 and 1875.

Brouwerij Girardin

Hanssens Artisanaal

Food Pairing

Serve as an aperitif	Mussels	Oysters	Goat's cheese

Fruit Lambic

Origin: Belgium
Colour: 3-7 SRM
(varies with fruit)
ABV: 5-7%
IBU: 0-10
Glassware: flute

A beer that's hard to believe is a beer, this style has a punch of fruit to balance the tartness.

A REFRESHING DESSERT DRINK

Much of the basic lambic story is the same here as for gueuze (see page 94). The base beer, before fruit is added, is typically a blend of young and old lambics. Once the brewer has found that perfect marriage of the two, fruit is added and the secondary fermentation begins. The specific fruit used is up to the brewer, but the most common are cherries, raspberries, blackcurrants, apples and peaches. The result is a product of the specific fruit addition, but will be a complex mélange of tart, fruity, dry, effervescent and crisp. This style is refreshing and can be delicious paired with dessert or served alone.

Three Beers to Try

KRIEK BOON A brilliantly red body and a light pink head, the nose is all cherry. The tartness continues on the palate, balanced by just enough sweetness.

CANTILLON ROSÉ DE GAMBRINUS
A framboise made by Cantillon, one of the world's great crafters of lambic beers. A beautiful deep pink with upfront tartness and well-rounded fruit.

LINDEMANS PÊCHE The nose is immediately peaches, the palate is tangy peach with a hint of earthiness.

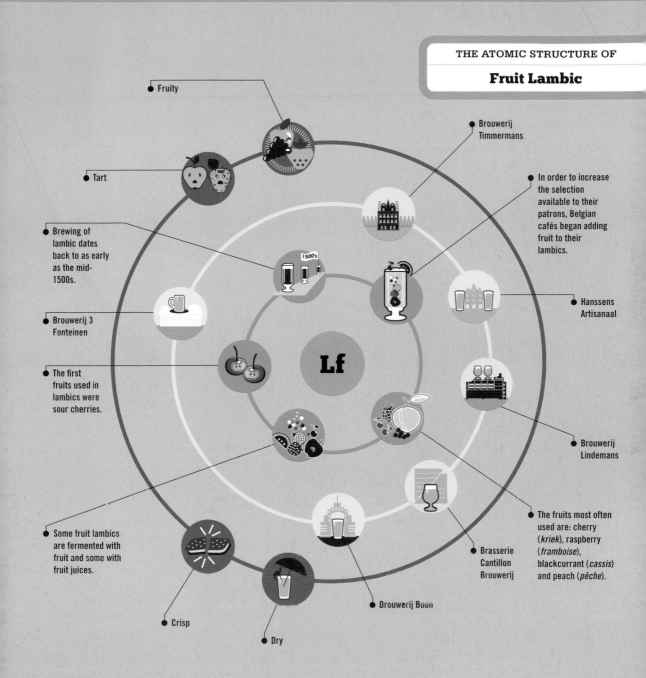

Fruity

Tart

Brewing of lambic dates back to as early as the mid-1500s.

Brouwerij 3 Fonteinen

The first fruits used in lambics were sour cherries.

Some fruit lambics are fermented with fruit and some with fruit juices.

Crisp

Dry

Brouwerij Timmermans

In order to increase the selection available to their patrons, Belgian cafés began adding fruit to their lambics.

Hanssens Artisanaal

Brouwerij Lindemans

The fruits most often used are: cherry (*kriek*), raspberry (*framboise*), blackcurrant (*cassis*) and peach (*pêche*).

Brasserie Cantillon Brouwerij

Drouwerij Boon

Lf

Food Pairing

| Chocolate desserts | Cheesecake | Sweet cheeses |

Belgian IPA

Origin: Belgium
Colour: 3–19 SRM
ABV: 6–10.5%
IBU: 50–80
Glassware: tulip

The beauty of beer is that it is ever changing. This style, new to the craft brewing scene, is one such tasty example.

BELGIAN YEAST AND HOPS

With the rise in popularity of IPAs worldwide, Belgian brewers, who traditionally had not produced hop-forward beer, began to experiment. The blend of the famed Belgian yeast strains with a hop-heavy palate was a dream match. From the outset it is impressive: a golden to amber body, hazy but brilliant, punctuated with a bright white cap. The nose continues the intrigue, an impossible blend of hops and earthy, biscuity, distinct yeast. Keeping the combination in balance becomes the key – American brewers lean more on the hops, while Belgians tend to be more focused on the yeast. A developing style, it is worth doing your own research.

Three Beers to Try

ACHOUFFE HOUBLON CHOUFFE   Brewed in 2006 by Achouffe for the first time, it was a pioneer. Bright gold, puffy white head with an immediate hop punch. The Belgian influence leans towards tripel. An incredible combination.

DUVEL TRIPLE HOP   Moortgat's famous golden ale now has a stronger, hoppier version, brewed with Amarillo, Saaz and Styrian Goldings that lend an immense spicy and peppery hop note.

DE RANKE XX BITTER   A spicy, floral, hoppy nose emits from a body of hazy apricot. Big, bitter hops and a nicely spicy yeast strain are present throughout.

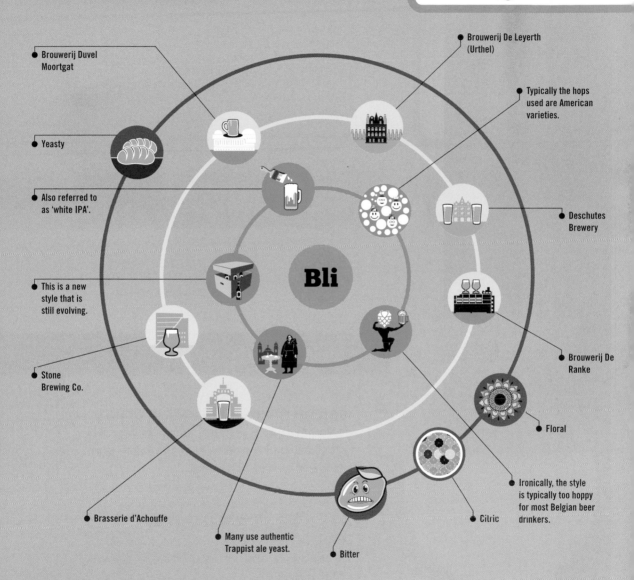

- Brouwerij Duvel Moortgat
- Brouwerij De Leyerth (Urthel)
- Typically the hops used are American varieties.
- Yeasty
- Also referred to as 'white IPA'.
- Deschutes Brewery
- This is a new style that is still evolving.
- Bli
- Brouwerij De Ranke
- Stone Brewing Co.
- Floral
- Brasserie d'Achouffe
- Ironically, the style is typically too hoppy for most Belgian beer drinkers.
- Many use authentic Trappist ale yeast.
- Bitter
- Citric

Food Pairing

| Fried chicken | Spicy seafood | Gorgonzola | Thai food |

Saison

Origin: Belgium
Colour: 5-14 SRM
ABV: 4.5-8%
IBU: 20-45
Glassware: tulip

A style with seemingly limitless boundaries, saisons give the brewer freedom to create and the drinker freedom to enjoy.

A SUMMER BREW

While the characteristics of this style vary, the history is relatively consistent. Traditionally brewed in late winter or early spring, saison (meaning 'season') beers, were meant to last the farmer-brewer from March to October. The summer months brought warm weather and difficult brewing conditions, so what was brewed in the spring was what would be consumed through the harvest.

The saison style is typically rustic and earthy, spicy and peppery. It varies in colour, but centres around a pale orange hue, with streaming carbonation and a buoyant vanilla head. Bright and refreshing, it finishes dry, with a pleasing and cleansing tart bite. Markedly bitter to survive the year, these beers are balanced enough to be perfectly quenching.

Three Beers to Try

SAISON DUPONT The flagship saison, this is one to be tried. A nose to die for, earthy, spicy with coriander, pepper and a veritable fruit feast. Pale golden and hazy, it becomes bitter, earthy, slightly sweet and wonderfully refreshing.

FANTÔME SAISON D'EREZÉE – PRINTEMPS Fantôme produces an array of saisons. This has lemon and hay aromas, and a light farmhouse funkiness. Light, refreshing and hopped.

SILLY SAISON Former farm brewery near the River Sille. A blend of young and matured beers, fruity and vinous with roasted malt notes and underpinned by spicy hops.

THE ATOMIC STRUCTURE OF
Saison

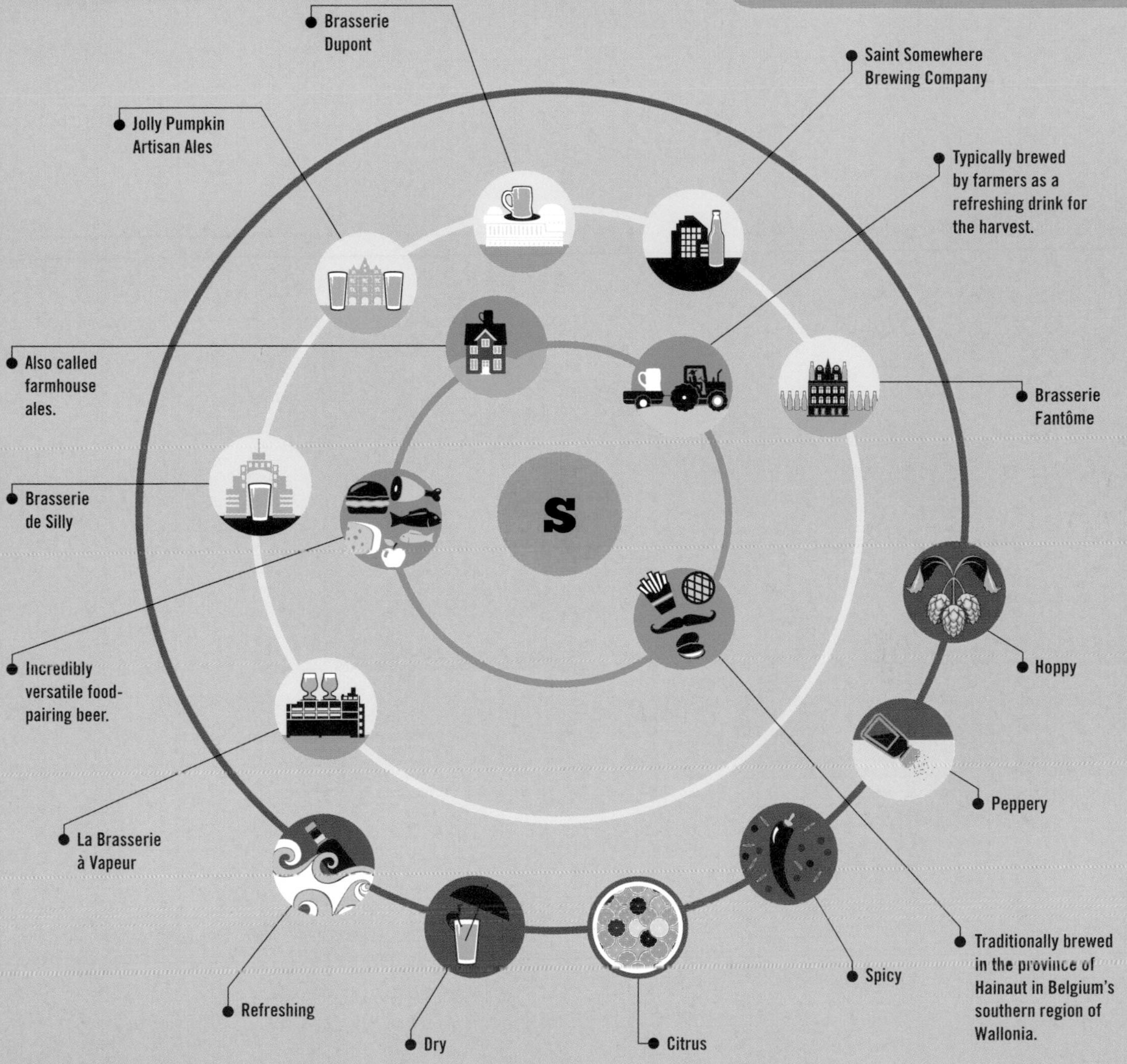

Brasserie Dupont

Saint Somewhere Brewing Company

Jolly Pumpkin Artisan Ales

Typically brewed by farmers as a refreshing drink for the harvest.

Also called farmhouse ales.

Brasserie Fantôme

Brasserie de Silly

S

Incredibly versatile food-pairing beer.

Hoppy

La Brasserie à Vapeur

Peppery

Spicy

Refreshing

Traditionally brewed in the province of Hainaut in Belgium's southern region of Wallonia.

Dry

Citrus

Food Pairing

| Crab cakes | Sausages | Thai food | Aged Gouda |

Bière de Garde

Origin: France
Colour: 6–19 SRM
ABV: 6–8.5%
IBU: 18–30
Glassware: tulip

The name of this farmhouse ale, which originated in northern France, means literally 'beer for keeping'.

A FREESTYLE BREW

This style can be formally divided into three subcategories according to colour: brown, blonde and amber. However, these subdivisions are at odds with the philosophy of the style, which emphasises artistic freedom and interpretation. Yet, a few lines must be drawn.

At its core is a soft maltiness, developed further by spiciness and mustiness and tactfully balanced by restrained hops. It checks in at 6–8.5 per cent alcohol and finishes crisp and refreshing. A musty, earthy complexity sets it apart as a most intriguing beer.

Three Beers to Try

JENLAIN AMBER This beer by Duyck kept the style from the grave. A bronzed amber with a velvety cap. A soft palate of sweet malt ends with a crisp finish.

CASTELAIN CH'TI BLONDE Brasserie Castelain uses lager yeast in its bières de garde. This well-balanced beer pours golden, with an earthy, slightly citric and spiced nose.

LA CHOULETTE BIÈRE DES SANS CULOTTES A lacy crown graces the deep gold body of this beer by La Choulette. Earthy notes on the nose and palate blend with spice and a refreshing hop bite.

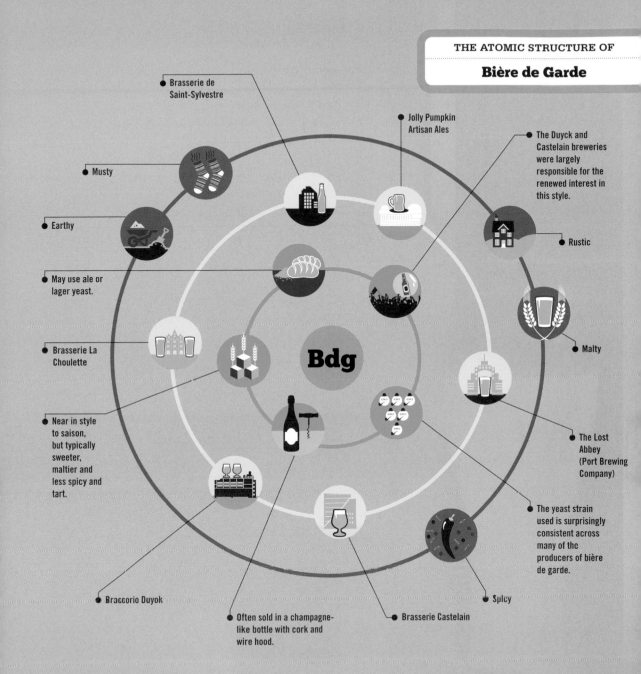

THE ATOMIC STRUCTURE OF
Bière de Garde

Brasserie de Saint-Sylvestre

Jolly Pumpkin Artisan Ales

The Duyck and Castelain breweries were largely responsible for the renewed interest in this style.

Musty

Earthy

Rustic

May use ale or lager yeast.

Malty

Brasserie La Choulette

Bdg

Near in style to saison, but typically sweeter, maltier and less spicy and tart.

The Lost Abbey (Port Brewing Company)

The yeast strain used is surprisingly consistent across many of the producers of bière de garde.

Braccorio Duyok

Often sold in a champagne-like bottle with cork and wire hood.

Brasserie Castelain

Spicy

Food Pairing

| Pungent French cheese | Sausages | Lamb chops | Turkey |

Dunkelweizen

Origin: Germany
Colour: 9-13 SRM
ABV: 4.5-6%
IBU: 10-18
Glassware: weizen

For a meatier version of Weissbier (page 86), Dunkelweizen hits the mark. Drinkable, refreshing and complex, there are many world-class beers in this category.

DEEPER AND DARKER

The towering head that typifies the Weissbier is no less impressive in its darker brother. Dunkelweizen's head is off-white and sponge-like; the body is a hazy, caramelly orange, with the signature carbonation streaking up the glass. The depth follows through on the nose, with just a slightly heavier undercurrent of wheat, malt and roastiness. There can be light notes of chocolate and fruit woven through a varied spiciness. Typically the mouthfeel is creamy and smooth, and the finish refreshingly crisp. With its richness and body, Dunkelweizen is a great choice as a cool-weather alternative to the more summery Weissbier.

Three Beers to Try

WEIHENSTEPHANER HEFEWEISSBIER DUNKEL Silky smooth without being cloying. Surprisingly refreshing with complex flavours.

AYINGER UR-WEISSE Malty nose and body with a cohesive blend of fruit, spice and malt. Creamy and rich.

FRANZISKANER HEFE-WEISSE DUNKEL Sweet and quite malty with a coating texture. Fruity and medium-bodied, it has a dry finish.

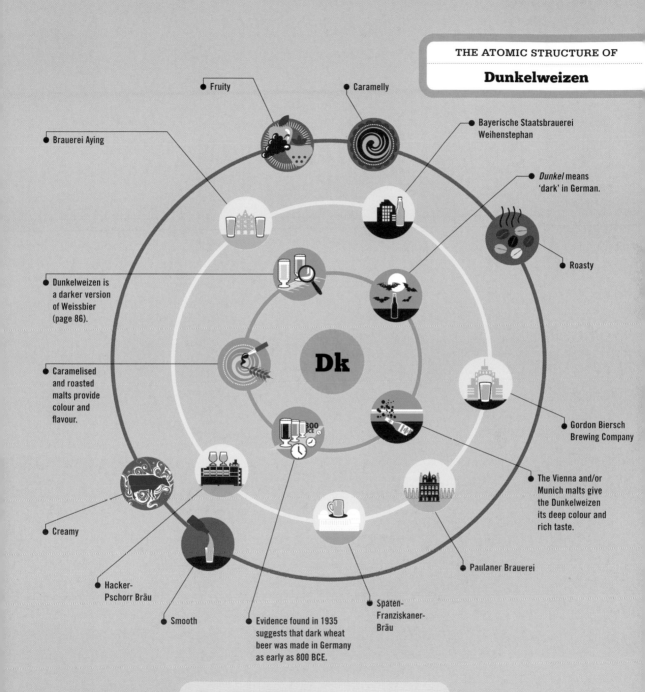

Fruity

Caramelly

Brauerei Aying

Bayerische Staatsbrauerei Weihenstephan

Dunkel means 'dark' in German.

Roasty

Dunkelweizen is a darker version of Weissbier (page 86).

Caramelised and roasted malts provide colour and flavour.

Dk

Gordon Biersch Brewing Company

The Vienna and/or Munich malts give the Dunkelweizen its deep colour and rich taste.

Creamy

Hacker-Pschorr Bräu

Smooth

Evidence found in 1935 suggests that dark wheat beer was made in Germany as early as 800 BCE.

Späten-Franziskaner-Bräu

Paulaner Brauerei

Food Pairing

| German food | Sausages | Enchiladas | Pulled pork |

Flanders Red

Origin: Belgium
Colour: 10-16 SRM
ABV: 4.5-6.5%
IBU: 10-25
Glassware: flute, tulip

A deceptive pour of soft garnet and brown, this beer is not for the faint of heart.

FUNKY FARMYARD FAVOURITE

Flanders red ale has its origins in the westernmost parts of Belgium. Unsurprisingly, it pours a deep reddish brown. It is intense in tartness and satisfying complexity. Typically the immediate impacts are earthiness, unusual yeasts and an intriguing balance of sweet and sour, but some can have hints of vanilla, oak, wet wool, lemons, sherry and cherries. It is normally the product of young and old blends and is aged for up to three years in unlined oak vats. During aging, wild yeast strains come to the fore, creating a barnyard funk that melds with sweet and fruity malt flavours. A bold style that, with an open mind, can become a favourite.

Three Beers to Try

RODENBACH GRAND CRU From the most famous producer of the style, this beer has an almost-brown body with a citrusy, earthy, funky nose. Malty, but tart and refreshing.

VERHAEGHE DUCHESSE DE BOURGOGNE Red with bronze lowlights and a bountiful head. The barnyard scent mixes with sour fruit and malt. The sour is tempered somewhat by earthiness, but is wonderfully balanced.

CUVÉE DES JACOBINS ROUGE Family-owned since 1892, the Brouwerij Bockor produces this brilliantly balanced sweet and sour red.

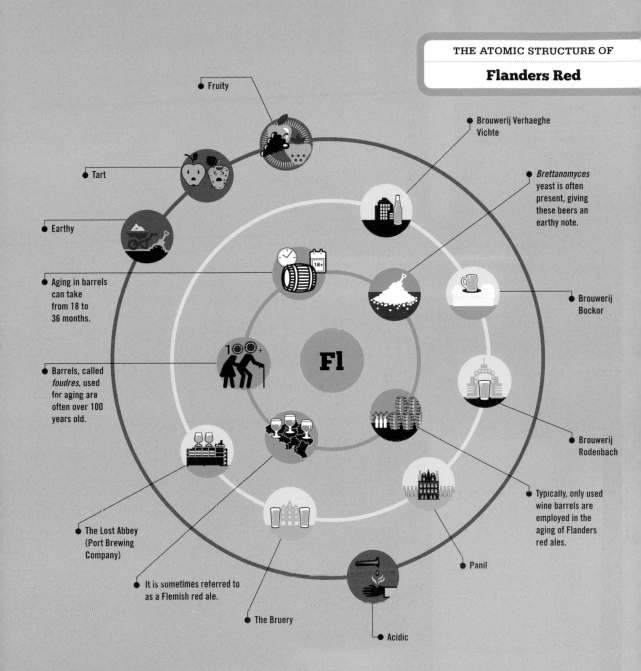

THE ATOMIC STRUCTURE OF

Flanders Red

Fl

Fruity

Tart

Earthy

Aging in barrels can take from 18 to 36 months.

Barrels, called *foudres*, used for aging are often over 100 years old.

Brouwerij Verhaeghe Vichte

Brettanomyces yeast is often present, giving these beers an earthy note.

Brouwerij Bockor

Brouwerij Rodenbach

Typically, only used wine barrels are employed in the aging of Flanders red ales.

Panil

The Lost Abbey (Port Brewing Company)

It is sometimes referred to as a Flemish red ale.

The Bruery

Acidic

Food Pairing

| Shellfish | Egg dishes | Mussels | Tangy cheese |

Altbier

Origin: Germany
Colour: 11-17 SRM
ABV: 4.5-5.2%
IBU: 35-50
Glassware: stange

Perhaps one of the world's oldest styles, Altbier still maintains a chic, hip reputation. Even today, it is a fine choice in any beer hall in Düsseldorf.

TANTALISING COPPER

In the idyllic brewing climate of Düsseldorf, Germany, Altbier has found a comfortable home. When the rest of Germany turned to lagers, this hybrid style borrowed the best from both worlds: it undergoes warm fermentation, then is cold-conditioned for several weeks. The body is clear, a tantalising copper with some versions nearing a deeper reddish brown. It is capped with a solid light brown head. The nose emits an undercurrent of the characteristic ale fruits, generally overshadowed by a soft malt body. A sip reveals a clean, crisp maltiness in tandem with the snappy bitterness of hops, all driving to a dry finish. Medium-bodied, smooth and drinkable, it is a great session beer.

Three Beers to Try

UERIGE ALT Known as one of the finest of the style, it has big aromatics and a bitter bite. It melds into rich malts, giving a friendly balance of bold flavours.

FRANKENHEIM ALT Boldly hop forward and highly drinkable. Caramelly malts balance before the hops return to the finish.

SCHLÜSSEL ALT The name means 'the keys', and the keys to Düsseldorf's gates are held at the brewery. The beer has a woody/grassy aroma and palate with hints of chocolate.

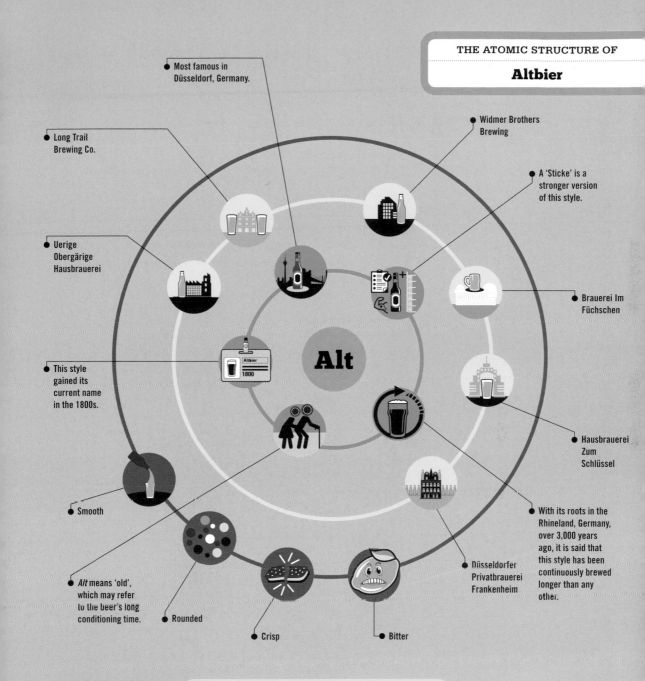

Most famous in Düsseldorf, Germany.

Long Trail Brewing Co.

Widmer Brothers Brewing

A 'Sticke' is a stronger version of this style.

Uerige Obergärige Hausbrauerei

Brauerei Im Füchschen

This style gained its current name in the 1800s.

Hausbrauerei Zum Schlüssel

Alt

Smooth

Alt means 'old', which may refer to the beer's long conditioning time.

Rounded

Crisp

Bitter

Düsseldorfer Privatbrauerei Frankenheim

With its roots in the Rhineland, Germany, over 3,000 years ago, it is said that this style has been continuously brewed longer than any other.

Food Pairing

| Roasted chicken | Grilled salmon | Pork | Burgers |

Roggenbier

Origin: Germany
Colour: 14-19 SRM
ABV: 4.5-6%
IBU: 10-20
Glassware: mug

An invention of the brewers of Regensburg, Bavaria, Germany, Roggenbier is essentially a Dunkelweizen (see page 104), but with malted rye replacing a portion of the wheat. That addition makes for a spicy, refreshing choice.

AN EXILE RETURNS

In 1516 Roggenbier fell out of production when rye was exiled from the brewhouse by beer purity laws, which limited the ingredients used in beer production to water, barley, yeast and hops. However, following a slow comeback in the 1980s, a few well-crafted examples of the Roggenbier style exist today.

In colour, this style runs from light orange to a coppery brown. A firm, creamy head caps a typically unfiltered body. Aromas of freshly baked rye bread, soft spices, earth and yeast predict the palate. Mild fruits mingle with the rye and the bready, yeasty and spicy centre. The finish is tangy, slightly bitter and dry.

Three Beers to Try

WOLNZACHER ROGGENBIER Yeast on the nose of banana and cloves, continues on the palate, with sweet bread and slightly funky earthiness.

THURN UND TAXIS ROGGEN Now brewed by the Paulaner brewery, it pours a dark amber with a beautiful off-white head. Pronounced characteristics of Weizen, with fruits and a smooth, malt centre.

ROGUENBIER RYE Made entirely from the brewer's – Rogue Ales – very own hops, barley and rye. Notes of rye, smoke, pepper and spice with light fruit throughout.

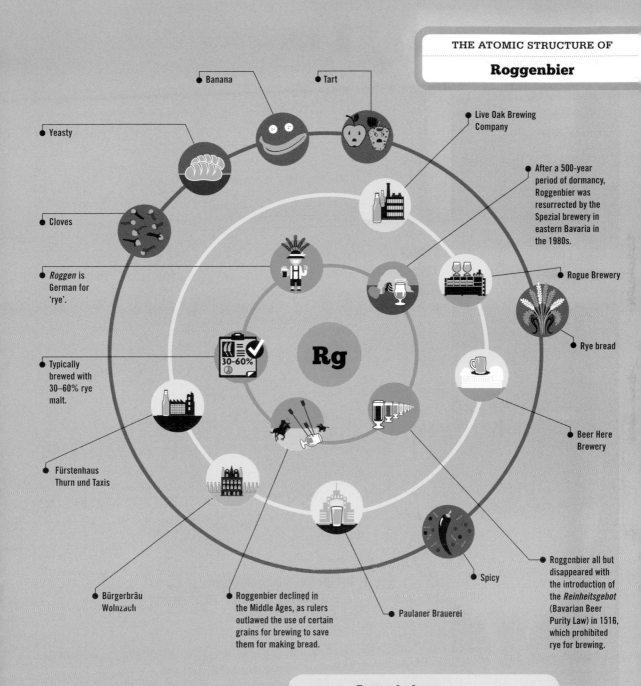

THE ATOMIC STRUCTURE OF
Roggenbier

Rg

- Banana
- Tart
- Yeasty
- Cloves
- *Roggen* is German for 'rye'.
- Typically brewed with 30–60% rye malt.
- 30-60%
- Fürstenhaus Thurn und Taxis
- Bürgerbräu Wolnzach
- Roggenbier declined in the Middle Ages, as rulers outlawed the use of certain grains for brewing to save them for making bread.
- Paulaner Brauerei
- Spicy
- Live Oak Brewing Company
- After a 500-year period of dormancy, Roggenbier was resurrected by the Spezial brewery in eastern Bavaria in the 1980s.
- Rogue Brewery
- Rye bread
- Beer Here Brewery
- Roggenbier all but disappeared with the introduction of the *Reinheitsgebot* (Bavarian Beer Purity Law) in 1516, which prohibited rye for brewing.

Food Pairing

| Barbecued pork | Sausages | Corned beef |

Dubbel

Origin: Belgium
Colour: 10-20 SRM
ABV: 6-7.8%
IBU: 15-25
Glassware: goblet

A cool evening and a warm meal make the perfect partners to the malty, spicy, fruity Belgian dubbel.

DARK FRUITS AND SPICE

Rich, robust, malty, yeasty, spicy, fruity and sweet. And that's just the beginning. Dubbel is an intricate and complex blend of flavours and textures, luring in the drinker from the outset. The aromatics can be fruity, with plums, figs, raisins and even cherry. The yeast profile on both the nose and the palate has notes of pepper, clove, cinnamon and nutmeg. A mahogany to russet-brown body is capped by a sticky light brown lace that laps the glass like a sturdy sea foam. A medium to full-bodied mouthfeel often blends chewiness with chocolate, rum notes, nuts, caramel, tawny port and a smooth layer of alcohol. Hops play a supporting role, used solely for balance.

Three Beers to Try

HALVE MAAN BRUGSE ZOT DUBBEL
Brewed by the Halve Maan — half moon — brewery in Bruges, it has spicy hops, toasted malt and rich chocolate on aroma and palate.

WESTMALLE DUBBEL   An initial tang, followed by chocolate and warming alcohol. It has a meaty mouthfeel like chestnuts and has a dry finish of lingering dark fruits and raisins.

TRAPPISTES ROCHEFORT 6   The bouquet is bready and spicy, with a thin layer of chocolate. Light and smooth mouthfeel underneath a caramel, fruity, slightly spicy palate.

THE ATOMIC STRUCTURE OF
Dubbel

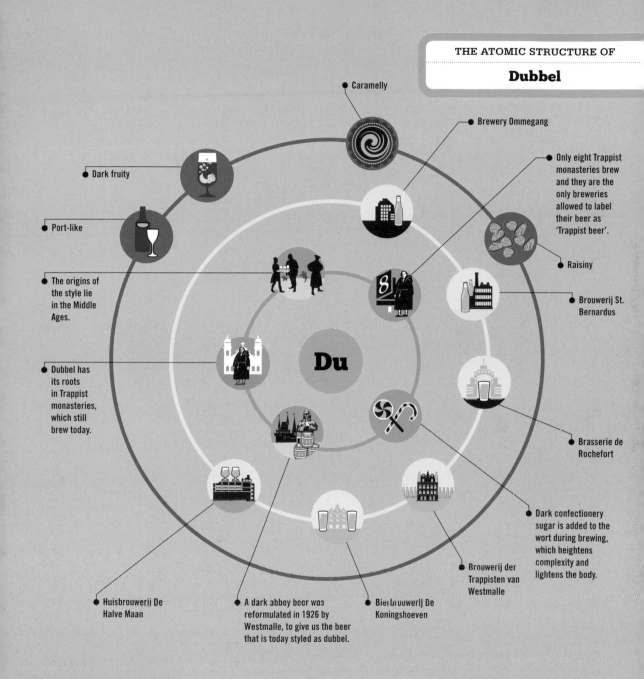

Caramelly

Brewery Ommegang

Only eight Trappist monasteries brew and they are the only breweries allowed to label their beer as 'Trappist beer'.

Dark fruity

Raisiny

Port-like

Brouwerij St. Bernardus

The origins of the style lie in the Middle Ages.

Du

Dubbel has its roots in Trappist monasteries, which still brew today.

Brasserie de Rochefort

Dark confectionery sugar is added to the wort during brewing, which heightens complexity and lightens the body.

Huisbrouwerij De Halve Maan

A dark abbey beer was reformulated in 1926 by Westmalle, to give us the beer that is today styled as dubbel.

Bierbrouwerij De Koningshoeven

Brouwerij der Trappisten van Westmalle

Food Pairing

| Beef stew | Game meats | Roasted chicken and pork | Olives |

Flanders Brown

Origin: Belgium
Colour: 12–18 SRM
ABV: 4.8–5.2%
IBU: 15–25
Glassware: flute, tulip

This style, also known as 'oud bruin', can be a shock to the unsuspecting, but with a little forewarning and an open mind, this Flemish specialty can be a treat.

MYSTERIOUS AND INTENSE

Blended to achieve different results, Flanders brown allows the brewer to become the artist. It pours brown, often with a hint of ruby, and is capped with a light brown head. The nose is a mysterious, intense blend: notes of chocolate, raisins, nuts, sherry, malts, dark fruits, barnyard, wet wool and leather can all stir together into a shockingly pleasant bouquet. The palate is simplified slightly from the aroma, but there is still an intense interplay of flavours, a forward tartness balanced by fruit and malt sweetness. Typically little bitterness is present, and the overall body is medium, with low carbonation. This outlier on the beer scene is definitely worth seeking out.

Three Beers to Try

LIEFMANS GOUDENBAND Each bottle of this crimson-brown liquid is wrapped in tissue paper. The funky, horsey nose blends with dark fruit and oak. Balanced fruit and tartness.

ROMAN ADRIAEN BROUWER Brewed by Roman of Oudenaarde and named after a local artist, it has roasted and toasted malt notes with hints of dark fruit and chocolate, and a late burst of hops.

PETRUS OUD BRUIN From Bavik, this beer has a complex barnyard nose with citrus highlights. It is lightly sour, balanced with fruity, malty sweetness, with a refreshingly tart finish.

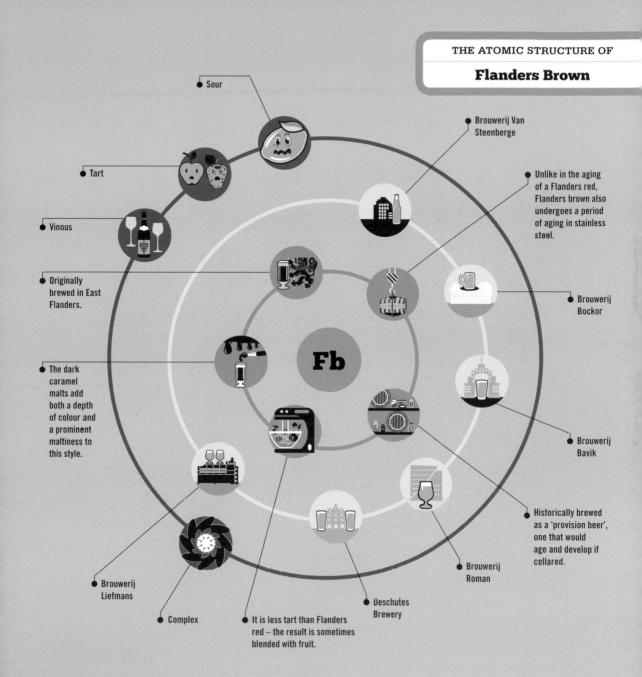

Sour

Tart

Vinous

Brouwerij Van Steenberge

Unlike in the aging of a Flanders red, Flanders brown also undergoes a period of aging in stainless steel.

Originally brewed in East Flanders.

Brouwerij Bockor

Fb

The dark caramel malts add both a depth of colour and a prominent maltiness to this style.

Brouwerij Bavik

Historically brewed as a 'provision beer', one that would age and develop if cellared.

Brouwerij Liefmans

Brouwerij Roman

Complex

It is less tart than Flanders red – the result is sometimes blended with fruit.

Deschutes Brewery

Food Pairing

Flemish stew	Game meats	Pork	Aged Cheddar

Belgian Strong Dark Ale

Origin: Belgium
Colour: 7-22 SRM
ABV: 7-11%
IBU: 20-50
Glassware: goblet

Seductive, complex and varied, into this category of dark, smooth and intense brews fall some of the world's greatest beers.

DARKLY COMPLEX

This beer is deep in colour, aromatic on the nose, tempting on the tongue and delicious on the palate. One brew from this category could crown the top spot on many a beer lover's list. While the style is truly a menagerie of breweries' artistic endeavors, there are a few factors that run throughout. Colours range from a dark amber to deeply brown with rocky heads of ecru to beige. The bouquet is bountiful: raisins, dates, spices, various fruits, caramel, bread, herbs and pepper. A malty backbone is prevalent and on this lie other ancillary flavours typically layered with a malty sweetness. The alcohol is wisely hidden, but warming and present nonetheless.

Three Beers to Try

CHIMAY GRANDE RÉSERVE　(Also called Chimay Blue Cap.) A pre-eminent example of this style. Sweet malts blend with dark fruit and spices to finish dry. Ages beautifully.

TRAPPIST WESTVLETEREN 12　An incredible example of the style, now becoming a bit more easily available.

TRAPPISTES ROCHEFORT 10　Deep brown with streaks of lace that crawl down the glass. The nose is bready and earthy with raisins, caramel and cloves. A sweet blend of maltiness on the palate and a dry finish, all concealing a big 11.3% ABV.

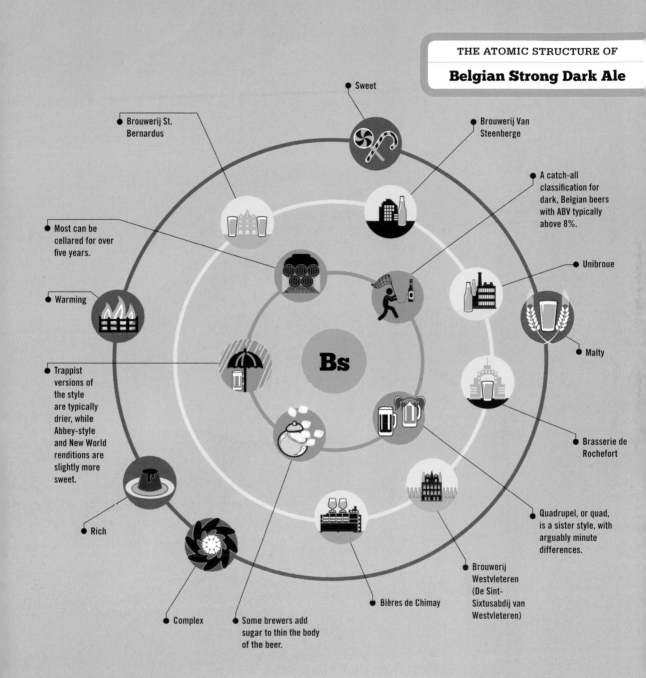

THE ATOMIC STRUCTURE OF
Belgian Strong Dark Ale

Sweet

Brouwerij St. Bernardus

Brouwerij Van Steenberge

A catch-all classification for dark, Belgian beers with ABV typically above 8%.

Most can be cellared for over five years.

Unibroue

Warming

Malty

Bs

Trappist versions of the style are typically drier, while Abbey-style and New World renditions are slightly more sweet.

Brasserie de Rochefort

Quadrupel, or quad, is a sister style, with arguably minute differences.

Rich

Brouwerij Westvleteren (De Sint-Sixtusabdij van Westvleteren)

Complex

Bières de Chimay

Some brewers add sugar to thin the body of the beer.

Food Pairing

Beef ribs	Game meats	Mushrooms	Washed-rind cheeses

Weizenbock

Origin: Germany
Colour: 15–20 SRM
ABV: 6–8.5%
IBU: 15–30
Glassware: weizen

With a relatively high alcohol content, this wheat beer fits the bill for a cold winter's eve.

WINTER WARMTH

From a Dunkelweizen to a Weizenbock, we continue to climb up the wheat-beer ladder of increasing alcoholic strength, darkness of colour and complexity of flavour. At the top of this scale, the Weizenbock is an intriguing brew. The fruity notes on the nose meld with the grains and yeast to form an immediate impression of depth. There are often the common notes of banana, cloves and spice, but with a pronounced caramel and malt character. While still highly drinkable and smooth, the blend of fruitiness, heavy maltiness and sweetish alcohol make this less a thirst-quenching brew than a comforting and warming winter drink.

Three Beers to Try

SCHNEIDER WEISSE TAP 6 UNSER AVENTINUS The characteristic banana and clove meld beautifully with rich caramel and sweet, warming alcohol.

WEIHENSTEPHANER VITUS Pours golden with a bursting nose of bread-like maltiness and hints of fruit and cloves. The palate reflects the nose, with a long and complex finish.

ERDINGER PIKANTUS Brewed by Erdinger, one of the major Bavarian wheat beer brewers, it has a liquorice, roasted malt, vanilla, dark fruit and spicy hop character.

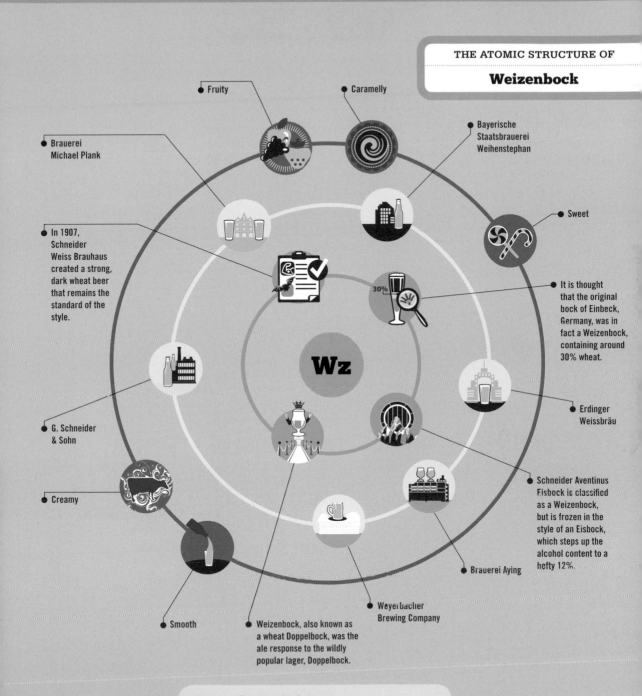

Fruity

Caramelly

Bayerische
Staatsbrauerei
Weihenstephan

Brauerei
Michael Plank

Sweet

In 1907,
Schneider
Weiss Brauhaus
created a strong,
dark wheat beer
that remains the
standard of the
style.

30%

It is thought
that the original
bock of Einbeck,
Germany, was in
fact a Weizenbock,
containing around
30% wheat.

Wz

Erdinger
Weissbräu

G. Schneider
& Sohn

Schneider Aventinus
Fisbock is classified
as a Weizenbock,
but is frozen in the
style of an Eisbock,
which steps up the
alcohol content to a
hefty 12%.

Creamy

Brauerei Aying

Weyerbacher
Brewing Company

Smooth

Weizenbock, also known as
a wheat Doppelbock, was the
ale response to the wildly
popular lager, Doppelbock.

Food Pairing

| Roasted meats | Grilled vegetables | Blue cheese | Apple desserts |

Belgian Black Ale

Origin: Belgium
Colour: 30–40 SRM
ABV: 4–6.2%
IBU: 20–40
Glassware: tulip, snifter, oversized wine glass

Not to be confused with Belgian strong dark ale (see page 116), this one is a true contradiction – smooth and light in texture, but deeply dark in the glass.

LIGHT AND DARK

Despite apparent references to the style dating back to the mid-1500s, Belgian black (also known as Belgian dark ale) has a hazy history. A couple of fairly standard features help to cohere the style: darkness of body and character eloquently blended with Belgian yeast. The result of this blend is a dark, smooth, rich brew, lightened in texture and taste by the fruity, sprightly, often zesty yeasts of Belgium. Spices appear such as anise, coriander, black pepper and cardamom. Hints of chocolate, coffee and toffee from the malt bill may be present as well. Highly drinkable, it is a pleasant surprise.

Three Beers to Try

BELLEVAUX BLACK A husband and wife team on a farm produce this black beer which has a rich liquorice character from dark malts. Burnt fruit, peppery hops and a dry finish.

3 SCHTENG Grain d'Orge produces this porter-style black beer with vinous fruits, hints of chocolate and coffee, touches of liquorice and molasses, and a peppery hop note.

TILBURG'S DUTCH BROWN ALE A richly complex brew by the Netherlands' only Trappist brewery, Koningshoeven. Notes of chocolate and toffee play through a sweet, creamy body.

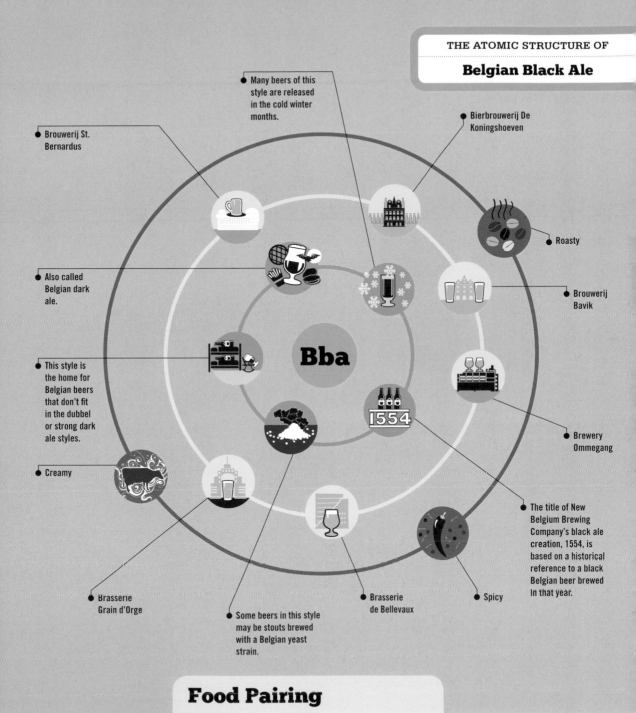

Many beers of this style are released in the cold winter months.

Bierbrouwerij De Koningshoeven

Brouwerij St. Bernardus

Roasty

Also called Belgian dark ale.

Brouwerij Bavik

Bba

This style is the home for Belgian beers that don't fit in the dubbel or strong dark ale styles.

Brewery Ommegang

Creamy

1554

The title of New Belgium Brewing Company's black ale creation, 1554, is based on a historical reference to a black Belgian beer brewed in that year.

Brasserie Grain d'Orge

Brasserie de Bellevaux

Spicy

Some beers in this style may be stouts brewed with a Belgian yeast strain.

Food Pairing

| Pork chops | Lamb | Meat sandwiches | Chocolate |

LAGERS OF CONTINENTAL EUROPEAN ORIGIN

LAGERS OF CONTINENTAL EUROPEAN ORIGIN

An oft-misunderstood category of beer, the lager family has a rich heritage, only recently overshadowed by mega-conglomerate brewing and its consistent, but uncreative, standardised products. The average beer drinker may think only of these undistinguished pale forms of lager, but there are a vast range of flavourful, clean, tantalising beers in this category to be discovered and enjoyed.

When categorising beer, each style falls into either the lager or the ale camp (save a few hybrid exceptions). While ales dominate in terms of varieties of styles, lagers have the stronghold on quantities consumed worldwide. It is this dominance, however, that has tainted the view of many ale fans, leading some to unfairly judge the whole style by its weakest members.

In general terms, a lager is labelled as such because of its cool fermentation, typically 4–7°C (40–45°F), and its extended period of 'lagering'. This term, which comes from *lager*, meaning 'store room' in German, illustrates one of the integral and defining features in the brewing process, separating it from those in the ale category. This longer period of cool aging and the use of bottom-fermenting lager yeast eliminates some of the characteristic fruity elements found in ales and rounds out harsher flavours, resulting in clean, clear flavours, behind which brewing imperfections cannot hide.

The most consumed styles of the world fall into the category of pale lagers. Despite American dominance in the style today, it was from Germany that the brews originated. In the 1400s, Bavarian brewers discovered that the storage of beer in cool caves resulted in a beer that kept well, even through warmer months. Soon, brewers took to fermenting and aging brews in caves, and by 1553 this practice was made law by the Bavarian Duke Albrecht V, the edict banning warm-weather brewing. This eventually all but eliminated the yeasts fermenting at warmer temperatures in the region and, in turn, lager brewing became the primary focus of the area's brewing activity. The first examples were dark, but with the rising popularity of pale ale elsewhere, German brewers, at home and abroad, followed suit and soon pilsner and helles were all the rage. These beers are beautifully clean and balanced, with solid malts, but spicy, sharp bitterness and a quenching, refreshing quality. Vienna lager – spawned from Bohemian pilsner – was akin to the Märzens and Oktoberfest brews of Germany. It is the bock family in which lagers start to pointedly stray from the lighter lager styles. The Maibock is light in colour, but richly malty. Bock takes on a bit more colour and malt, but is still smooth and satisfying. Doppelbock – the 'liquid bread' – comes in even stronger, but subtly so, and can be an almost black-brown. Eisbock is the strongest of the bock bunch, born from methods of freezing to produce a concentrated, sweet, alcoholic sipper. A drinker's preconceptions may be completely shattered with a sip of the darkest of the lager family, Schwarzbier, which, veiled in blackness, remains a clean, crisp and drinkable dark beer, with notes of bittersweet malt and nuts.

Lagers will not be as complex as ales, but are no less enjoyable. In their straightforward simplicity, the aromas are distinct, the appearance enticing and the taste delicious.

German Pilsner

Origin: Germany
Colour: 2-5 SRM
ABV: 4.5-5.2%
IBU: 25-45
Glassware: pilsner, flute, mug

When a bright golden lager was born in Bohemia (page 128), it didn't take long for German brewers to see its appeal. They embraced it and made it their own, and today it is the nation's most widely consumed style.

SHEER GOLD

German pilsner pours a beauty – from a crystal, pale straw to a sparkling gold, always capped with a dense puff of bright white. Its sheer, bright body presents a steady stream of carbonation, rushing to aid the lacing head. On the palate there is a crisp, refreshing, assertive hop bitterness. With little else to distract, the bitterness becomes the focal point, but not without a supporting bready malt character. It is an appetising blend that finishes satisfyingly dry. While similar to the Bohemian version from which it originated, German pilsner is typically more pale, dry and carbonated, with a slightly less aromatic nose.

Three Beers to Try

BITBURGER PREMIUM PILS Claiming the spot of Germany's number one draft beer, it is pale golden with a crisp, clean bitterness, yet not so much as to drown the pleasant German malt.

JEVER PILSENER Significant hops on the nose, layered with bready malts. A zippy, refreshing bitterness finishes incredibly dry.

VELTINS PILSENER A 19th-century, family-owned brewery in the North Rhine produces a beer with toasted malt, a touch of lemon, and spicy and floral hops.

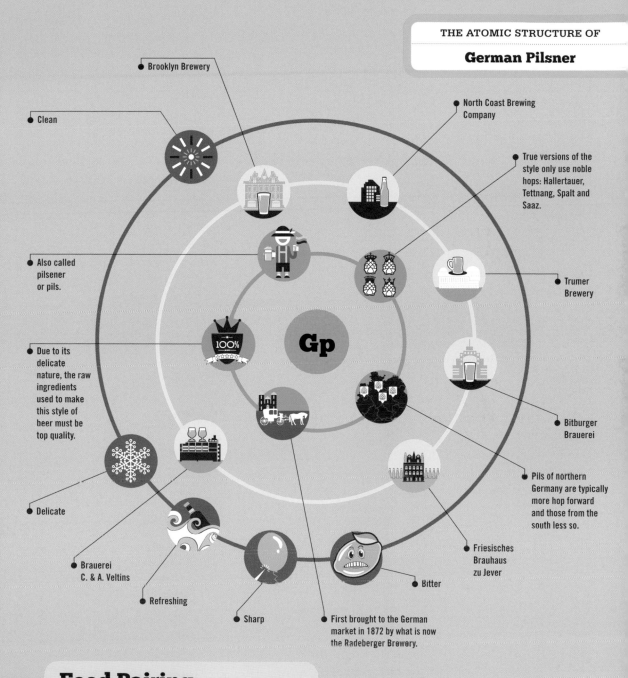

Brooklyn Brewery

Clean

North Coast Brewing Company

True versions of the style only use noble hops: Hallertauer, Tettnang, Spalt and Saaz.

Also called pilsener or pils.

Trumer Brewery

Due to its delicate nature, the raw ingredients used to make this style of beer must be top quality.

Gp

Bitburger Brauerei

Delicate

Pils of northern Germany are typically more hop forward and those from the south less so.

Brauerei C. & A. Veltins

Refreshing

Friesisches Brauhaus zu Jever

Sharp

Bitter

First brought to the German market in 1872 by what is now the Radeberger Brewery.

Food Pairing

Shellfish	Spicy sausages	Indian food	Fried fish	Jamaican food

Bohemian Pilsner

Origin: Bohemia (Czech Republic)
Colour: 3.5–6 SRM
ABV: 4–5.5%
IBU: 35–45
Glassware: pilsner, flute, mug

A Bavarian brewer and a city with a lot of bad beer spawned the world's most influential style.

A NAKED BEER

In 1842 in the city of Plzen (Pilsen), Bohemia, a Bavarian brewmaster created the palest malt of the age. It allowed the creation of a shining body of gold – highly flavourful and delicate. One of the more difficult beers to brew, it is often referred to as 'naked', as any brewing imperfections are immediately apparent. It has a characteristically creamy white head that sits atop a bubbling pale, sparkling body. Aromas of complex, bready malts blend with the spicy, floral hops, typically of the Saaz variety. German and Bohemian pilsners share many similarities, but the Bohemian version is slightly darker in colour, less carbonated and more aromatic than its sister style from Germany.

Three Beers to Try

PILSNER URQUELL *Urquell* means 'original source' in German. This classic, brewed by Plzensky Prazdroj, is full, flavourful and bitter with an eloquently balancing sweet malt.

GAMBRINUS Gambrinus is the neighbouring brewery to Pilsner Urquell in Pilsen, and is also owned by Plzensky Prazdroj . The beer is brewed with local malt and Saaz hops and has a fresh grass aroma, juicy malt in the mouth and a bitter finish.

SAMUEL ADAMS NOBLE PILS This offering from The Boston Beer Company is a bit more hoppy than is typical for the style, but is a perfectly refreshing, spicy, slightly citric blend.

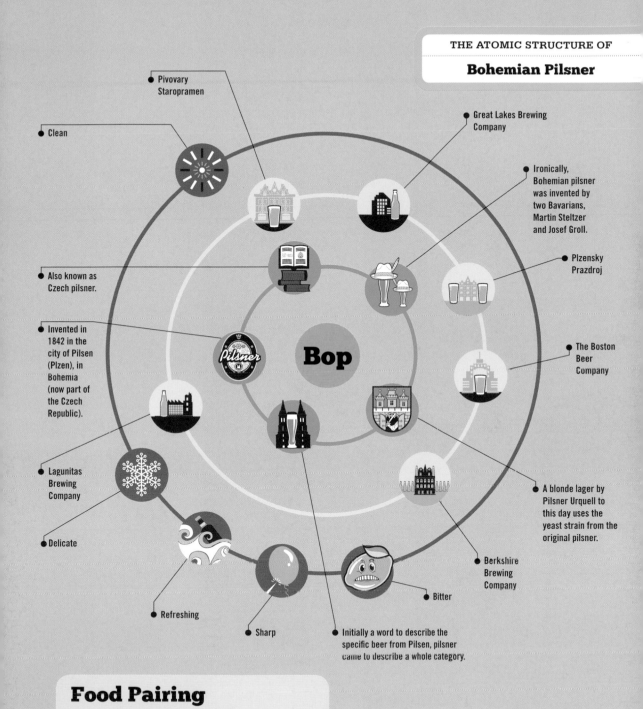

THE ATOMIC STRUCTURE OF

Bohemian Pilsner

Pivovary Staropramen

Clean

Great Lakes Brewing Company

Ironically, Bohemian pilsner was invented by two Bavarians, Martin Steltzer and Josef Groll.

Plzensky Prazdroj

Also known as Czech pilsner.

Invented in 1842 in the city of Pilsen (Plzen), in Bohemia (now part of the Czech Republic).

The Boston Beer Company

Lagunitas Brewing Company

Delicate

A blonde lager by Pilsner Urquell to this day uses the yeast strain from the original pilsner.

Berkshire Brewing Company

Refreshing

Sharp

Initially a word to describe the specific beer from Pilsen, pilsner came to describe a whole category.

Bitter

Bop

Pilsner

Food Pairing

| Shellfish | Spicy sausages | Indian food | Salmon | Ham |

Helles

Origin: Germany
Colour: 3–5 SRM
ABV: 4.7–5.4%
IBU: 16–22
Glassware: pilsner, flute, mug

Helles – meaning pale – is the everyday beer for Bavarian drinkers, quaffed in large mugs, with pilsner preferred for special occasions. It has a rich malt and gentle hop character.

A MUNICH MUGFUL

Pleasingly golden, a bright, shimmering body of translucent yellow, confidently capped with a rocky froth of white, helles makes for a picture-perfect pint. The sight is beautiful and the palate well balanced – having a quiet supporting note of hops, and a more spotlighted sweet, bready maltiness. The medium body and smooth mouthfeel clearly explain the popularity of this style in the beer halls of Munich. It is more malty and less bitter than its inspiration, pilsner, yet maintains a quaffable quality the whole mug through.

Three Beers to Try

WEIHENSTEPHANER ORIGINAL From the brewery founded in 1040 comes an example that typifies the style. Malt forward, but balanced, smooth and refreshing.

HOFBRÄU ORIGINAL Brewed by Munich's famous Hofbräuhaus, this beer is golden in colour and substantial, with a forward maltiness.

SPATEN MÜNCHNER HELL From the creator of the style, this beer has a bready, sweet malt body, balanced with a zip of hops.

THE ATOMIC STRUCTURE OF

Helles

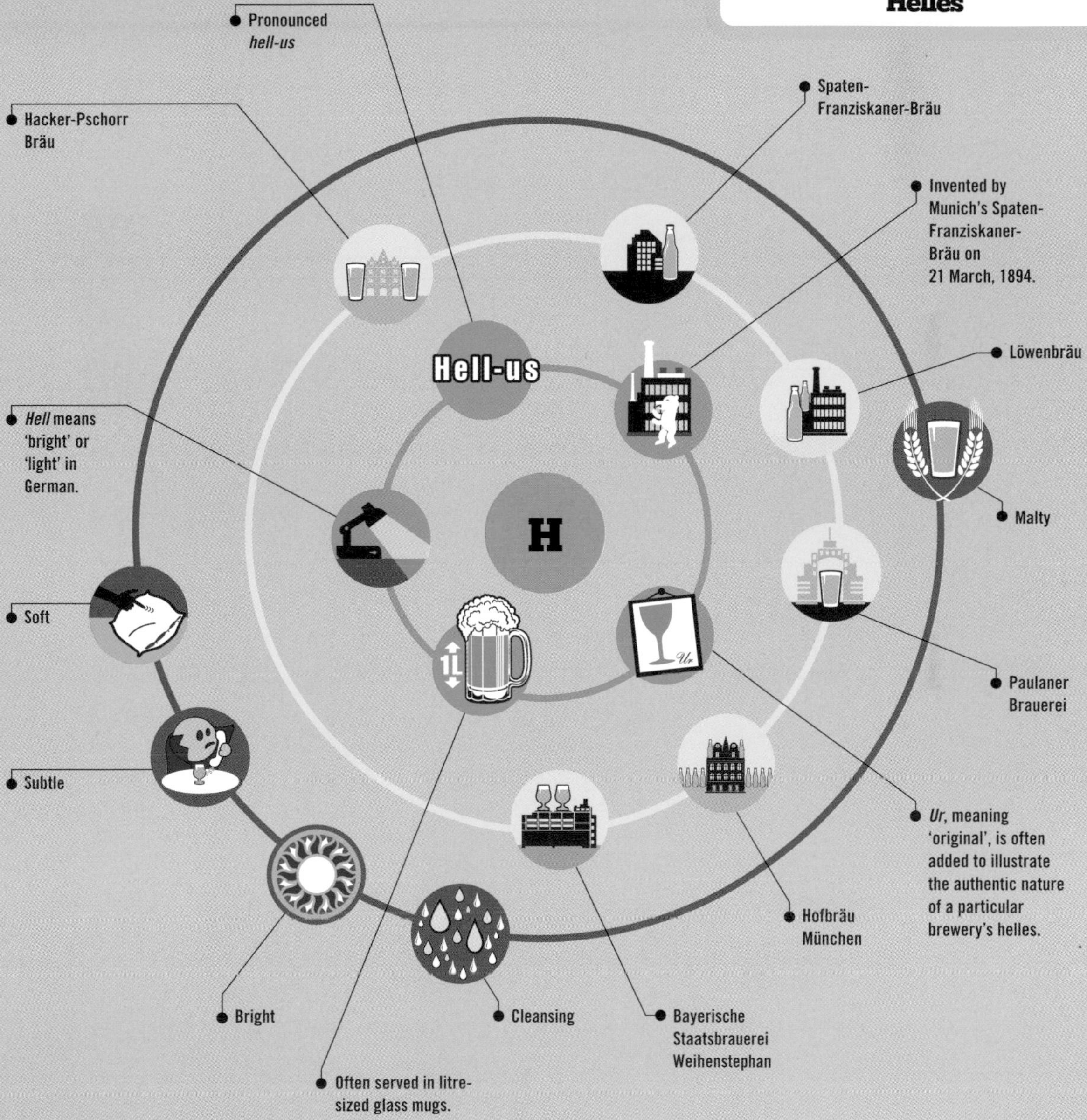

Pronounced *hell-us*

Hacker-Pschorr Bräu

Spaten-Franziskaner-Bräu

Invented by Munich's Spaten-Franziskaner-Bräu on 21 March, 1894.

Löwenbräu

Hell-us

Hell means 'bright' or 'light' in German.

H

Malty

Soft

Paulaner Brauerei

Subtle

Ur, meaning 'original', is often added to illustrate the authentic nature of a particular brewery's helles.

Bright

Hofbräu München

Often served in litre-sized glass mugs.

Cleansing

Bayerische Staatsbrauerei Weihenstephan

Food Pairing

| Light seafood | Sausages | Creamy egg dishes |

Dortmunder Export

Origin: Germany
Colour: 4-6 SRM
ABV: 4.8-6%
IBU: 23-30
Glassware: pilsner, flute, pint

From Dortmund, the largest city in Germany's industrial region of Ruhr, comes a hearty brew, crafted for the tough workers of the day.

HEARTY AND REFRESHING

A beer with a heritage always seems to taste better. In the industrial town of Dortmund in the 19th century, mining was king, and the miners thirsted for a hearty, yet refreshing brew. Dortmunder export is hoppier than a helles, but less so than a pilsner. The result is a well-balanced quencher. The body is typically a shade of gold with a lasting head, and the innocent aroma is a faint mixture of hops and slightly sweet malt. The balance continues on first sip, which evokes a rich, sometimes caramelly, malt character and a present, but not bold, layer of hops. Typically it racks in at about 5.5 per cent ABV, just enough to take the edge off after a hard day at the coal face.

Three Beers to Try

BALTIKA #7 EXPORT Russian interpretation that pours bright gold and has a pleasing, bready nose. Slight citrus and lemongrass hops guide a clean finish.

DAB ORIGINAL One of the few beers of this style still produced in Dortmund – light maltiness, clean and as balanced as it should be.

PINKUS SPECIAL Brewed in Münster, close to Dortmund, by Pinkus Müller, this is long-lagered beer with a massive fruity aroma of ripe pears, with toasted malt and floral hops.

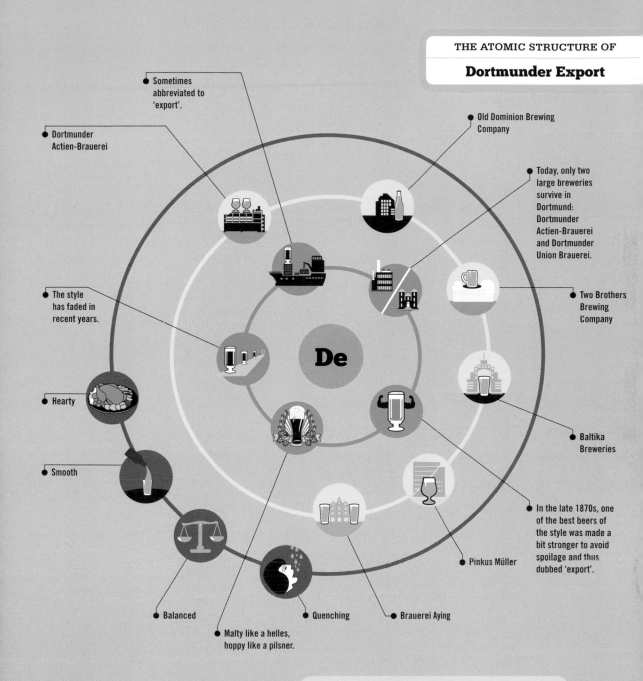

THE ATOMIC STRUCTURE OF
Dortmunder Export

Sometimes abbreviated to 'export'.

Dortmunder Actien-Brauerei

Old Dominion Brewing Company

Today, only two large breweries survive in Dortmund: Dortmunder Actien-Brauerei and Dortmunder Union Brauerei.

The style has faded in recent years.

Two Brothers Brewing Company

De

Hearty

Baltika Breweries

Smooth

In the late 1870s, one of the best beers of the style was made a bit stronger to avoid spoilage and thus dubbed 'export'.

Balanced

Pinkus Müller

Brauerei Aying

Quenching

Malty like a helles, hoppy like a pilsner.

Food Pairing

Steak	Burgers	Thai food

Maibock

Origin: **Germany**
Colour: **6–11 SRM**
ABV: **6.3–7.5%**
IBU: **23–35**
Glassware: **mug**

In the world of bocks, Maibock is a newcomer, but the changes that it has undergone since its birth have made it the perfect pint with which to usher in spring.

MALTY AND SATISFYING

With the origins of bock brewing in the 14th century (see traditional bock, page 144), Maibock was a relative latecomer. The malting innovations that came in the 19th century and affected the colour of many styles had an influence on this type of beer as well. Modern Maibocks are burnished gold to light amber in colour with a clear body and a lacy, creamy, white head. Rich maltiness is the focus, but tempered slightly by a touch more bitterness than others in the bock family. It is well-balanced in body and lacks any roasted or caramel notes. It aims to be satisfying and substantial without being heavy or overly complex.

Three Beers to Try

EINBECKER MAI-UR-BOCK This well-balanced, deeply amber brew is a testament to time-honoured tradition.

HOFBRÄU MAIBOCK This classic pours a glittering copper-red, thickly capped with a beige head. Rich, sweet malts harmonise with a hop note on the clean finish.

ULMER MAIBOCK Ulmer dates from the 19th century and ages its beer for six weeks. It has fruity and herbal aromas and flavours, with a big bitter note for the style.

THE ATOMIC STRUCTURE OF
Maibock

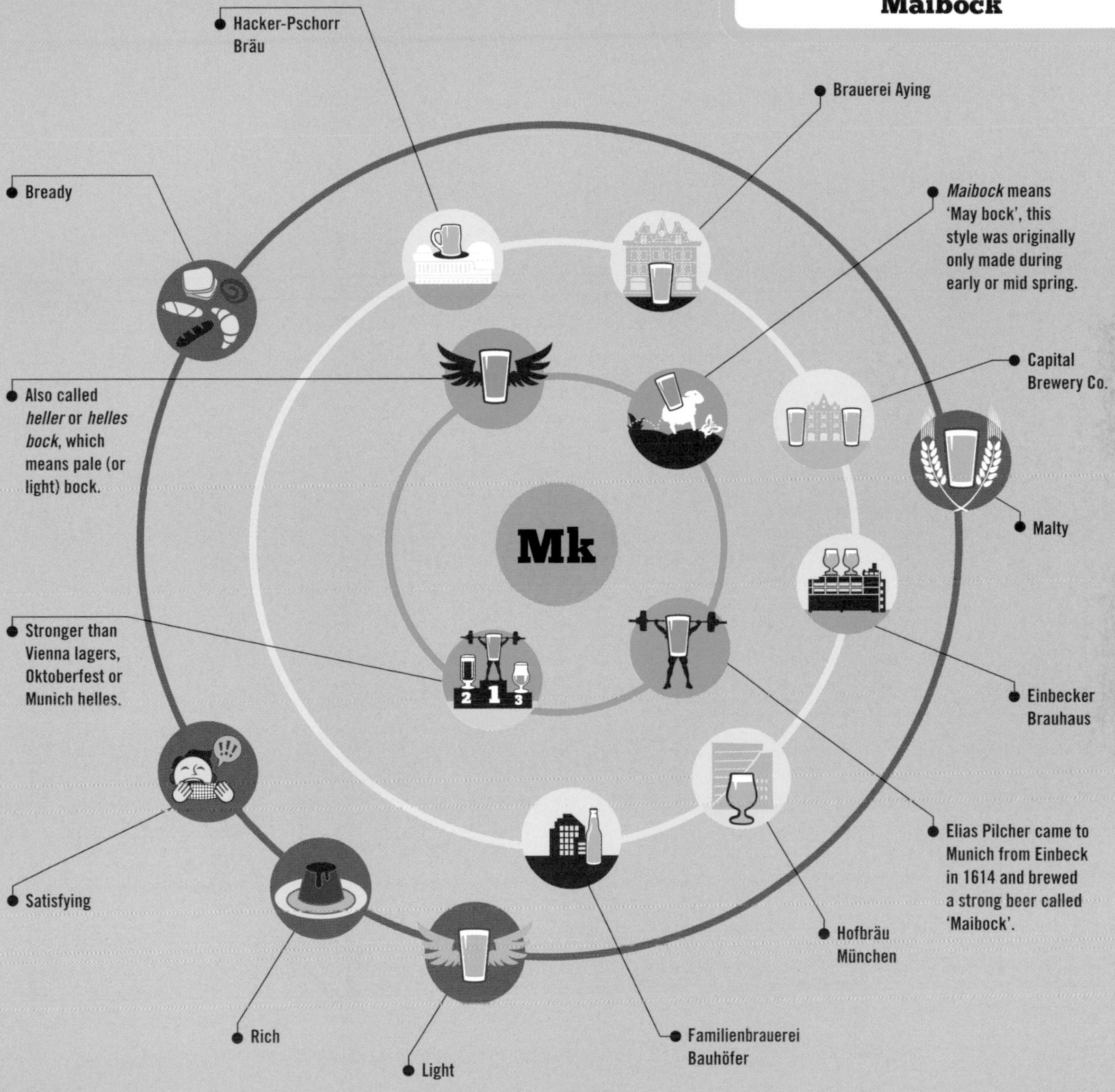

Hacker-Pschorr Bräu

Brauerei Aying

Maibock means 'May bock', this style was originally only made during early or mid spring.

Bready

Capital Brewery Co.

Also called *heller* or *helles bock*, which means pale (or light) bock.

Malty

Mk

Stronger than Vienna lagers, Oktoberfest or Munich helles.

Einbecker Brauhaus

Satisfying

Elias Pilcher came to Munich from Einbeck in 1614 and brewed a strong beer called 'Maibock'.

Rich

Hofbräu München

Light

Familienbrauerei Bauhöfer

Food pairing

Spicy Thai food	Roasted pork	Shellfish	Barbecue	Carrot cake

Märzen/Oktoberfest

Origin: Germany
Colour: 7–14 SRM
ABV: 4.8–5.9%
IBU: 20–28
Glassware: pint, mug

Brewed in March (Märzen) and stored until Oktoberfest, this style of beer is the perfect way to celebrate the turn of the seasons.

HISTORIES INTERTWINED

The fathers of this style and Vienna lager were fellow brewmasters, giving the two styles intertwined histories. Based on Anton Dreher's work with Vienna lager, the Sedlmayrs of the Spaten-Franziskaner-Bräu in Munich gave Märzen its fame.

The lines between Märzen and Oktoberfest have become blurred, so it makes sense to group them together. Both Märzen and Oktoberfest beers are rich in character, with prominence placed on the malts and just enough hop bitterness to balance. They are quite smooth with mixtures of freshly baked bread, toffee, malt sweetness and a dash of spiciness. The truest versions are clear and deep gold to reddish amber in colour with an off-white, rocky head. They are creamy, complex and satisfying.

Three Beers to Try

SPATEN OKTOBERFEST UR-MÄRZEN

Called *Ur-Märzen* (original Märzen), for a reason; the brewery that created the style brewed this one first. Pouring crystal clear copper, it is a hearty, balanced, satisfying classic.

AYINGER OKTOBER FEST-MÄRZEN

Another exemplary offering of the style. It is pure balance: malty with enough bitterness, rich, but clean and satisfying, and not heavy.

HACKER-PSCHORR ORIGINAL OKTOBERFEST
With a blend of toasty, sweet malts and fresh hops, this one is silky smooth with a clean finish.

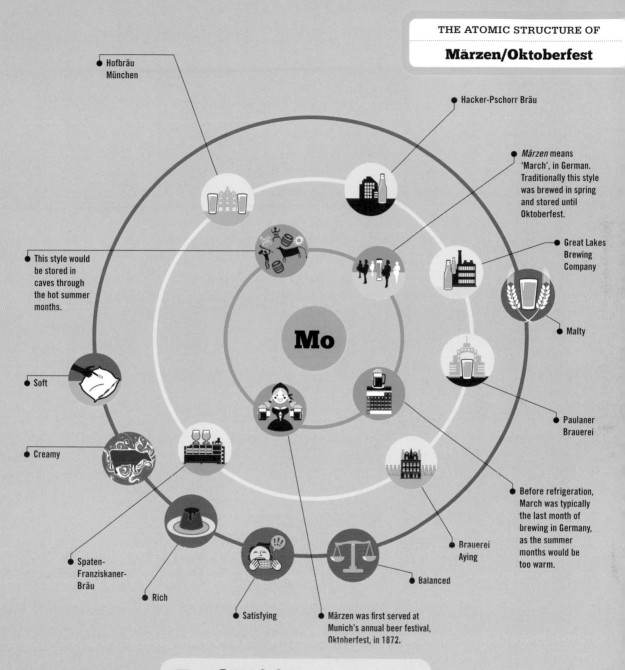

Hofbräu München

Hacker-Pschorr Bräu

Märzen means 'March', in German. Traditionally this style was brewed in spring and stored until Oktoberfest.

Great Lakes Brewing Company

This style would be stored in caves through the hot summer months.

Malty

Soft

Mo

Creamy

Paulaner Brauerei

Spaten-Franziskaner-Bräu

Before refrigeration, March was typically the last month of brewing in Germany, as the summer months would be too warm.

Rich

Brauerei Aying

Satisfying

Balanced

Märzen was first served at Munich's annual beer festival, Oktoberfest, in 1872.

Food Pairing

| Grilled foods | Pizza | Burgers | Sausages |

Vienna Lager

Origin: **Austria**
Colour: **10-16 SRM**
ABV: **4.5-5.9%**
IBU: **18-30**
Glassware: **mug, flute, pilsner, tulip**

Influenced by the pale beers of the early 19th century, Vienna lager was, in part, Austria's answer to Bohemian pilsner.

HOPPY AND DRY

With origins in Vienna, Austria, this style of lager has spread through the world and is now brewed elsewhere much more than in its birthplace. It is bright amber to copper in colour, with a sticky off-white to light brown head, and clean aromas of sweet malt and toastiness that emerge on the nose. While it and its German sister, the Märzen/Oktoberfest style (page 136), have a host of similarities, there are a few distinguishing factors. It is slightly lower in gravity, a bit more heavily hoppy and a little drier. Vienna lager leans less towards malt than a Märzen or Oktoberfest and is, in turn, slightly less rich.

Three Beers to Try

FREISTÄDTER ROTSCHOPF *Rot* means 'red' and this is a fine example of the Vienna style, with malty sweetness balanced by a fine floral and herbal hop bitterness in the finish.

WEITRA BRÄU HADMAR This Vienna lager was introduced in 1994 to rekindle interest in the style. It's copper coloured with a sweet, malty aroma with toasted malt building in the mouth and a bitter finish.

STIEGL GOLDBRÄU Austrians call this a 'Märzen bier' and it has an affinity to the style popular in Munich. Sweet malt is well balanced by a grassy hop note and a bitter finish.

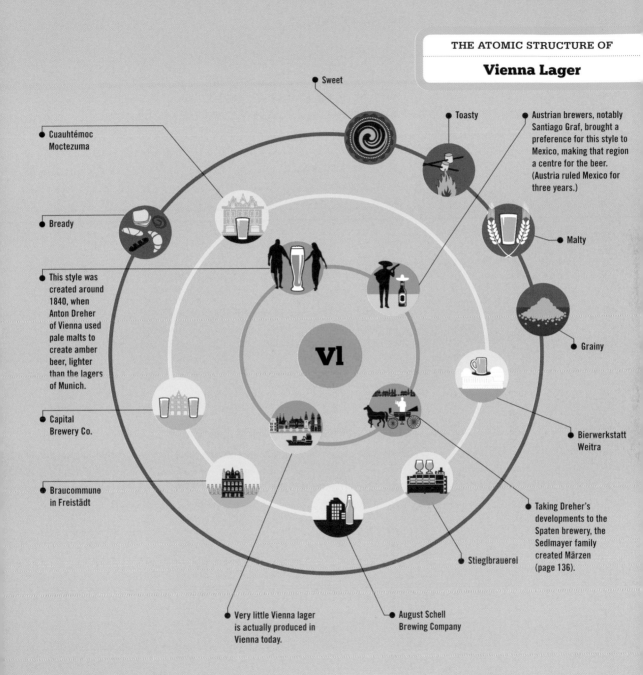

Sweet

Toasty

Austrian brewers, notably Santiago Graf, brought a preference for this style to Mexico, making that region a centre for the beer. (Austria ruled Mexico for three years.)

Cuauhtémoc Moctezuma

Bready

Malty

This style was created around 1840, when Anton Dreher of Vienna used pale malts to create amber beer, lighter than the lagers of Munich.

Grainy

Vl

Capital Brewery Co.

Bierwerkstatt Weitra

Braucommune in Freistädt

Taking Dreher's developments to the Spaten brewery, the Sedlmayer family created Märzen (page 136).

Stieglbrauerei

Very little Vienna lager is actually produced in Vienna today.

August Schell Brewing Company

Food Pairing

| Grilled meats | Grilled vegetables | Ham | Fried fish |

Kellerbier

Origin: Germany
Colour: 10-20 SRM
ABV: 5-5.5%
IBU: 25-35
Glassware: mug, stange

A rarity in today's beer world, Kellerbier's characteristic haze makes it distinctly different from a family of crystal clear lagers.

A CLOUDY BREW

A historical style, with its origins in Franconia, Germany, traditionally Kellerbier is brewed and then matured long, cool and slow in oak casks with the bung or stopper not completely closed. This allows the carbon dioxide that is created to escape as it is produced, leading to a cloudy, hazy brew, with very light carbonation. It has a deep amber body and most often the head is non-existent – when it is present it is a bright white layer of airy fluff. A delicate nose of aromatic, noble hops transitions to more intense hop bitterness on the palate. This beer is not pasteurised, which results in a short shelf life and means that there are only a few examples of Kellerbier generally available far from the breweries that make it.

Three Beers to Try

ST. GEORGEN BRÄU KELLER BIER Pours amber-brown with a nice head of beige. Complexly malty, the hops provide roundness and balance, and an earthy, hop bitterness.

HOFBRÄUHAUS TRAUNSTEIN 1612ER ZWICKELBIER This unfiltered beer is brewed by Hofbräuhaus Traunstein, which dates from 1612. The beer is amber-coloured with floral hops, toasted malt and a spicy yeast note.

BISCHOFSHOF ZOIGL *Zoigl* means a pointer that indicates when a brewery has a new batch ready. This version is hazy gold with a spicy aroma and a rich malty palate and gentle bitter finish.

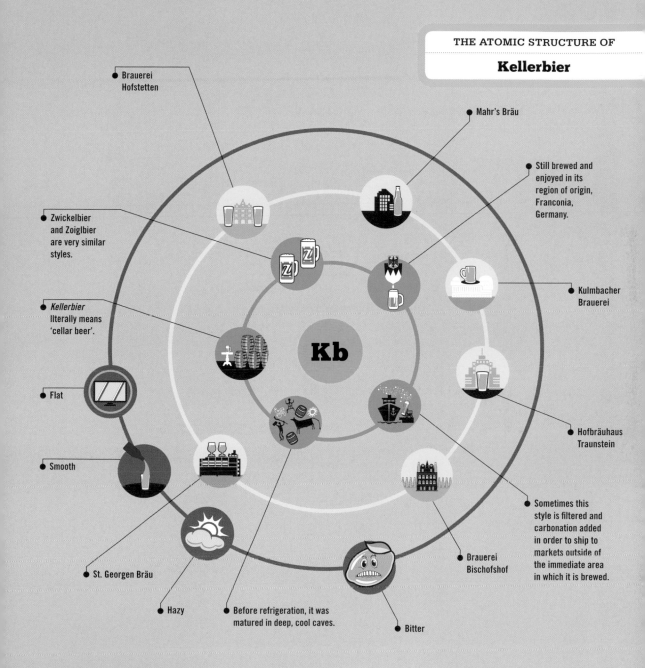

Kellerbier

Brauerei Hofstetten

Mahr's Bräu

Still brewed and enjoyed in its region of origin, Franconia, Germany.

Zwickelbier and Zoiglbier are very similar styles.

Kulmbacher Brauerei

Kellerbier llterally means 'cellar beer'.

Flat

Kb

Hofbräuhaus Traunstein

Smooth

St. Georgen Bräu

Sometimes this style is filtered and carbonation added in order to ship to markets outside of the immediate area in which it is brewed.

Brauerei Bischofshof

Hazy

Before refrigeration, it was matured in deep, cool caves.

Bitter

Food Pairing

| German food | Sausages | Burgers | Spicy food |

Rauchbier

Origin: Germany
Colour: 12-22 SRM
ABV: 4.8-6%
IBU: 20-30
Glassware: stange

Rauchbier is just one style of smoked beer, a category that encompasses a wide range of beers (including ales) brought together by a delicious undercurrent of smoke.

RETAINING THE SMOKE

In early brewing, all beer styles had a touch of smoke as a result of the kilning process. Following the introduction of techniques to eliminate the smoke, some brewers retained the smokiness by kilning the malt over wood fires, even increasing the degree to which smoke was present. Many smoke-influenced styles of today draw on this tradition. While Rauchbiers are lagers, many of today's smoked beers are ales.

The Rauchbier base is typically a darkened Märzen, bright copper to dark brown in colour. On the palate, a smoke layer gently filters through the sweet, toasted maltiness. It is medium-bodied and smooth, with the characteristically clean lager feel.

Three Beers to Try

AECHT SCHLENKERLA RAUCHBIER MÄRZEN   The aroma is immediately bonfire smokiness, followed by chewy malts and bold hops. The smoke layer lingers throughout, becoming more inviting with each sip.

EISENBAHN RAUCHBIER   Aromas of caramel, toffee and smoke are echoed by a similar flavour profile. A sweet, malty finish lingers, slightly more prominently than the smoke.

SPEZIAL RAUCHBIER MÄRZEN   Mellow smoke and toasty malt notes interplay through a smooth, medium-bodied brew. Long, dry, slightly smoky finish.

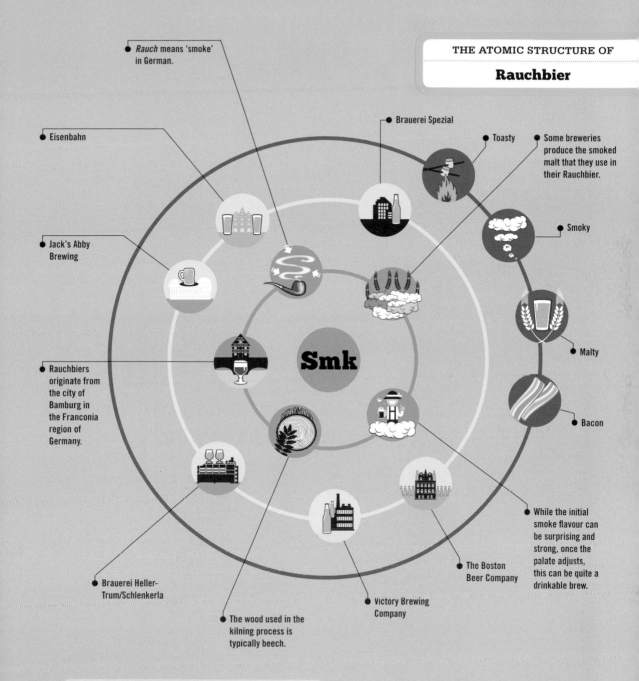

THE ATOMIC STRUCTURE OF

Rauchbier

Rauch means 'smoke' in German.

Eisenbahn

Jack's Abby Brewing

Rauchbiers originate from the city of Bamburg in the Franconia region of Germany.

Brauerei Spezial

Toasty

Some breweries produce the smoked malt that they use in their Rauchbier.

Smoky

Malty

Bacon

Smk

While the initial smoke flavour can be surprising and strong, once the palate adjusts, this can be quite a drinkable brew.

The Boston Beer Company

Brauerei Heller-Trum/Schlenkerla

The wood used in the kilning process is typically beech.

Victory Brewing Company

Food Pairing

| Barbecue | Bacon | Ham | Smoked salmon | Sausages |

Traditional Bock

Origin: Germany
Colour: 14–22 SRM
ABV: 6.2–7.2%
IBU: 20–27
Glassware: pokal, mug, stange

A rich, satisfying brew, this style became a Munich mainstay with a little help from a brewer from Einbeck.

HOP-RESTRAINED MALTINESS

Some people have the best of luck. Einbeck in central Germany has soft water, great hops, a historic cultivation of wheat and barley, quality malting techniques and brewers disciplined to know only to brew in winter. These are the ingredients that make for an incredible beer, one from which several sub-styles have stemmed over the years. Bock is almost entirely malt-focused, the hops reining it in just enough to avoid oversweetness. It is clear and typically copper to deep brown with a lacy, fluffy head. Long lagering produces a smooth, rich and creamy mouthfeel and the alcohol content makes for a strong, satisfying beer. It has a toasty, bready character with faint notes of caramel.

Three Beers to Try

EINBECKER UR-BOCK DUNKEL   Pours an amber-edged copper with a light brown head. On the palate are sweet malts, notes of caramel and toastiness. A firm bitterness balances and aids a lingering, dry finish.

AASS BOCK   With a brown body and a bursting bouquet of bready malts, this Norwegian brew transitions through a smooth mouthfeel of caramel and malts to a sweet finish.

KNEITINGER BOCK   A dark bock from Regensburg with floral hop notes, a rich, fruity palate and a dry biscuit malt and gentle hop finish.

THE ATOMIC STRUCTURE OF

Traditional Bock

Sweet

Breckenridge Brewery

Sprecher Brewing Co.

In around 1612, Einbeck brewer Elias Pilcher was brought in to improve Munich's bock production.

Bock also means 'billy goat' in German.

Anchor Brewing Company

Tb

Malty

The original bocks from Einbeck were renowned throughout Europe.

Brauerei Kneitinger

Smooth

The word *bock* probably stems from the name of the town where this style was created, Einbeck.

Aass Bryggeri

Rich

Bock is the style from which many sub-styles come: Doppelbock, Eisbock, Maibock and Hellesbock.

Einbecker Brauhaus

Food Pairing

Barbecue	Fried chicken	Game meats	Duck	Custard

Munich Dunkel

Origin: Germany
Colour: 14-28 SRM
ABV: 4.5-5.6%
IBU: 16-30
Glassware: pilsner, mug

Dunkels originated in Bavaria over 500 years ago. Complex, but not heavy or strong, beers of this style are delicious – after all, practice makes perfect.

MALTY COLOUR AND FLAVOUR

A beer from this long-brewed style is typically a deep reddish-brown blend, but sometimes deepening to a dark brown and crowned with a tan, sticky head. The colour is rich and stems from the use of Munich malt, which is often the sole malt used in a beer of this style. The aroma is mainly malt, with just a hint of hops. The palate can be beautifully complex, filled with blends of caramel and toffee notes, or hints of coffee and chocolate. There is a sweetness in the malt that is delicately balanced by the bitterness of the hops.

Three Beers to Try

AYINGER ALTBAIRISCH DUNKEL
A classic *Altbairisch*, meaning 'old Bavarian', is a ruby-edged mahogany. It is an intriguing contrast of sweet, flavourful malts and a refreshing mouthfeel.

SPATEN DUNKEL   Highly drinkable, this amber brew makes no bold decisions. It is balanced, malty, but not too sweet, and just enough bite of hops to make for a clean finish.

KÖNIG LUDWIG DUNKEL   The benchmark of the style, brewed by Prince Luitpold at his castle at Kaltenberg. It has roasted malt, figs, coffee and floral hop notes and a gentle, bitter finish.

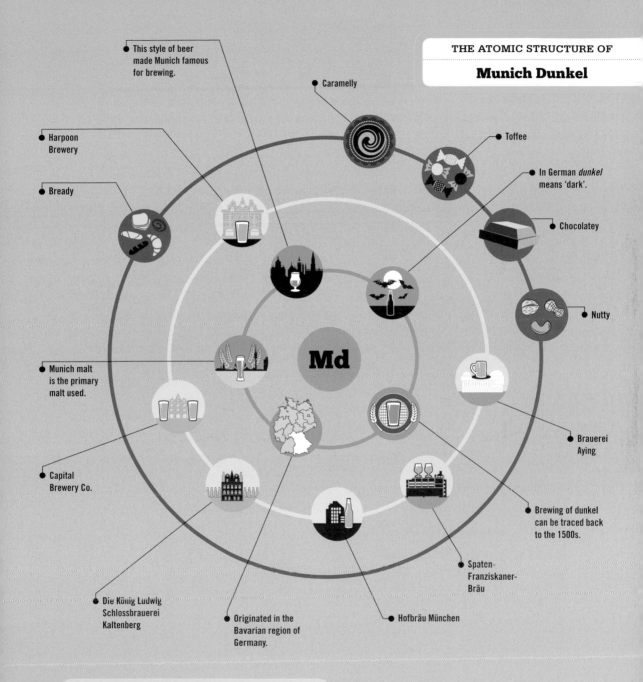

This style of beer made Munich famous for brewing.

Caramelly

Toffee

In German *dunkel* means 'dark'.

Chocolatey

Harpoon Brewery

Bready

Nutty

Munich malt is the primary malt used.

Brauerei Aying

Md

Capital Brewery Co.

Brewing of dunkel can be traced back to the 1500s.

Spaten-Franziskaner-Bräu

Die König Ludwig Schlossbrauerei Kaltenberg

Originated in the Bavarian region of Germany.

Hofbräu München

Food Pairing

| Pork | Sausages | Roasted chicken | Mushrooms | Chinese food |

Doppelbock

Origin: Germany
Colour: 15–30 SRM
ABV: 6.5–10%
IBU: 12–30
Glassware: pilsner, flute

While not literally double the strength of traditional bock, this strong, hefty version often sustained monks through Lent, earning it the title 'liquid bread'.

LENTEN FARE

Typically, Lent – the time in early spring between Ash Wednesday and Easter – is a time devoted to ridding vices from one's life. However, the Paulaner monks of the mid 1700s adopted a different type of fast. Forgoing any sustenance besides Doppelbock, they consumed pint after pint of this rich, malty, satisfying brew. Ranging from a deep mahogany to almost black, and often containing flashes of garnet, this malt-centred style is a meal in a glass. The strength hides slyly in a body of smooth, bread-like malts. The aroma is of a bakery morning, fresh loaves of grainy, rich bread waft from the glass. After one glass, you too may decide that a fast isn't such a bad idea.

Three Beers to Try

PAULANER SALVATOR The original of the style from Paulaner and still a classic. A light brown crown rests atop glowing amber, rich, sweet malts meld into a balancing bitter.

AYINGER CELEBRATOR DOPPELBOCK
A sticky, light brown head caps a body of very deep brown. Roasty, sweet malt flavours dominate, melding to a bitter, balancing finish.

SPATEN OPTIMATOR Spaten's contribution to the style. A light caramel weaves through the dark brown body in both bouquet and taste. Full and rich, a great representation.

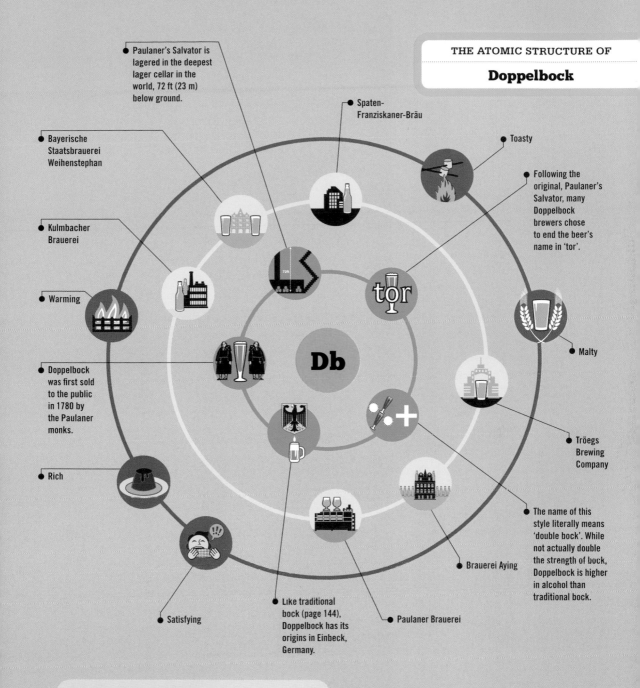

Paulaner's Salvator is lagered in the deepest lager cellar in the world, 72 ft (23 m) below ground.

Bayerische Staatsbrauerei Weihenstephan

Kulmbacher Brauerei

Warming

Doppelbock was first sold to the public in 1780 by the Paulaner monks.

Rich

Satisfying

Spaten-Franziskaner-Bräu

Toasty

Following the original, Paulaner's Salvator, many Doppelbock brewers chose to end the beer's name in 'tor'.

tor

Db

Malty

Tröegs Brewing Company

The name of this style literally means 'double bock'. While not actually double the strength of bock, Doppelbock is higher in alcohol than traditional bock.

Brauerei Aying

Paulaner Brauerei

Like traditional bock (page 144), Doppelbock has its origins in Einbeck, Germany.

Food Pairing

Ham	Roasted pork	Game meats	Duck	Chocolate cake

Eisbock

Origin: Germany
Colour: 18–30 SRM
ABV: 9–14%
IBU: 25–35
Glassware: snifter, flute, oversized wine glass, weizen

Eisbock entered the world by happy accident, but has since been crafted with extreme care, producing a deliciously complex brew.

ICY CONCENTRATION

While every story in beer lore has some debate around it, when it comes to the tale of Eisbock's origins, most sources agree on some form of the following account. A brewer or tavern keeper from the German town of Kulmbach left a barrel of bock – probably Doppelbock – outside overnight and when he came to serve it, he found that it was partially frozen. He served it anyway, and the result was a strong and desirable beer. The removal of the ice had concentrated the flavour and increased the alcohol content, creating an intense and flavourful lager. As with all bocks, malt is at its core, but with the high alcohol content there is also a residual warmth, mixed often with notes of sweetness, spices or fruit.

Three Beers to Try

KULMBACHER REICHELBRÄU EISBOCK
Seductively dark with a rich, thick head. A nose of blended caramel and dark fruits are indicative of the palate, too. Rich with a warming alcohol throughout.

EKU 28 Brewed by the Kulmbacher Brauerei that has merged with Reichelbräu. This 11% ABV amber beer has a big malty and fruity character with a long bittersweet finish.

EKU EISBOCK The companion to 28 (above). The brewery says its long, nine-month lagering leads to ice forming in the conditioning tank. Rich, malty but with a good balance of floral hops.

THE ATOMIC STRUCTURE OF

Eisbock

Eib
Sweet
Created initially by accident.
Southampton Publick House
Not to be confused with the 'ice beer' for which many Canadian breweries are famous.
Alcohol warmth
Malty
The strength of an Eisbock lends itself to being sipped like a fine liqueur.
Kuhnhenn Brewing Co.
Rich
Schneider Aventinus Weizen-Eisbock is a Weizenbock brewed in the Eisbock manner. As its base beer is a Weizenbock, it is classed as such, but it is also often categorised as an Eisbock.
Capital Brewery Co.
Complex
It is described as an 'ice strong beer'.
Kulmbacher Brauerei

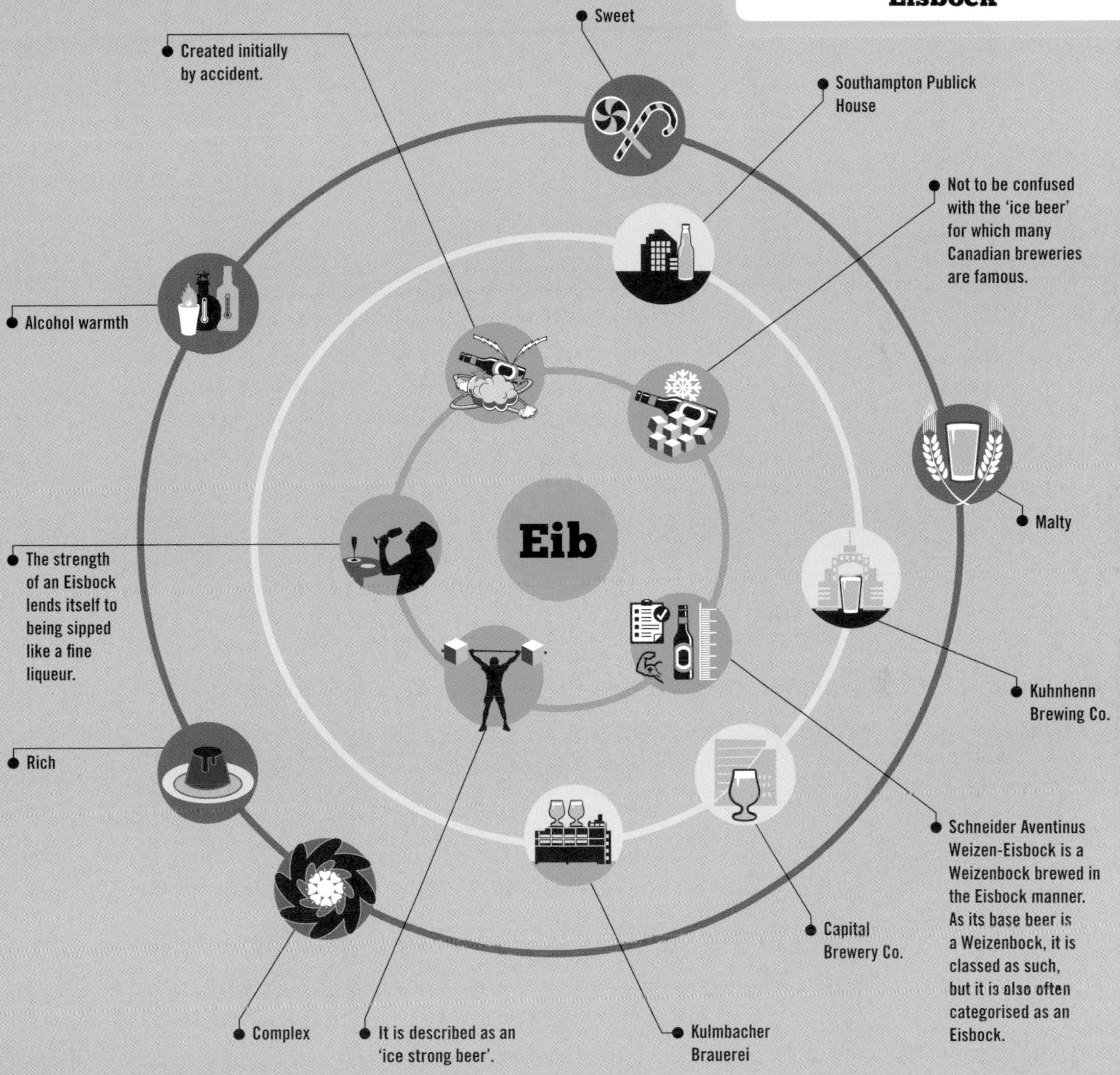

Food Pairing

Game meats	Roasted pork	Rich desserts	Crème brûlée

Schwarzbier

Origin: Germany
Colour: 25–30 SRM
ABV: 3–4.9%
IBU: 22–30
Glassware: flute, pilsner, pint

This beer is one of the oldest in the world, and yet is still surprisingly underappreciated.

BLACK LAGER

Meet Schwarzbier, the lager family's version of a stout. The roasty quality of this beer adds richness and heartiness to a clean, drinkable brew, and separates it from the rest of the lager pack. Similar to Irish dry stout (page 58), it lacks the harshness characteristic of that style. It is typically very dark, and while nearing black, often has ruby edges that denote something just on the brink of pure darkness. It has a delicate and contradictory balance between bitter and sweet, heavy and crisp and dark colour and light feel. Often there are notes of nuttiness, toffee and sweetness, balanced by enough hop bitterness to avoid a sticky, syrupy body. Very drinkable, it is complex while maintaining a highly sessionable quality.

Three Beers to Try

ALTENBURGER SCHWARZE From the former East Germany. It's deep black in colour, with a sweet, fruity aroma and palate but balanced by a light hop note in the finish.

KÖSTRITZER SCHWARZBIER A dry, dusty, earthy malt core is surrounded by a soft, smooth mouthfeel and slightly tangy finish.

MÖNCHSHOFF SCHWARZBIER Bold in flavour, this one, dubbed 'the original black', melds coffee, chocolate and roasty malts with a brisk snap of hops. By Kulmbacher.

THE ATOMIC STRUCTURE OF
Schwarzbier

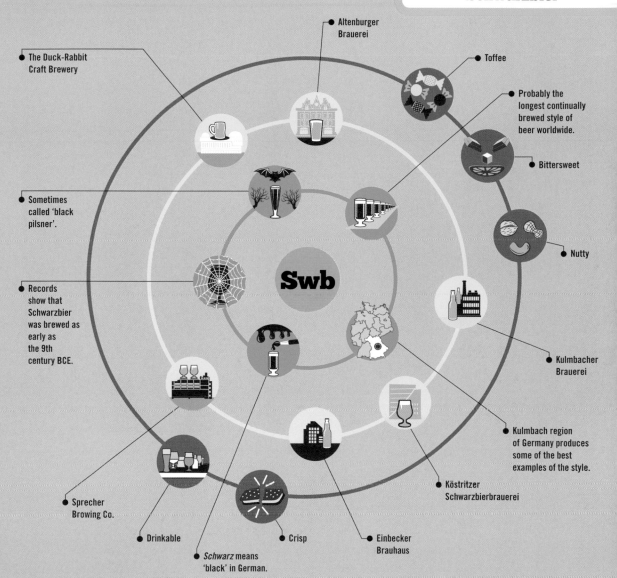

- Altenburger Brauerei
- The Duck-Rabbit Craft Brewery
- Toffee
- Probably the longest continually brewed style of beer worldwide.
- Bittersweet
- Sometimes called 'black pilsner'.
- Nutty
- Records show that Schwarzbier was brewed as early as the 9th century BCE.
- Kulmbacher Brauerei
- Kulmbach region of Germany produces some of the best examples of the style.
- Sprecher Browing Co.
- Köstritzer Schwarzbierbrauerei
- Drinkable
- Einbecker Brauhaus
- *Schwarz* means 'black' in German.
- Crisp

Swb

Food Pairing

| Barbecue | Roasted meats | Steak | Blackened chicken | Bread pudding |

BEERS OF AMERICAN ORIGIN

4

BEERS OF AMERICAN ORIGIN

American beer has a sordid but influential past. Today's most consumed style of beer worldwide is essentially an American brainchild. Yellow, light, fizzy and nearing flavourless, this American adjunct has grown to dominate beer culture globally. And yet, running parallel to the mega brewing conglomerates of the land, smaller scale producers have always been a persistent, passionate bunch – today a healthy, vibrant group with a growing influence on the world of craft beer.

If faced with the American version of a beer style, a likely bet is that the result is an amped-up, stronger, hoppier version of the original style. In some categories, an extreme artistic bent has spawned entirely new and intriguing styles, and has helped make the American beer landscape one of the most interesting in the world. The first resurgence of interest in craft beer came in the late 1970s, sparked by the legalisation of home brewing. Slow growth through the 80s and 90s has now gained incredible momentum and while large, domestic light lagers still dominate, drinkers are demanding more quality and more choice every day.

Ale styles with origins in America are often confusingly named the same as their British cousins, but frequently the similarities end there. Brown ales of the American tradition are bolder and hoppier. American pale ale is snappy and bursting with citrus, grapefruit and pine. The IPA is nearly unrecognizable, with copious amounts of American hops, bursting with upfront bitterness. This style is arguably the greatest source of American influence in the brewing world. America's obsession with hops has spread through the craft beer world, where the palates have continually culled the most bitter of brews, birthing the much-loved imperial or double IPA. Following in Belgian footsteps, American brewers have boldly experimented with wild yeast strains, developing some of the funkiest, most complex and most interesting beers in the industry. The American stout category becomes a catch-all for black, viscous, rich brews, but often the distinctions within the style can be wide, individual varieties focusing on coffee, chocolate and even fruit. Barrel aging these beers has become an American signature, defined separately and more specifically on pages 208–209.

Beyond the world-dominating American lager style, the nation has birthed two additions to the lager family: the long-lost pre-Prohibition lager, whose steady rise in American craft pubs across the nation has garnered it a bit of attention, and the best-forgotten American malt liquor, a high gravity, boozy bomb of a beer.

Most beers are classed as either an ale or a lager, and yet a couple of pure American inventions use the best of both worlds, resulting in unique hybrids. Cream ale, born from climactic conditions that disallowed typical lager brewing, is brewed with top-fermenting ale yeast then cold-conditioned, resulting in a clean, refreshing quencher. California common, known broadly as steam beer, is another such American brainchild. This uses bottom-fermenting lager yeast – specifically California lager yeast that works best at warmer, ale-like temperatures.

American Lager

Origin: United States
Colour: 2–3 SRM
ABV: 2.8–4.2%
IBU: 5–14
Glassware: pint

Snubbed by many in the craft beer community, this, the world's most consumed style, has its place in the world of beer.

CLEAN AND BRIGHT

As would be supposed, this style – the style that many worldwide automatically call to mind when they think of beer – is light: in body, aroma, flavour, colour, calories and alcohol. The craft beer world scowls at its inherent non-flavour and heavy use of cost-cutting adjuncts, but there is no denying the prevalence of the style.

This light and refreshing beer is pale straw yellow with a bright white, frothy head that quickly disappears. It goes down easily, with carbonation enough to cleanse and few dominant flavours. There are perhaps just hints of a floral hop. This sessionable brew might feel like it hits the spot on a hot summer's day, but there can be so much more to beer!

Three Beers to Try

 MILLER LITE   Introduced in 1975, this is one of the original low-calorie beers.

 BUDWEISER   First brewed in 1876, Budweiser is now brewed by Anheuser-Busch, the world's largest brewer. Dubbed the 'king of beers', it is a bestselling beer.

 RED STRIPE JAMAICAN LAGER   Its brand owned by Diageo (Guinness's owner), this version of the style receives broader acceptance by the beer-drinking community than some others in this category. Brewed by Desnoes & Geddes.

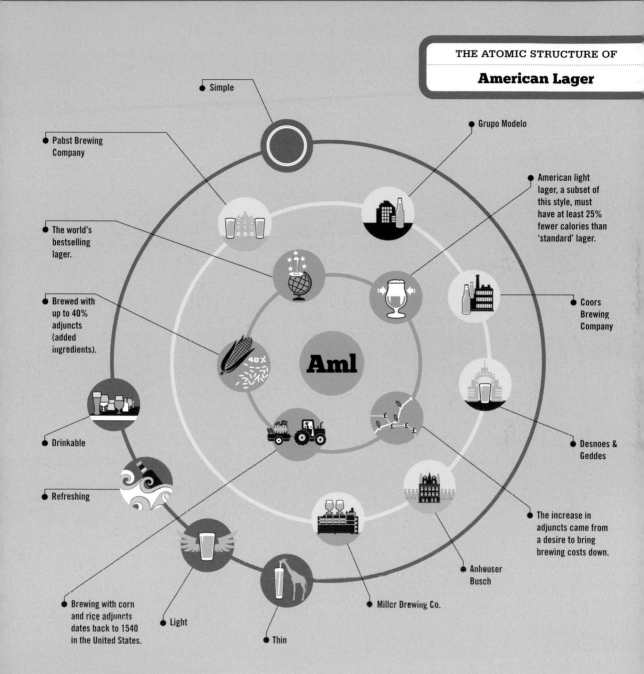

Simple

Pabst Brewing Company

Grupo Modelo

American light lager, a subset of this style, must have at least 25% fewer calories than 'standard' lager.

The world's bestselling lager.

Brewed with up to 40% adjuncts (added ingredients).

Coors Brewing Company

Aml

Drinkable

Desnoes & Geddes

Refreshing

The increase in adjuncts came from a desire to bring brewing costs down.

Brewing with corn and rice adjuncts dates back to 1540 in the United States.

Light

Thin

Miller Brewing Co.

Anheuser Busch

Food Pairing

| Salad | Barbecue | Pizza | Burgers |

Pale Lager

Origin: United States
Colour: 2–8 SRM
ABV: 4.3–5%
IBU: 13–23
Glassware: pilsner, pint

A stepped-up version of typical American lagers, this style has a bit more build, but remains ultimately easy-drinking and refreshing in character.

MORE MALT, MORE STRENGTH

With an ambiguous name and just a few simple differentiating factors, pale lager is a close kin to American lager. However, with a higher malt bill, sometimes no adjuncts at all, and a higher alcoholic strength, this style has garnered a following with a claim to more refined tastes. With globalisation and consolidation, European versions have become as popular in the United States as domestic ones. In appearance, this style has much the same straw-yellow colour as American lager and a white, diminishing head. It is refreshing, carbonated and slightly more alcoholic than its cousin, with a more complex hop profile and a bit of malt sweetness.

Three Beers to Try

LONGBOARD ISLAND LAGER Produced by Kona since 1998, this malty refresher has notes of spicy hops.

KIRIN ICHIBAN Billed as 'all-malt', this Japanese beer – meaning 'number one' – has a crisp body and a clean finish.

STELLA ARTOIS Brewed in Leuven, Belgium. Clear, pale straw in colour with a billowing bright white head.

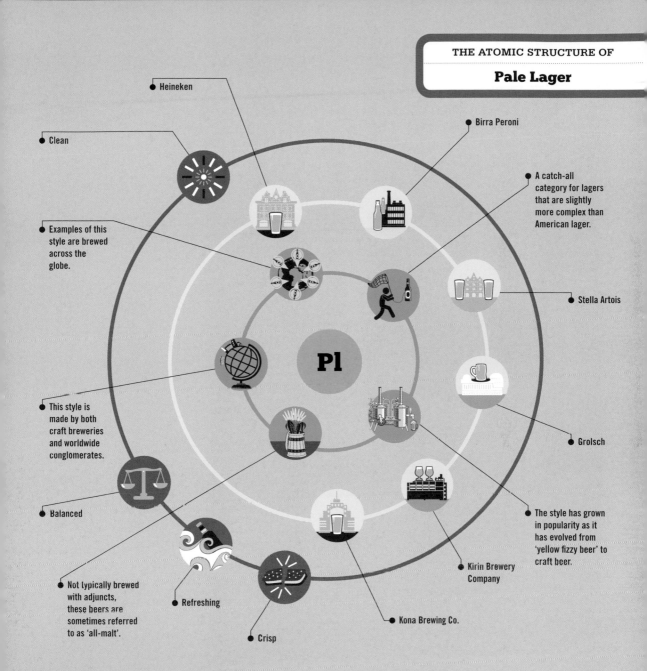

THE ATOMIC STRUCTURE OF
Pale Lager

Heineken

Birra Peroni

Clean

A catch-all category for lagers that are slightly more complex than American lager.

Examples of this style are brewed across the globe.

Stella Artois

This style is made by both craft breweries and worldwide conglomerates.

Pl

Grolsch

Balanced

The style has grown in popularity as it has evolved from 'yellow fizzy beer' to craft beer.

Not typically brewed with adjuncts, these beers are sometimes referred to as 'all-malt'.

Refreshing

Kirin Brewery Company

Kona Brewing Co.

Crisp

Food Pairing

| Salads | Light fish dishes | Burgers |

American Malt Liquor

Origin: United States
Colour: 2-5 SRM
ABV: 6.25-9%
IBU: 12-23
Glassware: pint, mug

With a primary purpose of getting more alcohol per ounce, this style is generally cheap, boozy and dry.

ADDED SUGAR, HIGHER ALCOHOL

Along similar lines to American lager, this style amps up the alcohol, giving a light-looking brew a substantially boozy kick. With the addition of significant amounts of adjuncts – often simply straight sugar – the simple beer gains in alcoholic strength up to 9 per cent. Typically quite cheaply produced, in the United States it is often served in 40-ounce bottles (just over two pints). It is light, pale yellow to light golden in colour. A whiff of grains and alcohol on the nose and palate are typical. There is sometimes a hint of bitterness and some residual sweetness. The low quality, high gravity nature of this style does not lend itself to being paired with food. Its primary mission is the most booze for the buck.

Three Beers to Try

STEEL RESERVE Also called '211', this example attempted to distance itself from the malt liquor style by describing itself as a 'high gravity lager'.

PABST COLT 45 MALT LIQUOR One of the first of the style to move away from high-end marketing to promoting the alcoholic kick.

MILLER OLDE ENGLISH 800 Clear yellow with a lacking head. Smells of grain and slightly of alcohol. Bitter, metallic and boozy.

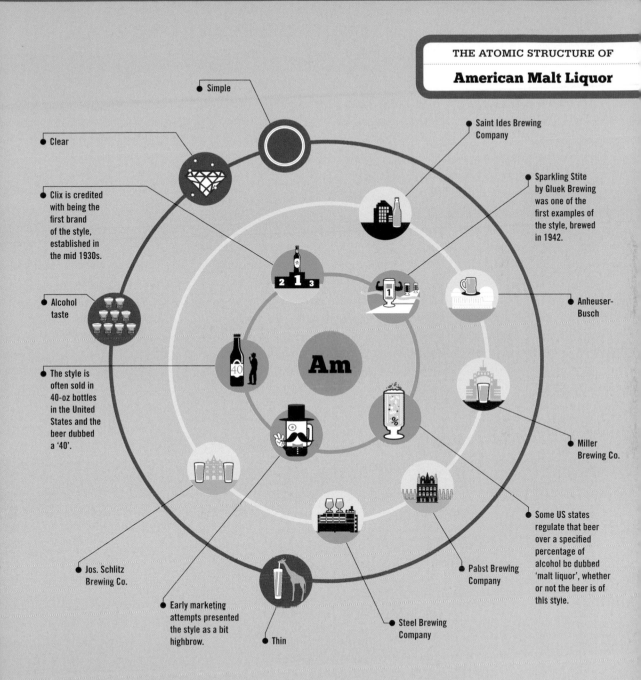

THE ATOMIC STRUCTURE OF
American Malt Liquor

Simple

Clear

Clix is credited with being the first brand of the style, established in the mid 1930s.

Alcohol taste

The style is often sold in 40-oz bottles in the United States and the beer dubbed a '40'.

Jos. Schlitz Brewing Co.

Early marketing attempts presented the style as a bit highbrow.

Thin

Am

Saint Ides Brewing Company

Sparkling Stite by Gluek Brewing was one of the first examples of the style, brewed in 1942.

Anheuser-Busch

Miller Brewing Co.

Some US states regulate that beer over a specified percentage of alcohol be dubbed 'malt liquor', whether or not the beer is of this style.

Pabst Brewing Company

Steel Brewing Company

Not usually consumed with food.

Pre-Prohibition Lager

Origin: United States
Colour: 3-5 SRM
ABV: 3.5-6%
IBU: 25-40
Glassware: pilsner, pint

The criticisms aimed at much American lager today have been unduly applied to this style, which is now enjoying a resurgence in craft breweries across the United States.

A REDISCOVERED STYLE

16 January, 1920 would forever change the landscape of American beer. With the advent of Prohibition and then its end, 13 years later, lager in the United States became weaker, thinner and brewed with much higher proportions of adjuncts. However, as the craft beer scene has begun to thrive again, the brews of old have started to stage a comeback.

With higher hop rates, this pale yellow to light amber beer comes with a bitter punch much greater than the standard American lager of today. While adjuncts are still used, typically of rice or corn, it is still more full-bodied and malty. A well-built, refreshing alternative to thinner, weaker brews.

Three Beers to Try

FULL SAIL SESSION LAGER Served in a 'stubby' 11-oz (half pint) bottle, this smooth throwback has both flavour and refreshment. Lemon notes clean the palate to a light, zesty finish.

SCHELL'S DEER BRAND Formerly 'Original', the brewery's flagship has been brewed since before Prohibition. Crisp, clean and simple.

COORS BATCH 19 A 21st-century version of the lager brewed before Prohibition times. This new take on the style is deep gold and balanced with a nice hop snap.

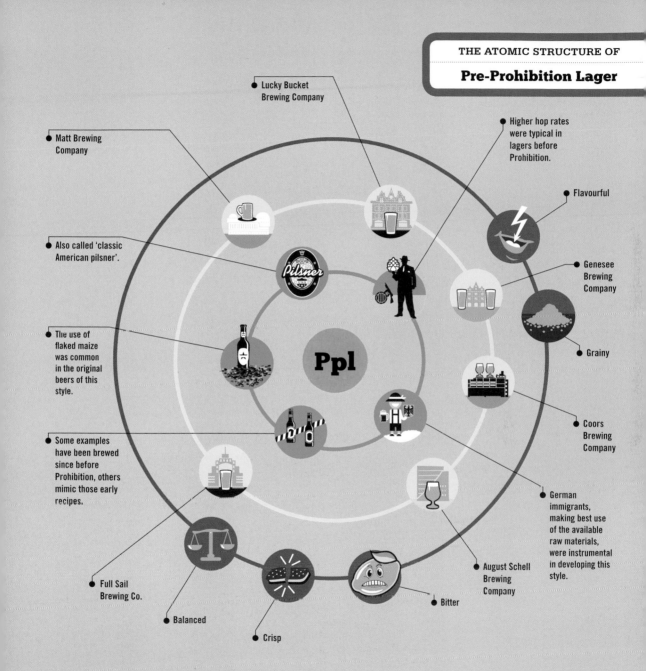

- Lucky Bucket Brewing Company

- Matt Brewing Company

- Higher hop rates were typical in lagers before Prohibition.

- Flavourful

- Also called 'classic American pilsner'.

- Genesee Brewing Company

Ppl

- Grainy

- The use of flaked maize was common in the original beers of this style.

- Coors Brewing Company

- Some examples have been brewed since before Prohibition, others mimic those early recipes.

- German immigrants, making best use of the available raw materials, were instrumental in developing this style.

- Full Sail Brewing Co.

- August Schell Brewing Company

- Balanced

- Bitter

- Crisp

Food Pairing

Sausages	Burgers	Salads	Cajun dishes

American Blonde/Golden Ale

Origin: United States
Colour: 3–6 SRM
ABV: 3.8–6%
IBU: 15–28
Glassware: pint, mug

Here's another candidate to choose for converting a stubborn palate from fizzy, yellow beer to something more substantial and satisfying.

SUMMERTIME QUENCHER

From first glance to last sip, this style seems built for refreshment – a sublime drink for a summer's day. A bright golden clarity invites the drinker to quench. Upon first gulp it is smooth, well-carbonated and refreshing. There is an underlying malt sweetness layered with a tempered hop flavour, often of lemongrass and florals, and very little bitterness. Approachable, versatile and well-built, this style is simple and direct in its object: to quench and refresh. This style is comparable to Kölsch (page 78).

Three Beers to Try

VICTORY SUMMER LOVE ALE This beer is an ideal summer quencher. Slightly hoppy, with floral and lemon notes.

NEW BELGIUM SOMERSAULT ALE Slightly cloudy, its golden body and fluffy head are a picture of a summer sky. Nicely citric with floral and grassy hop notes.

DESCHUTES TWILIGHT SUMMER ALE
A perfect balance of flavour and refreshment. The hops of this ale are of grass and lemon, and the finish is clean.

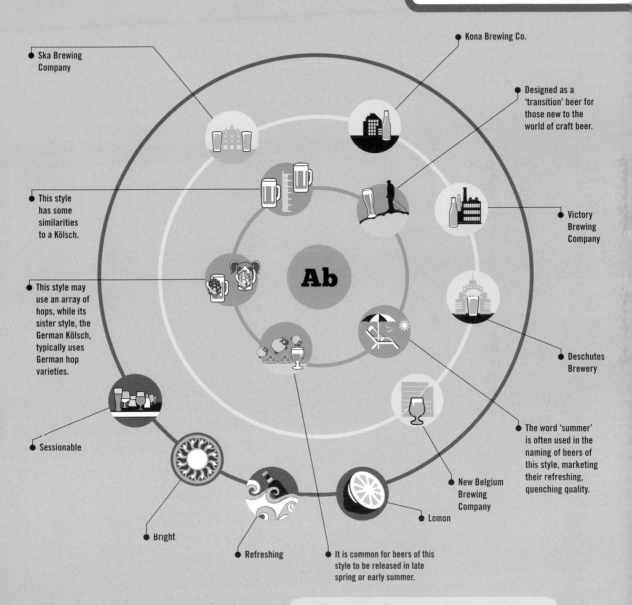

THE ATOMIC STRUCTURE OF
American Blonde/Golden Ale

Kona Brewing Co.

Designed as a 'transition' beer for those new to the world of craft beer.

Ska Brewing Company

Victory Brewing Company

This style has some similarities to a Kölsch.

Ab

This style may use an array of hops, while its sister style, the German Kölsch, typically uses German hop varieties.

Deschutes Brewery

Sessionable

The word 'summer' is often used in the naming of beers of this style, marketing their refreshing, quenching quality.

New Belgium Brewing Company

Bright

Refreshing

Lemon

It is common for beers of this style to be released in late spring or early summer.

Food Pairing

Salads	Light foods	Fish

Cream Ale

Origin: United States
Colour: 3–10 SRM
ABV: 4.5–5.5%
IBU: 15–25
Glassware: pint

Essentially an American lager brewed as an ale, this version was born when typical lagering wasn't an option.

REVIVAL OF PRE-PROHIBITION STYLE

Prohibition wreaked havoc on beer production in the United States and cream ale was one of the victims. What had been a lively, carbonated and refreshingly crisp ale alternative to American lagers in pre-Prohibition years, became just another fizzy, yellow and forgettable brew. However, with microbreweries' interest in the style, there has been a new generation of well-crafted examples.

Cream ales are light, ranging from pale, clear yellow to a gentle medium gold. The nose is mild with just hints of hops and fruit. The taste is crisp and clean, characteristically refreshing with slight bitterness. While not overly complex or especially interesting, it can be a good partner to a day spent in the sun.

Three Beers to Try

NEW GLARUS SPOTTED COW One of the style's finest examples, it is a surprisingly complex brew, with initial wafts of fruit and hops finishing through a malt core to a refreshing end.

ANDERSON VALLEY SUMMER SOLSTICE Self-styled as the 'cream soda for adults', this beer is incredibly drinkable, smooth and refreshingly simple.

SIXPOINT SWEET ACTION From Brooklyn, New York, comes a hybrid of a hybrid. While it doesn't fit squarely in any category, it is closest here, where the spicy, fruity complexity is trumped only by its perfect drinkability.

THE ATOMIC STRUCTURE OF
Cream Ale

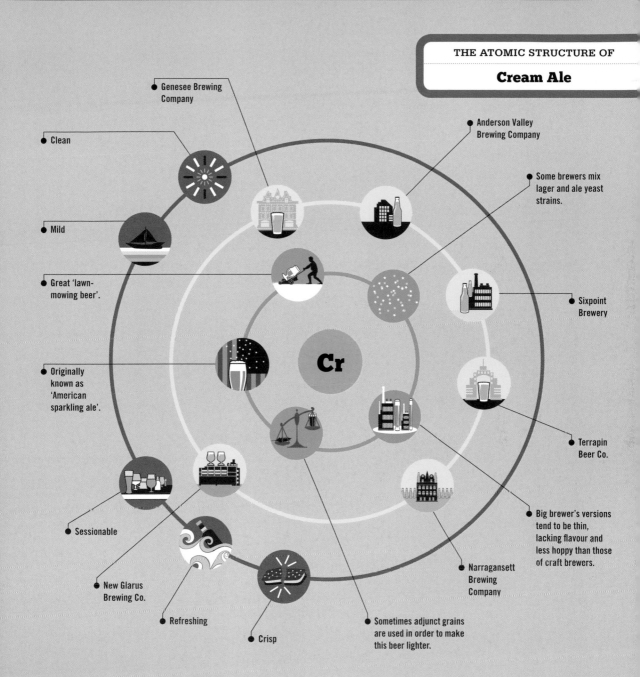

Clean

Genesee Brewing Company

Anderson Valley Brewing Company

Some brewers mix lager and ale yeast strains.

Mild

Great 'lawn-mowing beer'.

Sixpoint Brewery

Originally known as 'American sparkling ale'.

Cr

Sessionable

Terrapin Beer Co.

New Glarus Brewing Co.

Big brewer's versions tend to be thin, lacking flavour and less hoppy than those of craft brewers.

Refreshing

Crisp

Narragansett Brewing Company

Sometimes adjunct grains are used in order to make this beer lighter.

Food Pairing

| Salads | Light fish dishes | Burgers |

Gluten-free

Origin: As base style
Colour: As base style
ABV: As base style
IBU: As base style
Glassware: As base style

With the increasing demand for gluten-free foods, it was simply a matter of time before brewers created a range of beers to suit the dietary needs of many beer drinkers.

TASTE WITHOUT GLUTEN

Much to the relief of the gluten-intolerant beer drinker, beers brewed without gluten are not only growing in popularity, but are becoming available in an increasing range of base styles. Many beer drinkers with a gluten intolerance are only able to consume beer in which the gluten content is less than 20 parts per million. Unfortunately, in early versions, many of the beers that were made low in gluten were also not very flavourful. Recently, however, a few breweries have begun to focus on producing offerings that are both acceptable for gluten-intolerant drinkers and downright tasty.

Three Beers to Try

TWO BROTHERS PRAIRIE PATH GOLDEN ALE   This refreshing barley-based golden ale is bready with floral, grassy hops. Very drinkable.

SPRECHER SHAKPARO ALE   Brewed from sorghum and millet and marketed as African-style, this beer is sweet and fruity. Perfect for warmer months: refreshing, light and sessionable.

OMISSION PALE ALE   A fine choice for a pale ale, whether you're gluten-free or not. It pours orange, and the palate is initially hoppy, with citrus and caramel malts trailing behind.

THE ATOMIC STRUCTURE OF

Gluten-free

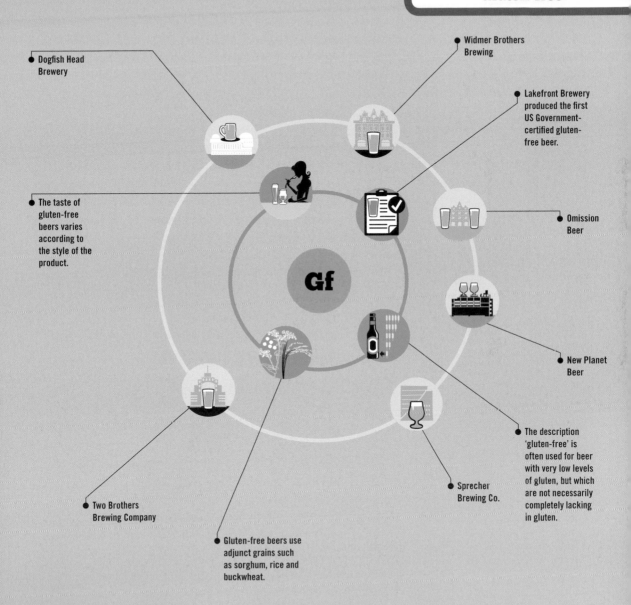

Dogfish Head Brewery

Widmer Brothers Brewing

Lakefront Brewery produced the first US Government-certified gluten-free beer.

The taste of gluten-free beers varies according to the style of the product.

Omission Beer

Gf

New Planet Beer

Two Brothers Brewing Company

Sprecher Brewing Co.

The description 'gluten-free' is often used for beer with very low levels of gluten, but which are not necessarily completely lacking in gluten.

Gluten-free beers use adjunct grains such as sorghum, rice and buckwheat.

This entry doesn't include food pairings or tasting notes, as these depend on the beer's base style. Try looking up the style of your gluten-free beer for food pairing suggestions.

American Style Wheat

Origin: United States
Colour: 3-6 SRM
ABV: 4-5.5%
IBU: 15-30
Glassware: weizen, pint

For a nation that continues its transition to drinking better beer, this take on the German Weissbier style makes a great bridge to the world of craft beers.

A RUSHING STREAM

Light, refreshing, crisp and drinkable. That's what many Americans have always wanted from their pint of beer, and, with this style, that's exactly what you get. And more. The pour is a pale straw to bright golden, the head a voluminous tuft of white. At its centre, a rushing stream of carbonation. The nose is bright, lightly hoppy with hints of fruit, but lacks the clove or banana esters of its German cousin. It is crisp and refreshing with a smooth, creamy feel. Hops are more noticeable than in a Weissbier (page 86), but they are not heavy or overbearing. This beer has won over many a convert.

Three Beers to Try

ANCHOR SUMMER BEER Filtered, clean and crisp, this refresher is the yardstick for the style.

GOOSE ISLAND 312 URBAN WHEAT
An inviting golden with a thick foam. Freshly baked bread, citrus, nuts and earthiness from start to finish.

LAGUNITAS LITTLE SUMPIN' SUMPIN' ALE A marriage of hops and wheat in this smooth, hoppy, easy-drinking offering from the Lagunitas Brewing Company.

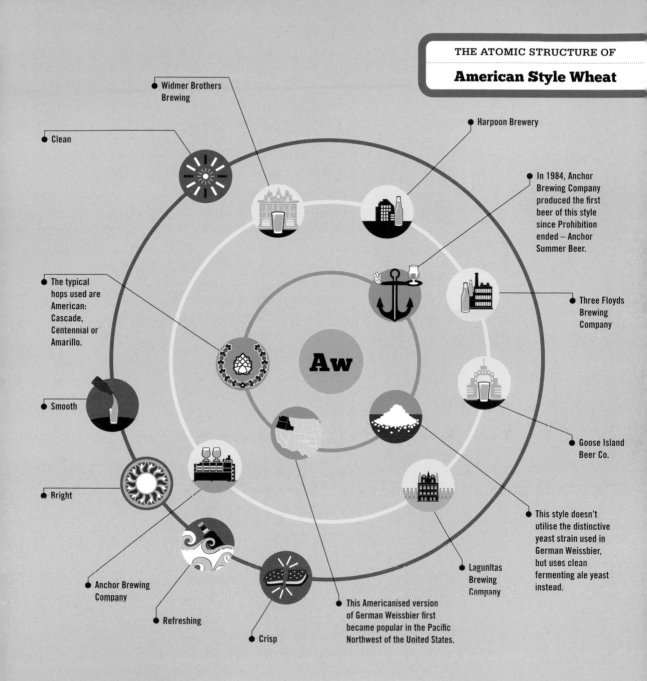

Widmer Brothers Brewing

Harpoon Brewery

Clean

In 1984, Anchor Brewing Company produced the first beer of this style since Prohibition ended – Anchor Summer Beer.

The typical hops used are American: Cascade, Centennial or Amarillo.

Three Floyds Brewing Company

Aw

Smooth

Goose Island Beer Co.

Bright

This style doesn't utilise the distinctive yeast strain used in German Weissbier, but uses clean fermenting ale yeast instead.

Anchor Brewing Company

Lagunitas Brewing Company

Refreshing

Crisp

This Americanised version of German Weissbier first became popular in the Pacific Northwest of the United States.

Food Pairing

| Salads | Mexican food | Thai food | Light seafood |

Rye Beer

Origin: United States
Colour: 3-6 SRM
ABV: 4-9%
IBU: 15-30
Glassware: pint

With influences from ancient rye beer styles, US brewers have used the spicy grain to develop an original and distinct category of beer.

MEETING THE CHALLENGE

When faced with a challenge in brewing, rather than shirking from it, brewers tend to revel in it. Malted rye presents just such a challenge. During the brewing process rye, which has no husk, can cause the mash to become sticky and gummy. Brewers – in particular US brewers – have taken to this speciality grain and utilised its strengths to produce a distinctive product. As rye may be added to a variety of base recipes, the colour can range from light golden to chestnut, with varying coloured heads, all generally dense and creamy. The distinctive feature is the slight tang that provides a crisp and refreshing quality. Some examples can be quite hoppy, most have a nice malty centre and a refreshing, often sharp, finish.

Three Beers to Try

FOUNDERS RED'S RYE PA Caramel, toast and spicy rye dominate a malty first impression from this beer. The hops ease in, a bright, piney bitterness, and linger through the finish.

BOULEVARD RYE-ON-RYE At 12% ABV, this beer tips the alcohol scale for the style. Citrus hops balance the spicy, malty and rye body. Whiskey-barrel aging lends notes of wood and complex fruits.

TWO BROTHERS CANE AND EBEL An amber rye, this brew is superbly balanced and drinkable, alternating between citrus, sweet malt and the tang of spicy rye.

THE ATOMIC STRUCTURE OF
Rye Beer

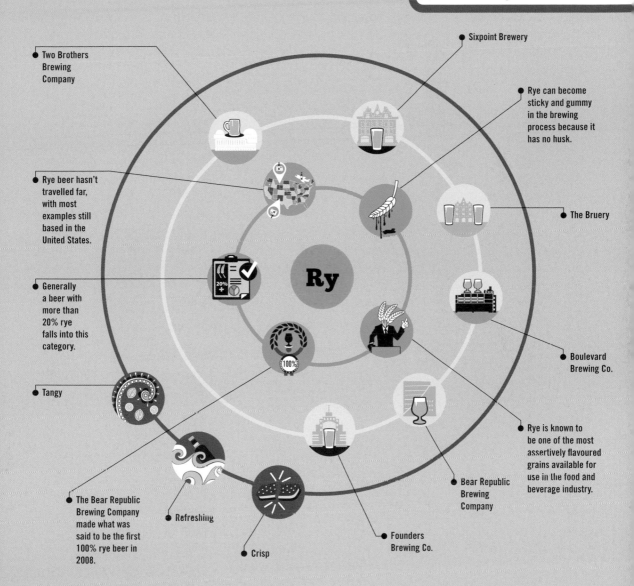

Ry

Sixpoint Brewery

Two Brothers Brewing Company

Rye can become sticky and gummy in the brewing process because it has no husk.

Rye beer hasn't travelled far, with most examples still based in the United States.

The Bruery

Generally a beer with more than 20% rye falls into this category.

Boulevard Brewing Co.

Tangy

Rye is known to be one of the most assertively flavoured grains available for use in the food and beverage industry.

The Bear Republic Brewing Company made what was said to be the first 100% rye beer in 2008.

Refreshing

Bear Republic Brewing Company

Crisp

Founders Brewing Co.

Food Pairing

| Jerk chicken | Spicy Thai food | Burgers | Roasted pork |

American Pale Ale

Origin: United States
Colour: 5–14 SRM
ABV: 4.5–6.2%
IBU: 30–45
Glassware: pint, mug

A brash, bold, yet refreshing style. Americans took the English pale ale and created a brew that is entirely their own.

AN AMERICAN STAPLE

In 1980, Sierra Nevada Brewing Company created the pale ale, upon whose shoulders would stand every American pale ale to come. Giving rise to a craft beer renaissance, this style has become a staple in almost every American brewery's arsenal. Pouring from a deep golden to a near-copper colour and bursting with hops, there can be notes of oranges, grapefruit, lemon, pine and grass, some with a bitterness that stretches from first sip to last swallow. There is a definite and firm malt backbone showing some caramel, which supports the hops with a solid balance. Overall, it is a refreshing beer, bursting with flavour.

Three Beers to Try

SIERRA NEVADA PALE ALE The classic continues to impress. Smooth with a hoppy blend of citrus fruit, pine and floral notes.

GREAT LAKES BURNING RIVER In this pale ale, bitter Cascade hops – punching pine and citrus – rest on a foundation of sweet malts and hints of caramel.

DESCHUTES MIRROR POND PALE ALE
A well-crafted blend in which an inviting nose of bread and citric hoppiness evokes interest and continues on through a clean, crisp body.

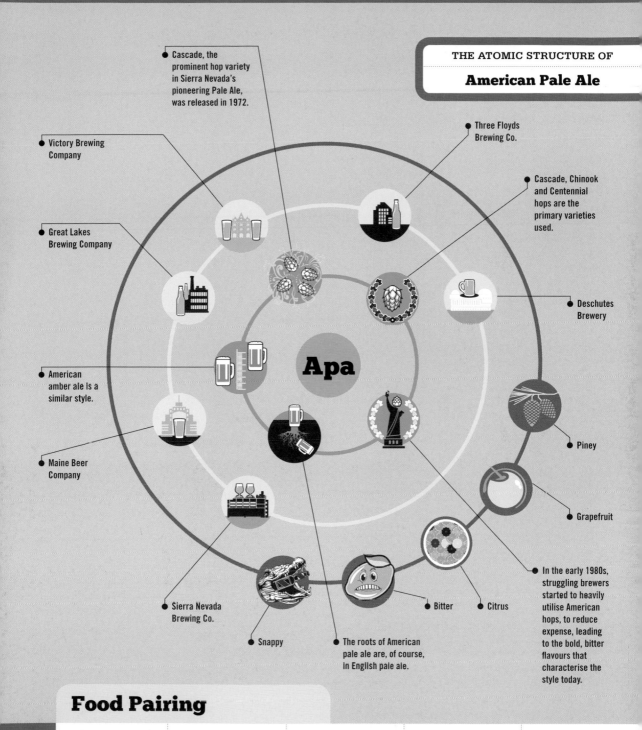

Cascade, the prominent hop variety in Sierra Nevada's pioneering Pale Ale, was released in 1972.

Victory Brewing Company

Great Lakes Brewing Company

American amber ale Is a similar style.

Maine Beer Company

Three Floyds Brewing Co.

Cascade, Chinook and Centennial hops are the primary varieties used.

Deschutes Brewery

Apa

Piney

Grapefruit

In the early 1980s, struggling brewers started to heavily utilise American hops, to reduce expense, leading to the bold, bitter flavours that characterise the style today.

Sierra Nevada Brewing Co.

Snappy

The roots of American pale ale are, of course, in English pale ale.

Bitter

Citrus

Food Pairing

| Citrus salads | Thai food | Burgers | Spicy crab cakes | Mexican food |

American IPA

Origin: United States
Colour: 6–15 SRM
ABV: 5.5–7.5%
IBU: 40–70
Glassware: pint, IPA glass

With roots deep in the English IPA style, America's belle of the beer ball is more brash and bitter than its ancestor, and embodies the new craft beer culture.

UNBALANCED AND ASSERTIVE

Today, the American craft beer scene has been overrun with India pale ales (IPAs). And what a good problem to have. Brewers are rising to the competition, making some bitterly assaulting, assertive brews.

In this style 'unbalanced' becomes an asset, where the bitterness can be enjoyably abrasive. In colour it is deep gold to a ruby-bronze, typically topped with a frothy head. The resinous, citric, floral, piney hops burst on the bouquet. Hop forward on the palate, the aromas also meld on the tongue, balancing on a supportive malty backbone. The flash of malt in the centre moves quickly to a dry and often long and bitter finish.

Three Beers to Try

BELL'S TWO HEARTED ALE A beautifully balanced brew, it relies solely on Centennial hops for its citrus and pine notes. Enough malt to make the bitterness pleasantly drinkable.

STONE IPA A smooth mouthfeel softens an intensity of bitterness. Enough malt presence, but piney, spicy, bitter hops are the main event.

DOGFISH HEAD 60 MINUTE IPA Continuous hopping during the 60-minute boil gives this bitter beauty its name. Pine and citrus flavours are up front, but there is a sweet maltiness behind.

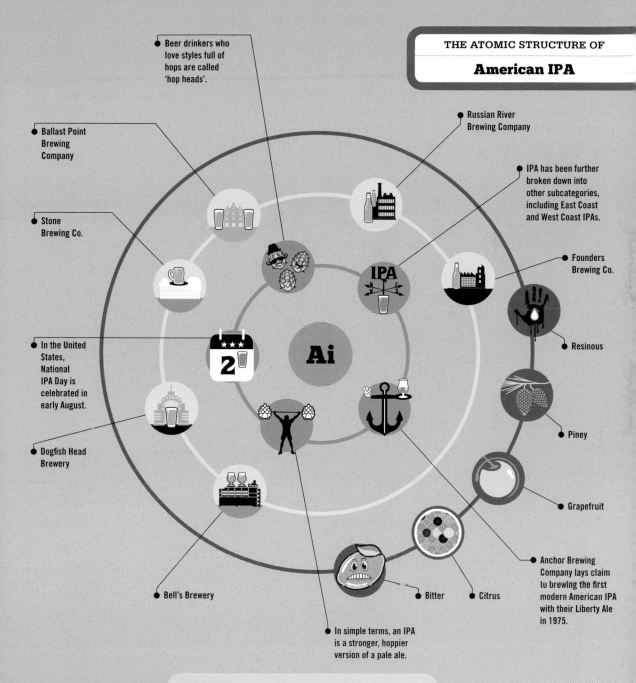

THE ATOMIC STRUCTURE OF
American IPA

Beer drinkers who love styles full of hops are called 'hop heads'.

Ballast Point Brewing Company

Stone Brewing Co.

Russian River Brewing Company

IPA has been further broken down into other subcategories, including East Coast and West Coast IPAs.

Founders Brewing Co.

Resinous

In the United States, National IPA Day is celebrated in early August.

Dogfish Head Brewery

Bell's Brewery

Piney

Grapefruit

Anchor Brewing Company lays claim to brewing the first modern American IPA with their Liberty Ale in 1975.

Bitter

Citrus

In simple terms, an IPA is a stronger, hoppier version of a pale ale.

Ai

IPA

Food Pairing

| Spicy Thai food | Indian curries | Jerk dishes | Carrot cake |

Wet Hop

Origin: United States
Colour: Varies
ABV: 5–7%
IBU: 35–70
Glassware: pint

A well-hopped addition to the American autumn beer lineup, these beers take advantage of the hop harvest and give the brew an extra fresh, hoppy boost.

FRESH FROM THE FIELD

The typical wet-hop beer is founded on a base of pale ale then amped up with fresh-from-the-field hops, often shipped overnight in order to be in the brewer's kettle within 24 hours of harvest. Instead of undergoing the typical drying process, the hops are thrown immediately into the wort, resulting in a fresh, hop-forward brew. While the specific results vary according to the underlying style, wet-hop beers typically have notes of pine, grapefruit, orange and earth. There is a succulent freshness on both the nose and the mouthfeel. The body can be deep golden to amber, and is topped with a dense, creamy head. Malt is in balance but takes a backseat, allowing the hops to showcase.

Three Beers to Try

SIERRA NEVADA NORTHERN HEMISPHERE HARVEST   A wet-hop classic, this beer has a bouquet of orange, grapefruit and pine, and a bitterness that lasts to the finish.

GREAT DIVIDE FRESH HOP   A lemongrass nose melts into a bitter, citrus centre on the palate of this wet-hop pale ale. Well-balanced malt and a solid mouthfeel.

DESCHUTES HOP TRIP   Notes of juicy citrus and earthy hops are well-balanced by sweet malts in this pale ale. Bitterness lingers through the finish.

THE ATOMIC STRUCTURE OF

Wet Hop

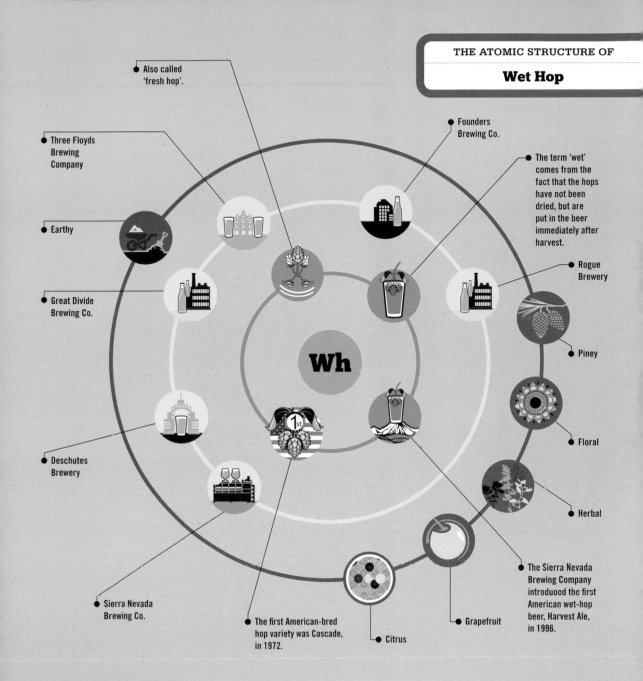

Also called 'fresh hop'.

Three Floyds Brewing Company

Earthy

Great Divide Brewing Co.

Deschutes Brewery

Sierra Nevada Brewing Co.

The first American-bred hop variety was Cascade, in 1972.

Citrus

Founders Brewing Co.

The term 'wet' comes from the fact that the hops have not been dried, but are put in the beer immediately after harvest.

Rogue Brewery

Piney

Floral

Herbal

Grapefruit

The Sierra Nevada Brewing Company introduood the first American wet-hop beer, Harvest Ale, in 1996.

Wh

Food Pairing

| Indian curries | Thai food | Cheddar cheese | Manchego cheese |

Single Hop IPA

Origin: United States
Colour: 6-15 SRM
ABV: 5.5-7.5%
IBU: 40-70
Glassware: pint, mug

Single hop IPAs are not so much a strict categorisation, but rather an interesting variation on a much-loved brewing style.

RESPONDING TO CRISIS

With the meteoric rise in popularity of IPA (page 32), brewers have crafted myriad imaginative examples of the style, and many different sub-styles have been created in the process. As hop growers continue to create new and hybrid varieties of hops, brewers have sought to produce single-hop beers, isolating and highlighting a specific hop variety.

Accelerating the development of this sub-style was the 'hop crisis' of 2007 and 2008, during which a shortage of hops drastically increased costs. This prompted further experimentation in the US brewhouses, and single-hop brews were a product of the trials.

Three Beers to Try

MIKKELLER SERIES This innovative Denmark-based brewery has a revolving single-hop series, in which each beer has an IBU of 100.

SIXPOINT SPICE OF LIFE SERIES
This series focuses on 12 hop varieties, one released each month — the base recipe and process are unaltered, only the hop strain changes.

THREE FLOYDS ZOMBIE DUST
Using only Yakima Valley-grown Citra hops, this pale ale is bursting with grapefruit, orange and mango.

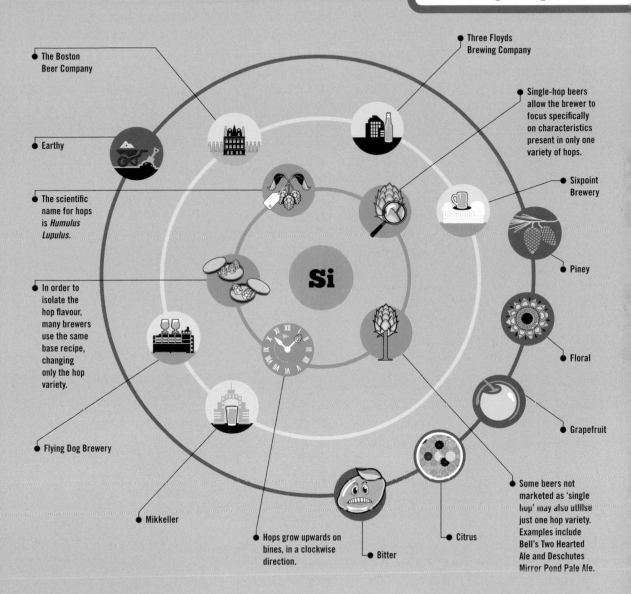

THE ATOMIC STRUCTURE OF
Single Hop IPA

The Boston Beer Company

Earthy

The scientific name for hops is *Humulus Lupulus.*

In order to isolate the hop flavour, many brewers use the same base recipe, changing only the hop variety.

Flying Dog Brewery

Mikkeller

Three Floyds Brewing Company

Single-hop beers allow the brewer to focus specifically on characteristics present in only one variety of hops.

Sixpoint Brewery

Piney

Floral

Grapefruit

Some beers not marketed as 'single hop' may also utilise just one hop variety. Examples include Bell's Two Hearted Ale and Deschutes Mirror Pond Pale Ale.

Si

Hops grow upwards on bines, in a clockwise direction.

Bitter

Citrus

Food Pairing

| Thai food | Burgers | Mexican food | Indian curries |

American Amber Lager

Origin: United States
Colour: 6-14 SRM
ABV: 4.8-5.5%
IBU: 18-30
Glassware: pint, pilsner, mug

With rebellion in their brew kettles, American craft brewers of the 1980s set out to brew a lager with character, to provide a response to pilsner's popularity.

AUSTRIAN ANCESTRY

A great big beer basket in which to throw amber-coloured American lagers, this category has become a bit of a blanket style. Its foundations lie in Vienna, but the beer has since taken an entirely American path. The malt is more caramelly than bready. The hops are crisply bitter and lean more on typically American pine and citrus notes. Usually light amber to copper in colour with an off-white head of varying strength and lacing, the degrees of distinction from Vienna lager vary and what one brewer may call an American amber lager, another may call Vienna lager (page 138).

Three Beers to Try

BROOKLYN LAGER Initial signature American hops of pine and florals ease into a creamy, caramel body that settles on the back of the tongue and finishes dry, with a tinge of bitter.

YUENGLING TRADITIONAL LAGER
From America's oldest brewery comes an iconic brew. It is a bright, clear amber and is smooth, with a sweet grain maltiness and clean hops, with slight notes of citrus.

LAKEFRONT RIVERWEST STEIN BEER
 A lasting head tops a creamy, amber base. Smooth on the palate with hop notes of citrus and wood, outweighed by the sweet, caramel

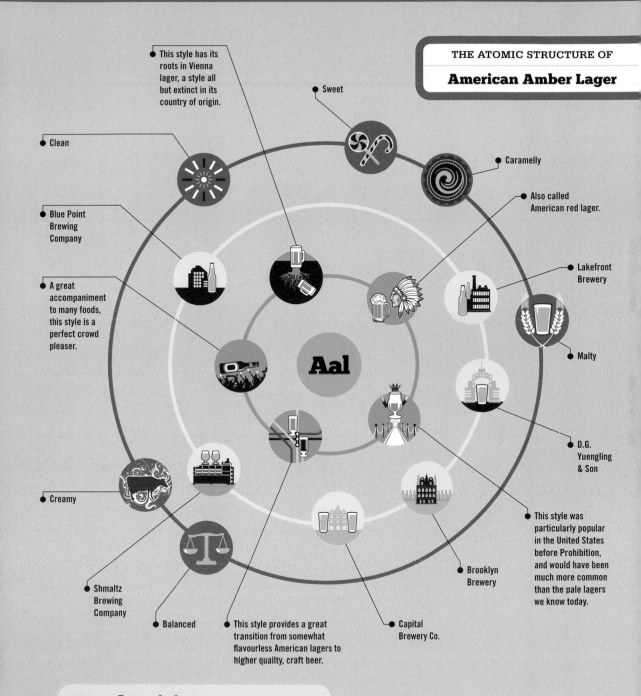

This style has its roots in Vienna lager, a style all but extinct in its country of origin.

Sweet

Clean

Caramelly

Also called American red lager.

Blue Point Brewing Company

Lakefront Brewery

A great accompaniment to many foods, this style is a perfect crowd pleaser.

Malty

Aal

D.G. Yuengling & Son

Creamy

This style was particularly popular in the United States before Prohibition, and would have been much more common than the pale lagers we know today.

Shmaltz Brewing Company

Brooklyn Brewery

Balanced

This style provides a great transition from somewhat flavourless American lagers to higher quality, craft beer.

Capital Brewery Co.

THE ATOMIC STRUCTURE OF
American Amber Lager

Food Pairing

| Pizza | Grilled meats | Roasted chicken | Aged Gouda | Barbecue |

Double/Imperial IPA

Origin: United States
Colour: 8–15 SRM
ABV: 7.5–10%
IBU: 60–120
Glassware: snifter, tulip, oversized wine glass, pint

From the country where more hop varieties are grown than in the rest of the world, comes this hop-heavy style. Big and bitter, with an imperial ABV, it is not for the faint of heart.

HOPS AND MORE HOPS

With the craft beer renaissance in the United States came the love of the IPA. As beer drinkers fell in love with hops, brewers saw room to push the envelope. Enter double IPA.

This style ranges in colour from an orange-tinted gold to copper, with a long-lasting, off-white cap of foam. An intensely hoppy bouquet of grapefruit, other citrus, pine and floral notes burst from the glass. The first sip is hoppy, the aromas melded in a delicious mixture of bitterness. All this adheres to a supportive caramel malt structure, present enough for balance alone. The alcohol is high, but typically well veiled and the finish is long lasting and bitter.

Three Beers to Try

RUSSIAN RIVER PLINY THE ELDER
A great example of the style, this beer is assertively hoppy. Bitterness is bold, with grapefruit, grass and clean pine woven throughout.

BELL'S HOPSLAM ALE From a stellar Midwest brewer, comes this winter seasonal. Citrus and floral notes erupt on the nose. The palate is introduced with a sweetish caramel that rushes to grapefruit and ends at bitingly bitter hops.

DOGFISH HEAD 90 MINUTE IPA Sitting comfortably between 60 and 120 in Dogfish Head's continuously hopped lineup, 90 Minute was the first. The showcase of complex hops is buoyed by a stiff, sweet, maltiness.

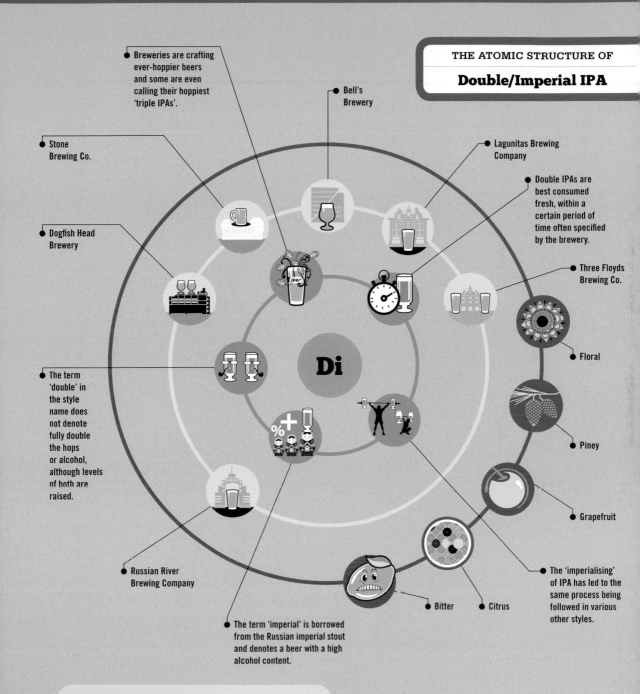

THE ATOMIC STRUCTURE OF
Double/Imperial IPA

Di

Breweries are crafting ever-hoppier beers and some are even calling their hoppiest 'triple IPAs'.

Bell's Brewery

Stone Brewing Co.

Lagunitas Brewing Company

Double IPAs are best consumed fresh, within a certain period of time often specified by the brewery.

Dogfish Head Brewery

Three Floyds Brewing Co.

Floral

The term 'double' in the style name does not denote fully double the hops or alcohol, although levels of both are raised.

Piney

Grapefruit

Russian River Brewing Company

The 'imperialising' of IPA has led to the same process being followed in various other styles.

Bitter

Citrus

The term 'imperial' is borrowed from the Russian imperial stout and denotes a beer with a high alcohol content.

Food Pairing

| Thai food | Cajun food | English Cheddar | Triple-cream cheese | Carrot cake |

Pumpkin Ale

Origin: United States
Colour: 6–12 SRM
ABV: 5–6%
IBU: 10–15
Glassware: pint

A uniquely American style, pumpkin ale can be spiced like hot cider or as sweet as pumpkin pie.

SEASONAL SPICE

As the leaves start to turn colour across the United States, the shelves begin to fill with Autumn seasonals, one of which is the coveted pumpkin ale.

With gains in popularity, so comes a creativity in brewing and a variety of takes on the style. Pumpkin ale can be light orange to rich copper in colour and is typically crowned with a nice light brown head. The nose pours out in blends of fresh spices, cinnamon, nutmeg, cloves, allspice, ginger and, of course, pumpkin. On the palate, there's a blend of the same with additions of caramel and perhaps brown sugar, all layered on a sweet malty backbone. Hops are typically quiet, but provide a bit of balance. A distinctive and delicious treat, to drink more than one is as easy as pie.

Three Beers to Try

SOUTHERN TIER PUMKING Sweet, almost confectionery-like, this brew is smooth and viscous. Pumpkin bread notes blend with sweet malt and disguise the 8.5% ABV.

DOGFISH HEAD PUNKIN ALE With origins before its brewery existed, this brew has reason to last. Smooth, sweet and spicy.

ELYSIAN NIGHT OWL PUMPKIN ALE
From a brewery with a gambit of the pumpkin style, comes its standard. Brewed with pumpkin and pumpkin seeds, it is well spiced and deliciously drinkable.

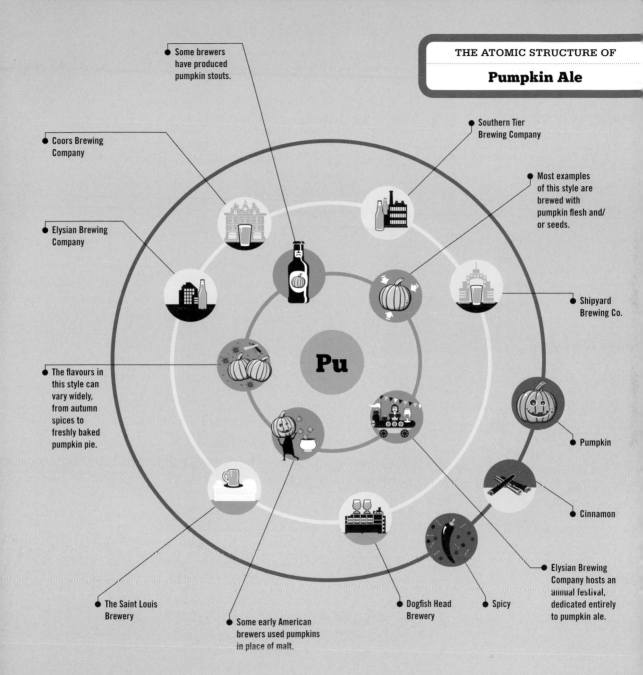

Some brewers have produced pumpkin stouts.

Southern Tier Brewing Company

Coors Brewing Company

Most examples of this style are brewed with pumpkin flesh and/or seeds.

Elysian Brewing Company

Shipyard Brewing Co.

Pu

The flavours in this style can vary widely, from autumn spices to freshly baked pumpkin pie.

Pumpkin

Cinnamon

The Saint Louis Brewery

Some early American brewers used pumpkins in place of malt.

Dogfish Head Brewery

Spicy

Elysian Brewing Company hosts an annual festival, dedicated entirely to pumpkin ale.

Food Pairing

| Turkey | Roasted vegetables | Sharp Cheddar |

American Amber

Origin: United States
Colour: 10–17 SRM
ABV: 4.5–6.2%
IBU: 25–40
Glassware: pint

As with many pale ale styles, the American amber (also called red ale) is a category that is home to – in this case, amber-hued – orphans that simply don't belong anywhere else.

RED AND MALTY

A style category created for darker, reddish pale ales, American amber ale does have a few defining characteristics. Besides its deeper, richer colouring, it has a more malty centre than pales, with toasty and caramel notes. The body is richer as well, and the malt moves slightly to the centre, sharing the spotlight with the hops. The hops used in this style are typical American varieties and showcase grapefruit, citrus, pine and flowery notes. It is a balanced, versatile beer with the ability to please a wide variety of palates.

Three Beers to Try

NEW BELGIUM FAT TIRE AMBER ALE
This is the beer that exploded craft beer onto the American market. It is smooth and mild, a great transition into the world of better beer.

TRÖEGS NUGGET NECTAR From Pennsylvania, comes a generously hopped amber. The Nugget variety hops lend bitterness while maintaining incredible drinkability.

NORTH COAST RUEDRICH'S RED SEAL ALE With a rich maltiness and an abundance of hops, this beer is balanced, flavourful and smooth. Nice notes of evergreen, citrus and caramel.

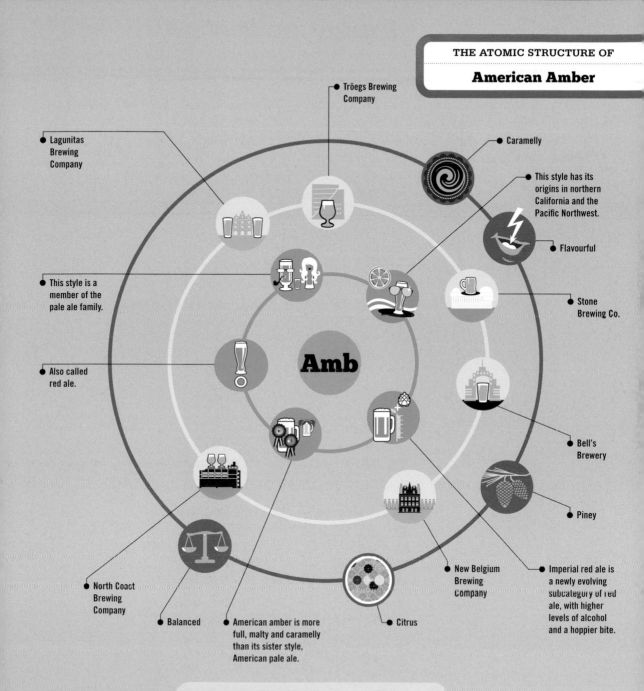

Tröegs Brewing Company

Caramelly

This style has its origins in northern California and the Pacific Northwest.

Lagunitas Brewing Company

Flavourful

This style is a member of the pale ale family.

Stone Brewing Co.

Amb

Also called red ale.

Bell's Brewery

Piney

North Coast Brewing Company

Balanced

American amber is more full, malty and caramelly than its sister style, American pale ale.

Citrus

New Belgium Brewing Company

Imperial red ale is a newly evolving subcategory of red ale, with higher levels of alcohol and a hoppier bite.

Food Pairing

| Burgers | Roasted chicken | Spicy cuisine | Mild Cheddar |

American Wild Ale

Origin: United States
Colour: 2–26 SRM
ABV: 5.5–10%
IBU: 20–40
Glassware: tulip, goblet, chalice

With a funky, intriguing and powerful palate, these brews draw a line in the sand. You either love 'em or hate 'em.

A RAINBOW OF COLOURS AND FLAVOURS

Time to meet another style-bending category. American wild ale is so-called because it utilises organisms other than *Saccharomyces cerevisiae*, the standard brewing ale yeast, in the brewing process. With the addition of these microorganisms comes an array of flavours, from subtle to brash, resulting in a very distinct and polarising brew. Colours run the rainbow, from golden to deep garnet to rich, dark brown. The head, too, varies hugely, but is typically fluffy with nice lace. The nose and palate are an intruiging medley, from tart and sour to an earthy, barnyard-like mustiness. Most American wild ales are complex and many are quite worth the venture.

Three Beers to Try

RUSSIAN RIVER SUPPLICATION An American pioneer of the style, Russian River, produces this beautiful blend of flavours: tart cherries, must and fruit. A beer you should try.

NEW BELGIUM LE TERROIR A hazy gold body produces a tart, funky nose. The palate melds sour and barnyard notes in pleasing harmony in this beer.

THE LOST ABBEY CUVEE DE TOMME
The base beer, a brown ale, follows the path of barrel aging with cherries and *Brettanomyces* yeast to arrive at a complex wild ale.

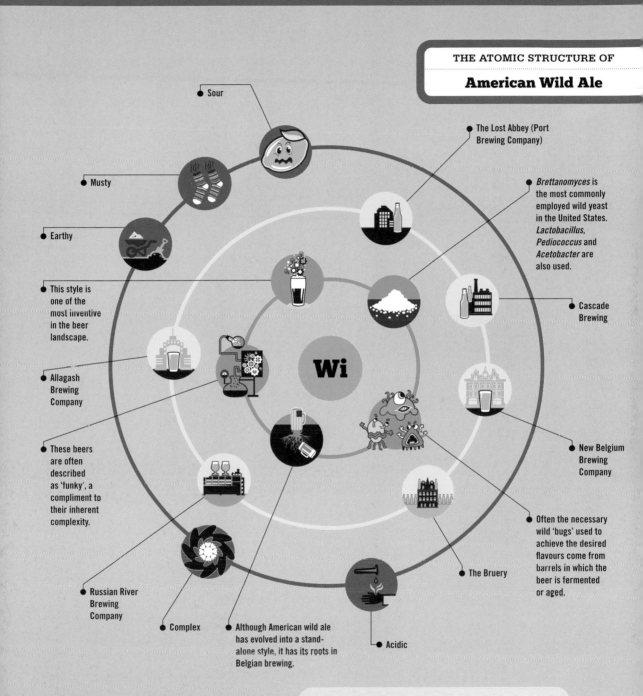

THE ATOMIC STRUCTURE OF

American Wild Ale

Sour

Musty

Earthy

The Lost Abbey (Port Brewing Company)

Brettanomyces is the most commonly employed wild yeast in the United States. *Lactobacillus*, *Pediococcus* and *Acetobacter* are also used.

This style is one of the most inventive in the beer landscape.

Cascade Brewing

Allagash Brewing Company

Wi

New Belgium Brewing Company

These beers are often described as 'funky', a compliment to their inherent complexity.

Often the necessary wild 'bugs' used to achieve the desired flavours come from barrels in which the beer is fermented or aged.

Russian River Brewing Company

The Bruery

Complex

Although American wild ale has evolved into a stand-alone style, it has its roots in Belgian brewing.

Acidic

Food Pairing

| Smoked meats | Creamy or tangy cheese | Salads |

California Common

Origin: United States
Colour: 10-14 SRM
ABV: 4.5-5.5%
IBU: 30-45
Glassware: pint

The invention of gold rush-era brewmasters, this style was a refreshing necessity for thirsty, and usually penniless, prospectors.

WARM FERMENTATION

During the California gold rush of the 1800s, refrigeration was a luxury unavailable to most. Brewers, forced to be creative, fermented beer in shallow vessels in order to cool it more quickly.

Despite the use of lager yeast, the warmer fermentation temperatures result in some ale-like fruit aromas and flavours in brews of this style. Usually deep gold to deep amber in colour, California commons have a rushing carbonation, typical of the first brews of this style ever created. California commons are smooth and brisk, with a medium body. Wood and earthy flavours of hops, as well as bitterness are present, but well-balanced by a juicy maltiness. Today, Anchor Steam Beer is the embodiment of the style, leaving little room for competition.

Three Beers to Try

ANCHOR STEAM BEER The only beer allowed to bear the term 'steam', it is a classic. The flavours are a rush, alternating between assertive hops, a malt centre and a long-lasting, bitter finish.

FULLSTEAM SOUTHERN LAGER With its aromatic nose of wood, toast, bread and caramel, this brew is sessionable, simple and refreshing.

STEAMWORKS STEAM ENGINE LAGER A small, Colorado-based brewery produces this classic. Spicy hops blend well with sweet, caramel maltiness.

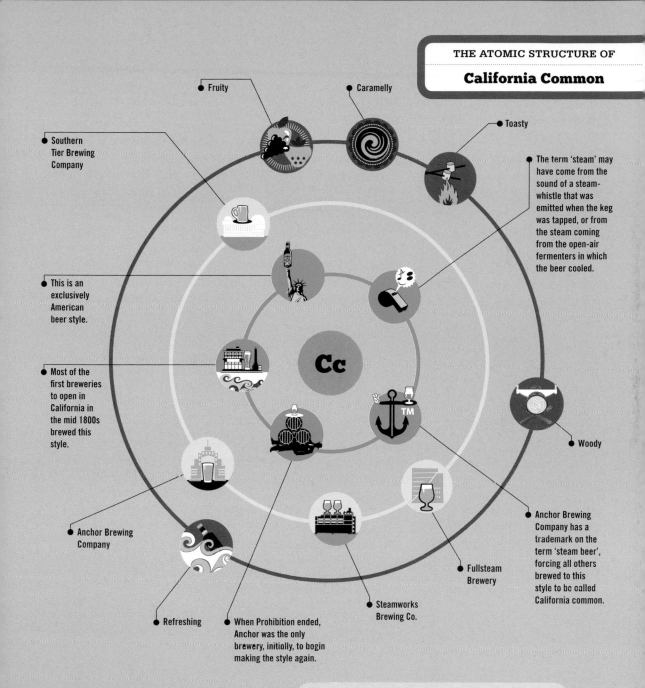

California Common

- Fruity
- Caramelly
- Toasty

Southern Tier Brewing Company

The term 'steam' may have come from the sound of a steam-whistle that was emitted when the keg was tapped, or from the steam coming from the open-air fermenters in which the beer cooled.

This is an exclusively American beer style.

Most of the first breweries to open in California in the mid 1800s brewed this style.

Cc

Woody

Anchor Brewing Company

Anchor Brewing Company has a trademark on the term 'steam beer', forcing all others brewed to this style to be called California common.

Fullsteam Brewery

Refreshing

When Prohibition ended, Anchor was the only brewery, initially, to begin making the style again.

Steamworks Brewing Co.

Food Pairing

Steak	Mexican food	Mellow cheese

Fruit Beers

Origin: United States
Colour: 5–50 SRM
ABV: 2.5–12%
IBU: 5–70
Glassware: pint, oversized wine glass, mug, flute

A category in which creativity blossoms, modern fruit beers have a spectrum of flavours, impacting the taste buds in a powerful way. Typically refreshing, these beers are a perfect summer choice.

A MARKET STALL IN A GLASS

Raspberries, strawberries, cherries and blueberries. Apricots and apples. Blackcurrant, tangerine and watermelon. While it sounds like a trip to the farmers' market, it's just another day in the beer aisle. From subtle hints and blends, to bold and bursting palates of fruit, this style can vary in flavour according to the limits of the brewer's imagination. Often intentionally unbalanced, these beers can taste very unlike a beer and can be sweet, fruity or puckeringly tart. An evolving sub-style, fruit wheat beers are common. The American style wheat lends itself particularly to fruit additions.

Three Beers to Try

NEW GLARUS RASPBERRY TART From the brewery renowned for this style, comes one bursting with flavour. Ruby with a delicate rose head, it is as advertised: bursting with raspberry and refreshingly tart.

SHIPYARD SMASHED BLUEBERRY Coffee, chocolate and blueberry form an unlikely, but delicious, partnership in this brew.

SAMUEL SMITH'S ORGANIC APRICOT ALE Apricot flavours are balanced by a slight tartness and sufficient bready yeast, so you don't forget it's a beer.

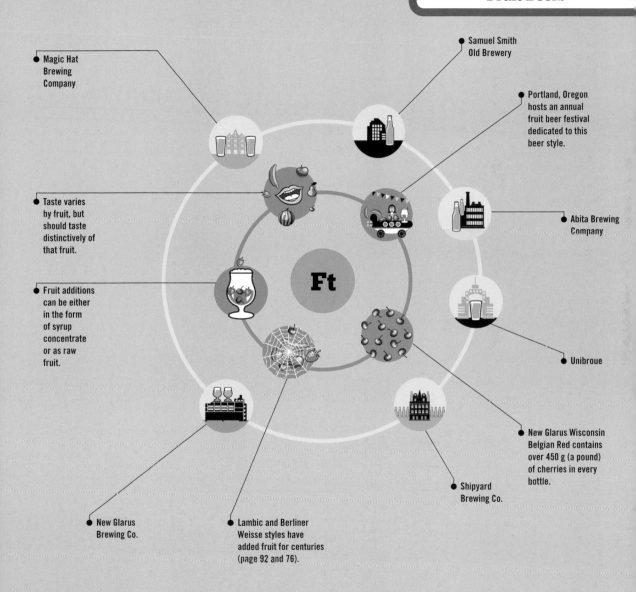

Samuel Smith
Old Brewery

Magic Hat
Brewing
Company

Portland, Oregon
hosts an annual
fruit beer festival
dedicated to this
beer style.

Taste varies
by fruit, but
should taste
distinctively of
that fruit.

Abita Brewing
Company

Ft

Fruit additions
can be either
in the form
of syrup
concentrate
or as raw
fruit.

Unibroue

New Glarus Wisconsin
Belgian Red contains
over 450 g (a pound)
of cherries in every
bottle.

Shipyard
Brewing Co.

New Glarus
Brewing Co.

Lambic and Berliner
Weisse styles have
added fruit for centuries
(page 92 and 76).

Food Pairing

This beer doesn't have tasting notes — it
depends on the fruit used in the brewing.

| Various cheeses | Desserts | |

American Barley Wine

Origin: United States
Colour: 10-19 SRM
ABV: 8-12%
IBU: 50-120
Glassware: snifter

In typical American brewer fashion, American barley wine takes the more tempered English version and douses it with hops and greater alcoholic strength.

MALTY SWEET CORE

A bold, strong brew with depth and complexity, American barley wine typically ranges in colour from light amber to a deep copper, with some brews being even a bit darker on the scale. Viscous, with a velvet-smooth mouthfeel, it has 'legs' that drip from the top of the glass when slowly swirled. Maltiness is at its core, sweetness, caramel and bread notes are common.

The hop profile has more variety. Some of this style retain just enough bitterness to balance out the tremendous malt forefront, but others have a brash, assertive hop bite, usually in pine and citrus, that carry through to the finish.

Three Beers to Try

SIERRA NEVADA BIGFOOT BARLEYWINE STYLE ALE Rich from first glance to final sip, the flavour medley ranges from a malty nose to an oncoming hop-heavy centre, to a lingering and bitter finish in this beer.

THREE FLOYDS BEHEMOTH Big, sweet and malty, this January seasonal makes the cold winter a bit warmer with an ABV of 10.5%.

GREAT DIVIDE OLD RUFFIAN This barley wine is hugely hopped, but not light on the fruity, caramelly malts either. Creamy and smooth, it is a timeless sipper.

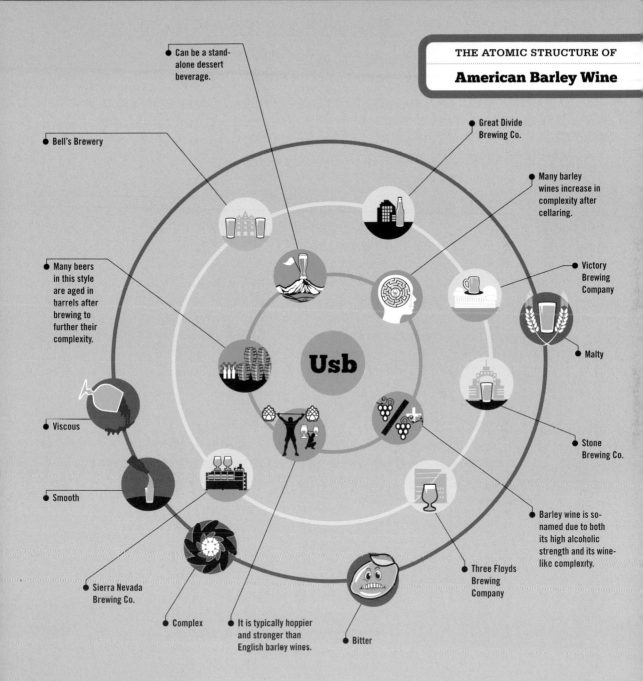

Can be a stand-alone dessert beverage.

Bell's Brewery

Great Divide Brewing Co.

Many barley wines increase in complexity after cellaring.

Many beers in this style are aged in barrels after brewing to further their complexity.

Victory Brewing Company

Usb

Malty

Viscous

Smooth

Stone Brewing Co.

Sierra Nevada Brewing Co.

Barley wine is so-named due to both its high alcoholic strength and its wine-like complexity.

Complex

It is typically hoppier and stronger than English barley wines.

Bitter

Three Floyds Brewing Company

Food Pairing

| Hearty foods | Stilton cheese | Bread pudding | Crème brûlée |

American Strong Ale

Origin: United States
Colour: 15–35 SRM
ABV: 7.5–13%
IBU: 45–80
Glassware: snifter

A close relative of English old ale, across the Atlantic the style is given a typical American twist of a heftier hop bill.

BIG BEER, HIGH ALCOHOL

This category is a slippery one: vague in specifics, but with a few common threads. American strong ale has become a catch-all category for those dark, viscous, boozy misfits that don't belong anywhere else. Typically it is dark brown to almost black in colour, often with ruby highlights. Most examples have a chewy, caramel-sweet malt centre, balanced by hops but without overly bitter notes. However, some hugely hopped imperial IPAs have somehow landed in this bucket as well. Essentially, a big beer with high alcohol is about as pinned-down as this style comes. Prepare for a complex, boozy brew.

Three Beers to Try

STONE ARROGANT BASTARD ALE   This is an oddly perfected balance of sweet, caramel maltiness and brash, bold hops.

LAGUNITAS BROWN SHUGGA   What was almost a ruined batch of Olde GnarlyWine has become a seasonal favourite. Copious amounts of brown sugar make this a sweet, malty treat.

ROGUE XS DEAD GUY   From a base of Rogue's Maibock, this amped-up, hopped-up copper brew envelopes the palate with creamy caramel and sweet breadiness, blended with citrus and bitter, yet balancing, hops.

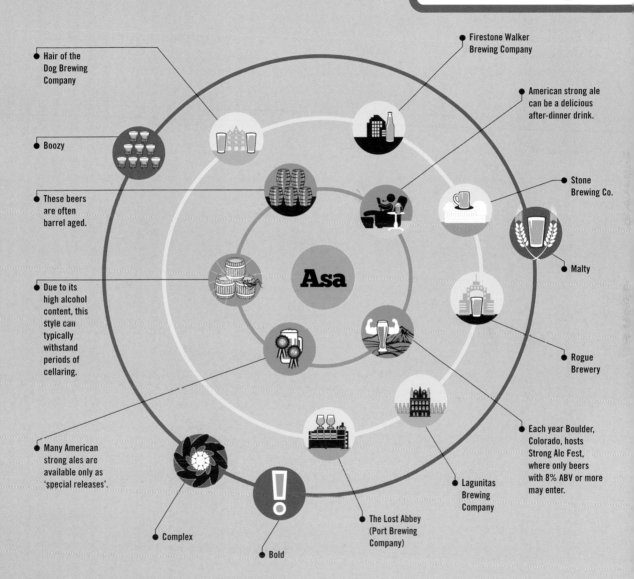

Firestone Walker
Brewing Company

American strong ale
can be a delicious
after-dinner drink.

Hair of the
Dog Brewing
Company

Boozy

Stone
Brewing Co.

These beers
are often
barrel aged.

Malty

Asa

Due to its
high alcohol
content, this
style can
typically
withstand
periods of
cellaring.

Rogue
Brewery

Each year Boulder,
Colorado, hosts
Strong Ale Fest,
where only beers
with 8% ABV or more
may enter.

Many American
strong ales are
available only as
'special releases'.

Lagunitas
Brewing
Company

Complex

The Lost Abbey
(Port Brewing
Company)

Bold

Food Pairing

| Meat stew | Strong cheese | Desserts |

American Brown Ale

Origin: United States
Colour: 18–35 SRM
ABV: 4.3–6.2%
IBU: 20–40
Glassware: pint

Based on the more conservative English rendition of the style, United States brewers have amped up the classic, to create a style that is distinctly American.

SWEET AND NUTTY

Despite the robust step up from English browns, the American version maintains the soft, sweet, nutty character that makes the style so inviting. It ranges in colour, but is most comfortable as a dark russet graced with a thin beige head. Immediately the aroma tells a tale of big malt and hop bills; sweet notes of chocolate, nuts and caramel mingle with the scent of fresh, citrus hops. The palate reveals an equally appealing combination of flavours, at times adding cocoa and coffee, and bitterness becomes a significant part of the equation. Balancing itself between English brown ale and light porter, American brown ale justifies its own perfectly delicious niche.

Three Beers to Try

BROOKLYN BROWN ALE Claiming to be a blend of northern and southern English brown styles, this brew is a smooth and drinkable mosaic, with complexities of fruit, chocolate, caramel and coffee. All washing down with a lingering, clean bitterness.

DOGFISH HEAD INDIAN BROWN ALE
Big on hops and alcohol, this beer still achieves a balance with caramel notes and floral hoppiness.

SURLY BENDER Smooth and complex, this brown ale toes the line of sweet and bitter with notes of vanilla and chocolate balanced by a bitter hop bite.

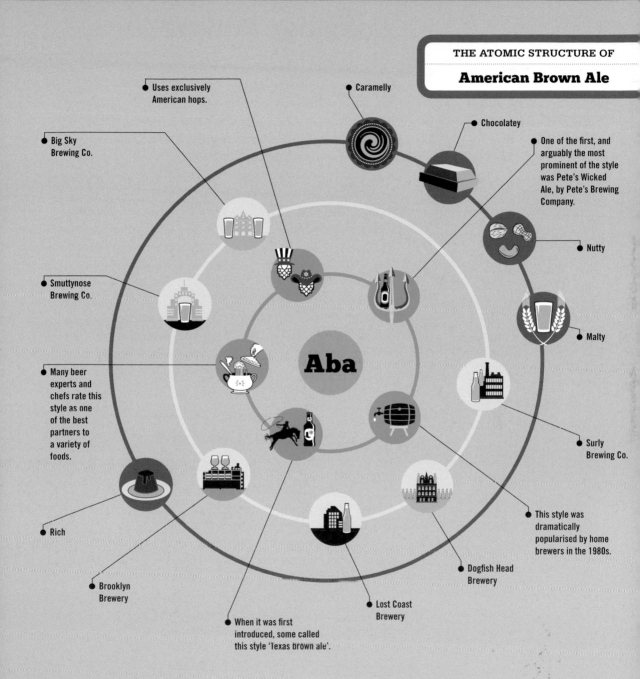

THE ATOMIC STRUCTURE OF
American Brown Ale

Uses exclusively American hops.

Caramelly

Chocolatey

One of the first, and arguably the most prominent of the style was Pete's Wicked Ale, by Pete's Brewing Company.

Big Sky Brewing Co.

Nutty

Smuttynose Brewing Co.

Malty

Many beer experts and chefs rate this style as one of the best partners to a variety of foods.

Aba

Surly Brewing Co.

Rich

This style was dramatically popularised by home brewers in the 1980s.

Brooklyn Brewery

Dogfish Head Brewery

When it was first introduced, some called this style 'Texas brown ale'.

Lost Coast Brewery

Food Pairing

Burgers	Steak	Manchego cheese	Barbecue	Cajun food

American Porter

Origin: United States
Colour: 22–35 SRM
ABV: 4.8–6.5%
IBU: 25–50
Glassware: pint, nonic pint

Its origins are in the slightly more basic English porter, but with American inventiveness, this style has evolved to house a wide array of distinctive flavours.

AROMATIC AND VERSATILE

Balancing somewhere between medium brown and almost black, many American porters push the envelope in every direction. While most often rich with aromas of roastiness, caramel, coffee and chocolate, some may even possess a shocking hop bouquet. In typical American style, brewers have embraced this style as an essentially blank canvas, and have painted it with everything from bitter hops, to sweet vanilla or campfire-like smoke. The best versions of this style have a medium-full mouthfeel and a complex flavour profile.

Three Beers to Try

GREAT LAKES EDMUND FITZGERALD PORTER Very deep brown, nearing on black, with a cap of light brown foam. Chocolate, coffee, roasted malts and floral hops blend into a beautifully big and bitter end.

FOUNDERS PORTER Lusciously creamy, a blend of dark, roasted coffee and chocolate create a balance with hop bitterness.

ALASKAN SMOKED PORTER Brewed just once each year, this exclusive beer – credited with sparking the smoked beer phenomenon in the US – is worth the wait. The sweet smokiness is not overwhelming and perfectly suited to the style.

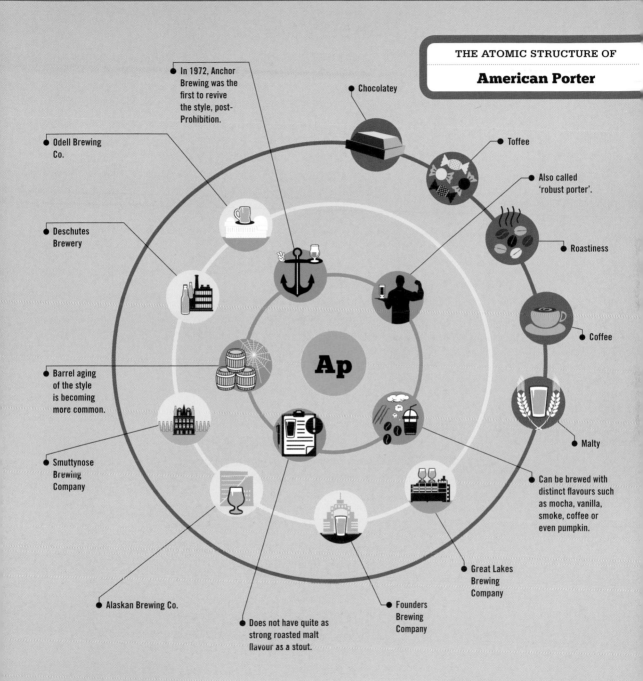

In 1972, Anchor Brewing was the first to revive the style, post-Prohibition.

Odell Brewing Co.

Deschutes Brewery

Barrel aging of the style is becoming more common.

Smuttynose Brewing Company

Alaskan Brewing Co.

Does not have quite as strong roasted malt flavour as a stout.

Chocolatey

Toffee

Also called 'robust porter'.

Roastiness

Coffee

Malty

Can be brewed with distinct flavours such as mocha, vanilla, smoke, coffee or even pumpkin.

Great Lakes Brewing Company

Founders Brewing Company

Ap

Food Pairing

| Barbecue | Grilled meats | Gruyère cheese | Cheesecake |

Black IPA

Origin: United States
Colour: 25–35+ SRM
ABV: 6–9%
IBU: 50–80
Glassware: pint

A newly coined category, this innovative, seemingly contradictory creation has created a rapidly filling bandwagon of enthusiasts.

DARK ROASTINESS

Black and bitter, this style demonstrates the creativity and willingness to invent in the US brewing community.

The American palate has always loved big, robust flavour profiles, on either end of the hop-malt spectrum. This style combines dark roastiness and chocolate with the notorious resinous, citrus hops of the Pacific Northwest, and produces a pleasingly competing battle of flavours: bitterness, orange and pine blend with layers of chocolate, roastiness, coffee and even black liquorice. Black IPA has proved a surprising success – yet another beer-making risk that was well worth taking.

Three Beers to Try

STONE SUBLIMELY SELF-RIGHTEOUS ALE Brewed in 2007 as a one-off, it soon became available all year round. Opaque black, with huge hops from the nose to the finish.

SOUTHERN TIER INIQUITY This beer is a shocking contrast of dark colour and light body. The huge pine and citrus reveal its style status. The brew's big 9% ABV is well hidden.

FIRESTONE WALKER WOOKEY JACK Bitter citrus notes on the forefront of this ale lean back through the centre as a spicy rye emerges. Balanced and quite drinkable.

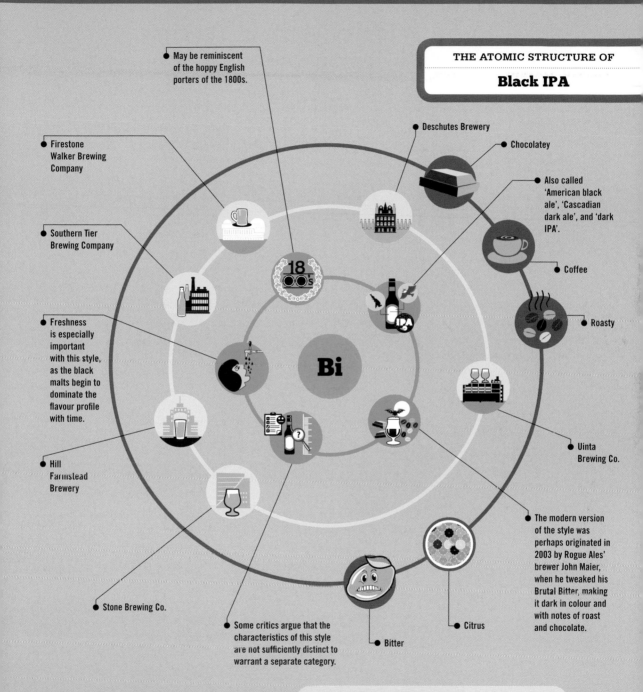

May be reminiscent of the hoppy English porters of the 1800s.

Firestone Walker Brewing Company

Southern Tier Brewing Company

Freshness is especially important with this style, as the black malts begin to dominate the flavour profile with time.

Hill Farmstead Brewery

Stone Brewing Co.

Some critics argue that the characteristics of this style are not sufficiently distinct to warrant a separate category.

Deschutes Brewery

Chocolatey

Also called 'American black ale', 'Cascadian dark ale', and 'dark IPA'.

Coffee

Roasty

Uinta Brewing Co.

The modern version of the style was perhaps originated in 2003 by Rogue Ales' brewer John Maier, when he tweaked his Brutal Bitter, making it dark in colour and with notes of roast and chocolate.

Citrus

Bitter

Bi

Food Pairing

| Ribs | Cajun food | Barbecue |

Barrel-aged Beers

Origin: United States
Colour: 10-50 SRM
ABV: 5-15%
IBU: 40-100
Glassware: snifter, tulip

Not every beer aged in a barrel has a place in this category, but the explosion of interest in the craft beer sector in this method of brewing justifies the differentiation of this style.

BARRELS OF FLAVOUR

Barrel aging is an increasingly widespread method of production, resulting in some complex and inventive brews. The basic concept is simple: a base beer is brewed, typically all the way through fermentation, then moved to wooden barrels for a period of aging. From appearance to aroma to flavour profile, the character of the final beer stems from two main sources: the style of the base beer and the barrel in which it was aged. Base styles can be lagers or ales, light or dark, hoppy or malty. Generally, however, dark, rich, strong beers are best suited to barrel aging. The barrels, most often made of oak, provide hints of the previous resident and can alter the base beer in amazing ways.

Three Beers to Try

GOOSE ISLAND BOURBON COUNTY STOUT One of the first in American craft brewing to experiment with barrel aging, this barrel-aged Russian imperial stout is an intense mix of charred oak, chocolate, vanilla, caramel, and smoke.

RUSSIAN RIVER BEATIFICATION Famous for its use of wild yeast strains, Russian River has a solid lineup of barrel-aged brews, including this offering aged in oak wine barrels.

JOLLY PUMPKIN LA ROJA Brewed in the traditions of a Flanders ale (page 106), this American wild ale is aged in oak barrels and pours a hazy, red-brown. Well-balanced, its flavours move seamlessly from sweet to tart.

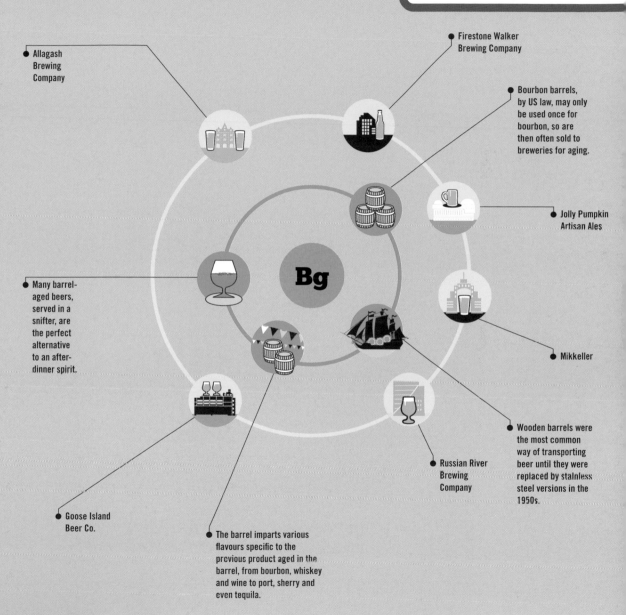

THE ATOMIC STRUCTURE OF
Barrel-aged Beers

Firestone Walker Brewing Company

Bourbon barrels, by US law, may only be used once for bourbon, so are then often sold to breweries for aging.

Allagash Brewing Company

Jolly Pumpkin Artisan Ales

Bg

Many barrel-aged beers, served in a snifter, are the perfect alternative to an after-dinner spirit.

Mikkeller

Goose Island Beer Co.

Russian River Brewing Company

Wooden barrels were the most common way of transporting beer until they were replaced by stainless steel versions in the 1950s.

The barrel imparts various flavours specific to the previous product aged in the barrel, from bourbon, whiskey and wine to port, sherry and even tequila.

This entry doesn't include food pairings or tasting notes, as these depend on the beer's base style. Try looking up the style of your barrel-aged beer for food pairing suggestions.

Imperial and Hyper Beers

Origin: United States
Colour: 8-55 SRM
ABV: 7-40%
IBU: 30-100
Glassware: varies (imperial); snifter (hyper)

With big flavour profiles and characteristic levels of alcohol, these beers start strong and can even approach extreme.

EXTREME BEER

In the modern craft beer world, many have come to think that bigger means better. Imperial Russian stouts (page 66) and imperial IPAs (page 186) have garnered almost cult-like followings. With this desire for bigger and bolder beers, brewers have decided to dabble, bolstering other styles such as brown ales, porters, bocks and even pilsners to create 'imperial' versions. Imperialising typically means that the beer has a substantially greater amount of malt and hops, and a higher alcohol content. When done well these beers can be a bolder, more complex version of the base beer. When a brewer takes imperialising to the next level, a hyper beer is created. Hyper beers have an ABV of over 14 per cent and can occasionally reach a spirit-like 40 per cent.

Three Beers to Try

ARCADIA SHIPWRECK PORTER Complex, rich and silky smooth, many stouts don't approach this depth of colour, character and body. This brew has an ABV of 12%.

DOGFISH HEAD 120 MINUTE IPA The label evokes images of a hop bomb, yet the end product is sweet, fruity and smooth, hiding the 18% ABV surprisingly well.

BREWDOG TACTICAL NUCLEAR PENGUIN BrewDog uses freezing to concentrate their base beer, Paradox, and increase the ABV of this incredibly alcoholic brew to 32%.

THE ATOMIC STRUCTURE OF
Imperial and Hyper Beers

Hyper brews are an ideal digestif. Both imperial and hyper beers make for a perfect after-dinner drink.

Boozy

Spirituous

Warming

Intense

Complex

The Boston Beer Company

Hyper beers often resemble a spirit more than a beer.

The Bruery

BrewDog

In 2010 BrewDog released 12 bottles of a brew named The End of History. The bottles for each beer were made out of taxidermied roadkill.

Arcadia Brewing Company

Hair of the Dog Brewing Company

Dogfish Head Brewery

Samuel Adams Utopias often sells for over £95 for a 70 cl bottle, and at 27% ABV, it was once the strongest beer in the world. It is presented in a ceramic bottle shaped like a copper-finished brewing kettle.

I

Not usually consumed with food.

American Stout

Origin: United States
Colour: 30–40 SRM
ABV: 5–12%
IBU: 35–75
Glassware: snifter, pint

The American response to English brews is generally straightforward: make it strong and make it hoppy. In the stout family, US brewers have taken a slightly different path.

A DEPTH OF CREATIVITY

This brew may look very much the same as its English cousin – dark as night, thick, rich and viscous – but the palate often shows a stark contrast, separating it into a category of its own. Creativity abounds in this style, with not only more hops, but strong additions of espresso, chocolate, vanilla, coffee, raspberry and cherry. A recent trend receiving resounding applause is the process of barrel aging, which draws out notes of bourbon, rum and whisky (see page 208). These nuances have made the brew unique, intriguing and often boldly different. The popular double stout is not fully double the strength, but has been 'imperialised' to add greater depth, flavour and a higher ABV (see page 210 for other imperialised beers).

Three Beers to Try

SIERRA NEVADA STOUT This stout hits all the high points. It is smooth and rich, delicately balancing a full hop bitterness with robust malt. A classic.

FOUNDERS BREAKFAST STOUT Brewed with Sumatra and Kona blends of coffee, it is smooth and rich. Roasty notes blend with dark chocolate, and the finish is a lingering, bitter delight.

ROGUE CHOCOLATE STOUT The centre of this brew is velvety smooth with strong chocolate flavours easing to a balanced bittersweet finish.

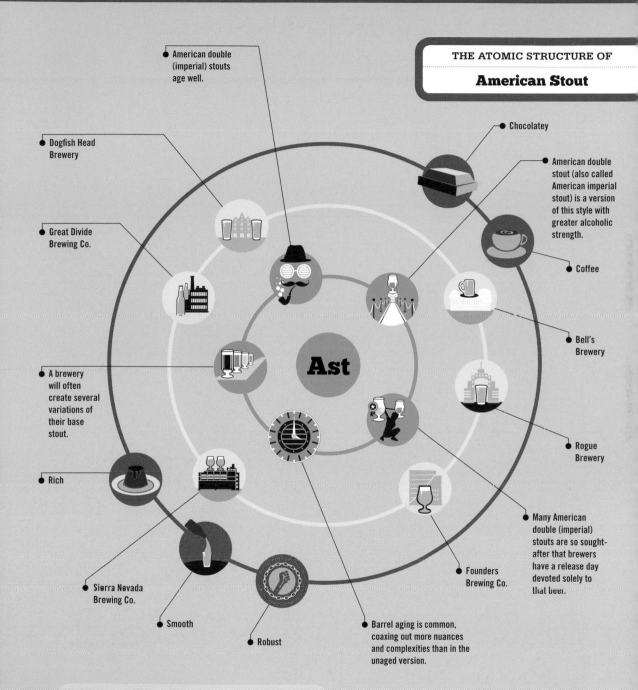

THE ATOMIC STRUCTURE OF
American Stout

American double (imperial) stouts age well.

Dogfish Head Brewery

Great Divide Brewing Co.

A brewery will often create several variations of their base stout.

Rich

Sierra Nevada Brewing Co.

Smooth

Robust

Chocolatey

American double stout (also called American imperial stout) is a version of this style with greater alcoholic strength.

Coffee

Bell's Brewery

Rogue Brewery

Many American double (imperial) stouts are so sought-after that brewers have a release day devoted solely to that beer.

Founders Brewing Co.

Barrel aging is common, coaxing out more nuances and complexities than in the unaged version.

Ast

Food Pairing

| Rich meat dishes | Triple-cream cheese | Mellow Cheddar cheese | Chocolate desserts | Crème brûlée |

Index of Beers

Index of Beers ... continued

Index of Breweries

continues on next page

Index of Breweries ... continued

Index of Food Pairing

CAMRA: The Campaign for Real Ale

CAMPAIGN FOR REAL ALE

CAMRA, the Campaign for Real Ale, is an independent, not-for-profit, volunteer-led consumer group. We promote good quality real ale and pubs, as well as lobbying the government to champion drinkers' rights and protect local pubs as centres of community life.

To achieve our goals **CAMRA** is dedicated to four key campaigns. We campaign to:
- Stop tax rates killing beer
- Secure an effective government support package for pubs
- Encourage people to try a range of real ales, ciders and perries
- Raise the profile of pub-going and increase the number of people using pubs regularly.

CAMRA has over 155,000 members from all ages and backgrounds, brought together by a common belief in the issues that CAMRA supports and their love of good quality British beer.

Join **CAMRA** today by visiting our website:
www.camra.org.uk/joinus
Or call **01727 867201**.

CAMRA Books is the publishing arm of the Campaign for Real Ale. We publish books on beer, pubs, brewing and beer tourism. We published the first *Good Beer Guide* in 1974, and this annual title has since gone on to become the UK's bestselling beer and pub guide. Our publishing list continues to grow with over 30 books in print, and with new titles being added to our list all the time. Our books are available to purchase direct from the CAMRA shop, or ask at your local bookstore. Visit our website: **www.camra.org.uk/books**, or call 01727 867201.

Author's Acknowledgements

Thanks to the team at Marshall Editions; Sorrel, Philippa and Lucy for your vision, guidance and eye for detail.

Thanks also to the team at The Perfectly Happy Man. The seed of my love for beer was sown there and grew only with the help of good friends and good brew.

Most importantly, I would like to thank my wife, Whitney, for her patience with my constant babbling about hops and malts, aromas and flavours, food pairings, glassware and styles. Her patience with a fridge full of beer and her constant encouragement has allowed me to pursue a dream.

Marshall Editions wishes to thank James Ashton-Tyler for his help initiating this book idea, Geoff Windram and Gareth Butterworth for additional design work, and Etty Payne for proofreading.

The publisher wishes to thank Paul Moorhouse, chair of CAMRA's beer tasting panel, for his advice on British and Irish beer styles.